MEDITERRANEAN DIET

COOKBOOK

for Beginners 2024

Simple & No-Stress Recipes, 28-Day Meal Plan to Help You
Build Healthy Habits for Living and Eating Well Every Day

Lena J. Kilgo

Copyright Statement and Disclaimer

Dear Reader,

Thank you for choosing to explore the culinary journey presented within the pages of this recipe book. We want to share our passion for food with you while also ensuring clarity about the rights, responsibilities, and expectations that come with using this book.

Copyright Notice

Warmest wishes,

Lena J. Kilgo

CONTENTS

VEGETABLE MAINS AND MEATLESS RECIPES 40

BEANS , GRAINS, AND PASTAS RECIPES 55

POULTRY AND MEATS RECIPES — 72

FISH AND SEAFOOD RECIPES — 86

FRUITS, DESSERTS AND SNACKS RECIPES   100

SHOPPING LIST   113

APPENDIX A: MEASUREMENT CONVERSIONS   115

APPENDIX B : RECIPES INDEX   117

INTRODUCTION

Hello there, I'm Lena J. Kilgo, a passionate chef with a deep-rooted connection to the Mediterranean region and its vibrant culinary traditions. After years of exploring and savoring the flavors of this enchanting part of the world, I'm thrilled to share my culinary journey with you through the pages of my Mediterranean Diet Cookbook.

My love for cooking and my extensive background in Mediterranean cuisine have led me to create this cookbook, which is not just a collection of recipes but a gateway to a healthier and more enjoyable way of eating. In these pages, you'll find a treasure trove of delectable dishes inspired by the sun-kissed shores of the Mediterranean, where fresh ingredients and time-honored techniques come together to create culinary magic.

The purpose of this cookbook is simple yet profound: to help you embrace the Mediterranean way of life—one filled with vibrant health, joyous gatherings, and unforgettable meals. Whether you're new to this dietary lifestyle or a seasoned enthusiast, you'll discover an array of dishes that celebrate the abundance of plant-based foods, the allure of healthy fats like olive oil, and the art of balancing flavors to perfection.

But this cookbook is not just about tantalizing your taste buds; it's about making the journey from page to plate as seamless as a Mediterranean breeze. You'll find step-by-step instructions that turn even the most intricate recipes into a delightful culinary adventure. I've included handy shopping lists, estimated cooking times, and pro tips to ensure your every endeavor in the kitchen is met with confidence and success.

So, whether you're yearning for the heart-healthy benefits of the Mediterranean Diet, eager to expand your culinary repertoire, or simply seeking the joy of sharing wholesome, delicious meals with loved ones, this cookbook is your passport to a world of flavor, health, and happiness. Welcome to a gastronomic odyssey where the Mediterranean sun meets your kitchen, and every meal is a celebration of life.

The Mediterranean Diet

The Mediterranean diet is a renowned dietary pattern characterized by an emphasis on fresh, wholesome foods commonly consumed in countries bordering the Mediterranean Sea. This heart-healthy diet centers around the consumption of fruits, vegetables, whole grains, olive oil, nuts, seeds, and legumes, with moderate intake of lean proteins such as fish and poultry, and limited consumption of red meat and processed foods. Its origins can be traced back to the traditional eating habits of Mediterranean populations, particularly in Greece, Southern Italy, and Spain. These dietary practices have evolved over centuries and are associated with numerous health benefits, including reduced risk of chronic diseases like heart disease, diabetes, and certain cancers, making it a globally recognized and adopted dietary model.

Mediterranean Diet Pyramid

MEDITERRANEAN DIET

The Mediterranean diet pyramid is the recommended proportions of the different food groups that should be consumed each day. At the bottom of the pyramid are foods such as fruits, vegetables, whole grains and olive oil, which are the basis of the diet and should be consumed in large quantities. Moving up the pyramid you will find foods such as nuts, seeds and legumes, followed by moderate consumption of fish, poultry and dairy products. Red meat and sweets are at the top of the pyramid and should be consumed sparingly. The Mediterranean Diet Pyramid emphasizes the importance of a balanced and varied intake of nutrient-dense foods, highlighting the potential benefits for heart health, longevity and overall well-being.

8 principles of the Mediterranean Diet

ABUNDANCE OF PLANT FOODS

The diet emphasizes the consumption of a wide variety of fruits and vegetables, which are rich in vitamins, minerals, antioxidants, and dietary fiber. These foods provide essential nutrients and promote overall health while reducing the risk of chronic diseases.

HEALTHY FATS

Olive oil is a staple in Mediterranean cuisine and is used for cooking and dressing salads. It contains monounsaturated fats and antioxidants, which have been associated with heart health and reduced inflammation. This principle promotes the replacement of saturated fats (found in butter and lard) with healthier fats.

MODERATE FISH AND POULTRY

Fatty fish like salmon, mackerel, and sardines are encouraged due to their high omega-3 fatty acid content, which supports heart health. Poultry, such as chicken and turkey, is also included but should be consumed in moderation. Red meat is limited to occasional consumption.

DAILY DAIRY

Dairy products, particularly yogurt and cheese, are a source of calcium, protein, and probiotics, which can contribute to gut health. However, these are consumed in moderate amounts, and low-fat or Greek yogurt is preferred over high-fat options.

NUTS AND LEGUMES

Nuts like almonds, walnuts, and pistachios provide healthy fats, protein, and fiber. Legumes such as lentils, chickpeas, and beans offer plant-based protein, fiber, and a variety of vitamins and minerals. Both are staples in the Mediterranean Diet and can be used in salads, stews, or as snacks.

HERBS AND SPICES

Herbs and spices like basil, oregano, garlic, and rosemary are used generously to season dishes, adding flavor without the need for excessive salt. These herbs and spices also provide antioxidants, which may have health benefits.

MODERATE WINE CONSUMPTION

If alcohol is consumed, red wine is favored for its potential cardiovascular benefits due to compounds like resveratrol. However, this principle emphasizes moderation, typically one glass a day for women and up to two glasses a day for men, and should not be seen as an encouragement to start drinking.

SOCIAL AND ENJOYABLE EATING

The Mediterranean Diet promotes the idea that meals should be enjoyed in the company of others, emphasizing the social and cultural aspects of dining. This principle recognizes that a positive relationship with food and a relaxed dining experience can contribute to overall well-being.

Reasons for recommending a Mediterranean Diet Cookbook

Health Benefits: A Mediterranean Diet Cookbook helps individuals adopt a diet associated with reduced risk of chronic diseases like heart disease, stroke, diabetes, and certain cancers due to its focus on nutrient-rich, plant-based foods and healthy fats.

Nutritional Guidance: These cookbooks provide information on the nutritional content of recipes, aiding in making informed choices and meeting dietary needs. This information is particularly valuable for those with specific dietary goals or health concerns.

Culinary Variety: Mediterranean cuisine is known for its diverse and flavorful dishes, and a cookbook introduces readers to a wide range of ingredients, cooking techniques, and flavor profiles, inspiring them to explore new culinary horizons.

Meal Planning: Many Mediterranean Diet cookbooks offer meal plans and shopping lists, simplifying the process of planning balanced and nutritious meals. This is especially helpful for busy individuals and families.

Cooking Skills: Mediterranean cuisine frequently involves cooking from scratch, enhancing cooking skills and encouraging a more hands-on approach to meal preparation. Cookbooks provide step-by-step instructions and tips for mastering these skills.

Weight Management: For those looking to manage their weight, these cookbooks offer recipes that are both satisfying and nutritious, making it easier to achieve and maintain a healthy weight while enjoying delicious meals.

28-DAY MEAL PLAN

DAY	BREAKFAST	LUNCH	DINNER
1	Easy Pizza Pockets 13	Spinach & Pea Salad With Rice 27	Stir-fried Kale With Mushrooms 41
2	Greek Vegetable Salad Pita 13	Cucumber & Spelt Salad With Chicken 27	Roasted Asparagus With Hazelnuts 41
3	Red Pepper Coques With Pine Nuts 13	Cauliflower Soup With Pancetta Crisps 27	Sautéed Cabbage With Parsley 41
4	Berry-yogurt Smoothie 14	Seafood Fideuà 28	Creamy Cauliflower Chickpea Curry 41
5	Easy Alfalfa Sprout And Nut Rolls 14	Turkey Egg Soup With Rice 28	Baked Honey Acorn Squash 42
6	Creamy Vanilla Oatmeal 14	Bell Pepper & Lentil Salad With Tomatoes 28	Quick Steamed Broccoli 42
7	Eggplant, Spinach, And Feta Sandwiches 14	Moroccan Lamb Soup 28	Eggplant And Zucchini Gratin 42
8	Baked Ricotta With Honey Pears 15	Brussels Sprout And Apple Slaw 29	Moroccan Tagine With Vegetables 42
9	Classic Shakshuka 15	Cherry & Pine Nut Couscous 29	Chargrilled Vegetable Kebabs 43
10	Spinach Frittata With Roasted Peppers 15	Simple Tuna Salad 29	Brussels Sprouts Linguine 44
11	Zucchini & Ricotta Egg Muffins 15	Cream Cheese Stuffed Cherry Tomatoes 29	Spinach & Lentil Stew 44
12	Pesto Salami & Cheese Egg Cupcakes 16	Green Bean And Halloumi Salad 30	Sweet Mustard Cabbage Hash 44
13	Banana-blueberry Breakfast Cookies 16	Summer Gazpacho 30	Cauliflower Steaks With Arugula 44
14	Cinnamon Oatmeal With Dried Cranberries 16	Fennel Salad With Olives & Hazelnuts 30	Chickpea Lettuce Wraps With Celery 45

DAY	BREAKFAST	LUNCH	DINNER
15	Fluffy Almond Flour Pancakes With Strawberries 16	Fruit Salad With Sesame Seeds & Nuts 30	Tasty Lentil Burgers 45
16	Morning Zinger Smoothie 17	Chorizo & Fire-roasted Tomato Soup 31	Zucchini Ribbons With Ricotta 45
17	Cheesy Kale & Egg Cupcakes 17	Arugula & Caper Green Salad 31	Roasted Caramelized Root Vegetables 46
18	Quick Pumpkin Oatmeal 17	Cucumber Salad With Mustard Dressing 31	Lentil And Tomato Collard Wraps 46
19	Creamy Peach Smoothie 17	Party Summer Salad 31	Hot Turnip Chickpeas 46
20	Avocado Bruschetta With Tomatoes 17	Favorite Green Bean Stir-fry 32	Grilled Eggplant "steaks" With Sauce 46
21	Lime Watermelon Yogurt Smoothie 18	Easy Roasted Cauliflower 32	Minty Broccoli & Walnuts 47
22	Ricotta Toast With Strawberries 18	Sautéed White Beans With Rosemary 32	Roasted Veggies And Brown Rice Bowl 47
23	Apple-tahini Toast 18	Corn & Cucumber Salad 32	Simple Zoodles 48
24	Spicy Tofu Tacos With Cherry Tomato Salsa 18	Tuscan-style Panzanella Salad 33	Eggplant Rolls In Tomato Sauce 48
25	Carrot & Pecan Cupcakes 19	Authentic Marinara Sauce 33	Mushroom & Cauliflower Roast 48
26	Tomato & Spinach Egg Wraps 19	Radicchio Salad With Sunflower Seeds 33	Simple Braised Carrots 48
27	Vegetable & Egg Sandwiches 19	Asparagus & Red Onion Side Dish 33	Asparagus & Mushroom Farro 49
28	Pecan & Peach Parfait 20	Chicken & Barley Soup 34	Stir-fry Baby Bok Choy 49

Breakfast Recipes

Breakfast Recipes

Easy Pizza Pockets

Servings:2
Cooking Time: 0 Minutes

Ingredients:
- ½ cup tomato sauce
- ½ teaspoon oregano
- ½ teaspoon garlic powder
- ½ cup chopped black olives
- 2 canned artichoke hearts, drained and chopped
- 2 ounces pepperoni, chopped
- ½ cup shredded Mozzarella cheese
- 1 whole-wheat pita, halved

Directions:
1. In a medium bowl, stir together the tomato sauce, oregano, and garlic powder.
2. Add the olives, artichoke hearts, pepperoni, and cheese. Stir to mix.
3. Spoon the mixture into the pita halves and serve.

Nutrition Info:
- Per Serving: Calories: 375;Fat: 23.5g;Protein: 17.1g;-Carbs: 27.1g.

Greek Vegetable Salad Pita

Servings:4
Cooking Time: 0 Minutes

Ingredients:
- ½ cup baby spinach leaves
- ½ small red onion, thinly sliced
- ½ small cucumber, deseeded and chopped
- 1 tomato, chopped
- 1 cup chopped romaine lettuce
- 1 tablespoon extra-virgin olive oil
- ½ tablespoon red wine vinegar
- 1 teaspoon Dijon mustard
- 1 tablespoon crumbled feta cheese
- Sea salt and freshly ground pepper, to taste
- 1 whole-wheat pita

Directions:
1. Combine all the ingredients, except for the pita, in a large bowl. Toss to mix well.
2. Stuff the pita with the salad, then serve immediately.

Nutrition Info:
- Per Serving: Calories: 137;Fat: 8.1g;Protein: 3.1g;Carbs: 14.3g.

Red Pepper Coques With Pine Nuts

Servings:4
Cooking Time: 45 Minutes

Ingredients:
- Dough:
- 3 cups almond flour
- ½ teaspoon instant or rapid-rise yeast
- 2 teaspoons raw honey
- 1⅓ cups ice water
- 3 tablespoons extra-virgin olive oil
- 1½ teaspoons sea salt
- Red Pepper Topping:
- 4 tablespoons extra-virgin olive oil, divided
- 2 cups jarred roasted red peppers, patted dry and sliced thinly
- 2 large onions, halved and sliced thin
- 3 garlic cloves, minced
- ¼ teaspoon red pepper flakes
- 2 bay leaves
- 3 tablespoons maple syrup
- 1½ teaspoons sea salt
- 3 tablespoons red whine vinegar
- For Garnish:
- ¼ cup pine nuts (optional)
- 1 tablespoon minced fresh parsley

Directions:
1. Make the Dough:
2. Combine the flour, yeast, and honey in a food processor, pulse to combine well. Gently add water while pulsing. Let the dough sit for 10 minutes.
3. Mix the olive oil and salt in the dough and knead the dough until smooth. Wrap in plastic and refrigerate for at least 1 day.
4. Make the Topping:
5. Heat 1 tablespoon of olive oil in a nonstick skillet over medium heat until shimmering.
6. Add the red peppers, onions, garlic, red pepper flakes, bay leaves, maple syrup, and salt. Sauté for 20 minutes or until the onion is caramelized.
7. Turn off the heat and discard the bay leaves. Remove the onion from the skillet and baste with wine vinegar. Let them sit until ready to use.
8. Make the Coques:
9. Preheat the oven to 500°F. Grease two baking sheets with 1 tablespoon of olive oil.
10. Divide the dough ball into four balls, then press and shape them into equal-sized oval. Arrange the ovals on the baking sheets and pierce each dough about 12 times.
11. Rub the ovals with 2 tablespoons of olive oil and bake

for 7 minutes or until puffed. Flip the ovals halfway through the cooking time.

12. Spread the ovals with the topping and pine nuts, then bake for an additional 15 minutes or until well browned.

13. Remove the coques from the oven and spread with parsley. Allow to cool for 10 minutes before serving.

Nutrition Info:
- Per Serving: Calories: 658;Fat: 23.1g;Protein: 3.4g;-Carbs: 112.0g.

Berry-yogurt Smoothie

Servings:1
Cooking Time:5 Minutes

Ingredients:
- ½ cup Greek yogurt
- ¼ cup milk
- ½ cup fresh blueberries
- 1 tsp vanilla sugar
- 2 ice cubes

Directions:
1. Pulse the Greek yogurt, milk, vanilla sugar, and berries in your blender until the berries are liquefied. Add the ice cubes and blend on high until thick and smooth. Serve.

Nutrition Info:
- Per Serving: Calories: 230;Fat: 8.8g;Protein: 16g;Carbs: 23g.

Easy Alfalfa Sprout And Nut Rolls

Servings:16
Cooking Time: 0 Minutes

Ingredients:
- 1 cup alfalfa sprouts
- 2 tablespoons Brazil nuts
- ½ cup chopped fresh cilantro
- 2 tablespoons flaked coconut
- 1 garlic clove, minced
- 2 tablespoons ground flaxseeds
- Zest and juice of 1 lemon
- Pinch cayenne pepper
- Sea salt and freshly ground black pepper, to taste
- 1 tablespoon melted coconut oil
- 2 tablespoons water
- 2 whole-grain wraps

Directions:
1. Combine all ingredients, except for the wraps, in a food processor, then pulse to combine well until smooth.
2. Unfold the wraps on a clean work surface, then spread the mixture over the wraps. Roll the wraps up and refrigerate for 30 minutes until set.
3. Remove the rolls from the refrigerator and slice into 16 bite-sized pieces, if desired, and serve.

Nutrition Info:

- Per Serving: Calories: 67;Fat: 7.1g;Protein: 2.2g;Carbs: 2.9g.

Creamy Vanilla Oatmeal

Servings:4
Cooking Time: 40 Minutes

Ingredients:
- 4 cups water
- Pinch sea salt
- 1 cup steel-cut oats
- ¾ cup unsweetened almond milk
- 2 teaspoons pure vanilla extract

Directions:
1. Add the water and salt to a large saucepan over high heat and bring to a boil.
2. Once boiling, reduce the heat to low and add the oats. Mix well and cook for 30 minutes, stirring occasionally.
3. Fold in the almond milk and vanilla and whisk to combine. Continue cooking for about 10 minutes, or until the oats are thick and creamy.
4. Ladle the oatmeal into bowls and serve warm.

Nutrition Info:
- Per Serving: Calories: 117;Fat: 2.2g;Protein: 4.3g;Carbs: 20.0g.

Eggplant, Spinach, And Feta Sandwiches

Servings:2
Cooking Time: 6 To 8 Minutes

Ingredients:
- 1 medium eggplant, sliced into ½-inch-thick slices
- 2 tablespoons olive oil
- Sea salt and freshly ground pepper, to taste
- 5 to 6 tablespoons hummus
- 4 slices whole-wheat bread, toasted
- 1 cup baby spinach leaves
- 2 ounces feta cheese, softened

Directions:
1. Preheat the grill to medium-high heat.
2. Salt both sides of the sliced eggplant, and let sit for 20 minutes to draw out the bitter juices.
3. Rinse the eggplant and pat dry with a paper towel.
4. Brush the eggplant slices with olive oil and season with sea salt and freshly ground pepper to taste.
5. Grill the eggplant until lightly charred on both sides but still slightly firm in the middle, about 3 to 4 minutes per side.
6. Spread the hummus on the bread slices and top with the spinach leaves, feta cheese, and grilled eggplant. Top with the other slice of bread and serve immediately.

Nutrition Info:
- Per Serving: Calories: 493;Fat: 25.3g;Protein: 17.1g;-Carbs: 50.9g.

Baked Ricotta With Honey Pears

Servings:4
Cooking Time: 22 To 25 Minutes

Ingredients:
- 1 container whole-milk ricotta cheese
- 2 large eggs
- ¼ cup whole-wheat pastry flour
- 1 tablespoon sugar
- 1 teaspoon vanilla extract
- ¼ teaspoon ground nutmeg
- 1 pear, cored and diced
- 2 tablespoons water
- 1 tablespoon honey
- Nonstick cooking spray

Directions:
1. Preheat the oven to 400°F. Spray four ramekins with nonstick cooking spray.
2. Beat together the ricotta, eggs, flour, sugar, vanilla, and nutmeg in a large bowl until combined. Spoon the mixture into the ramekins.
3. Bake in the preheated oven for 22 to 25 minutes, or until the ricotta is just set.
4. Meanwhile, in a small saucepan over medium heat, simmer the pear in the water for 10 minutes, or until slightly softened. Remove from the heat, and stir in the honey.
5. Remove the ramekins from the oven and cool slightly on a wire rack. Top the ricotta ramekins with the pear and serve.

Nutrition Info:
- Per Serving: Calories: 329;Fat: 19.0g;Protein: 17.0g;-Carbs: 23.0g.

Classic Shakshuka

Servings:2
Cooking Time: 30 Minutes

Ingredients:
- 1 tablespoon olive oil
- ½ red pepper, diced
- ½ medium onion, diced
- 2 small garlic cloves, minced
- ½ teaspoon smoked paprika
- ½ teaspoon cumin
- Pinch red pepper flakes
- 1 can fire-roasted tomatoes
- ¼ teaspoon salt
- Pinch freshly ground black pepper
- 1 ounce crumbled feta cheese (about ¼ cup)
- 3 large eggs
- 3 tablespoons minced fresh parsley

Directions:
1. Heat the olive oil in a skillet over medium-high heat and add the pepper, onion, and garlic. Sauté until the vegetables start to turn golden.
2. Add the paprika, cumin, and red pepper flakes and stir to toast the spices for about 30 seconds. Add the tomatoes with their juices.
3. Reduce the heat and let the sauce simmer for 10 minutes, or until it starts to thicken. Add the salt and pepper. Taste the sauce and adjust seasonings as necessary.
4. Scatter the feta cheese on top. Make 3 wells in the sauce and crack one egg into each well.
5. Cover and let the eggs cook for about 7 minutes. Remove the lid and continue cooking for 5 minutes more, or until the yolks are cooked to desired doneness.
6. Garnish with fresh parsley and serve.

Nutrition Info:
- Per Serving: Calories: 289;Fat: 18.2g;Protein: 15.1g;-Carbs: 18.5g.

Spinach Frittata With Roasted Peppers

Servings:4
Cooking Time:30 Minutes

Ingredients:
- 2 tbsp olive oil
- 1 cup roasted peppers, chopped
- ½ cup milk
- 8 eggs
- Salt and black pepper to taste
- 1 tsp oregano, dried
- ½ cup red onions, chopped
- 4 cups baby spinach
- 1 cup goat cheese, crumbled

Directions:
1. Beat the eggs with salt, pepper, and oregano in a bowl. Warm the olive oil in a skillet over medium heat and sauté onions for 3 minutes until soft. Mix in spinach, milk, and goat cheese and pour over the eggs. Cook for 2-3 minutes until the base of the frittata is set. Place in preheated to 360 F oven and bake for 10-15 minutes until the top is golden. Top with roasted peppers.

Nutrition Info:
- Per Serving: Calories: 260;Fat: 5g;Protein: 15g;Carbs: 5g.

Zucchini & Ricotta Egg Muffins

Servings:4
Cooking Time:20 Minutes

Ingredients:
- 3 tbsp olive oil
- ½ cup ricotta cheese, crumbled
- 1 lb zucchini, spiralized
- ¼ cup sweet onion, chopped
- 4 large eggs
- ½ tsp hot paprika

- 2 tbsp fresh parsley, chopped
- Salt and black pepper to taste

Directions:

1. Preheat oven to 350 F.Combine the zucchini and sweet onion with olive oil, salt, and black pepper in a bowl. Divide between greased muffin cups. Crack an egg in each one; scatter some salt and hot paprika. Bake for 12 minutes or until set. Serve topped with ricotta cheese and parsley.

Nutrition Info:

- Per Serving: Calories: 226;Fat: 4.6g;Protein: 11g;Carbs: 6.6g.

Pesto Salami & Cheese Egg Cupcakes

Servings:6
Cooking Time:25 Minutes

Ingredients:

- ½ cup roasted red peppers, chopped
- 1 tbsp olive oil
- 5 eggs, whisked
- 4 oz Italian dry salami, sliced
- 1/3 cup spinach, chopped
- ¼ cup ricotta cheese, crumbled
- Salt and black pepper to taste
- 1 ½ tbsp basil pesto

Directions:

1. Preheat the oven to 380 F. Brush 6 ramekin cups with olive oil and line them with dry salami slices. Top with spinach, ricotta cheese, and roasted peppers. Whisk the eggs with pesto, salt, and pepper in a bowl and pour over the peppers. Bake for 15 minutes and serve warm.

Nutrition Info:

- Per Serving: Calories: 120;Fat: 8g;Protein: 10g;Carbs: 2g.

Banana-blueberry Breakfast Cookies

Servings:4
Cooking Time: 13 Minutes

Ingredients:

- 2 medium bananas, sliced
- 4 tablespoons almond butter
- 4 large eggs, lightly beaten
- ½ cup unsweetened applesauce
- 1 teaspoon vanilla extract
- ⅔ cup coconut flour
- ¼ teaspoon salt
- 1 cup fresh or frozen blueberries

Directions:

1. Preheat the oven to 375ºF. Line a baking sheet with parchment paper.
2. Stir together the bananas and almond butter in a medium bowl until well incorporated.
3. Fold in the beaten eggs, applesauce, and vanilla and

blend well.
4. Add the coconut flour and salt and mix well. Add the blueberries and stir to just incorporate.
5. Drop about 2 tablespoons of dough onto the parchment paper-lined baking sheet for each cookie. Using your clean hand, flatten each into a rounded biscuit shape, until it is 1 inch thick.
6. Bake in the preheated oven for about 13 minutes, or until the top is golden brown and a toothpick inserted in the center comes out clean.
7. Let the cookies cool for 5 to 10 minutes before serving.

Nutrition Info:

- Per Serving: Calories: 264;Fat: 13.9g;Protein: 7.3g;-Carbs: 27.6g.

Cinnamon Oatmeal With Dried Cranberries

Servings:2
Cooking Time: 8 Minutes

Ingredients:

- 1 cup almond milk
- 1 cup water
- Pinch sea salt
- 1 cup old-fashioned oats
- ½ cup dried cranberries
- 1 teaspoon ground cinnamon

Directions:

1. In a medium saucepan over high heat, bring the almond milk, water, and salt to a boil.
2. Stir in the oats, cranberries, and cinnamon. Reduce the heat to medium and cook for 5 minutes, stirring occasionally.
3. Remove the oatmeal from the heat. Cover and let it stand for 3 minutes. Stir before serving.

Nutrition Info:

- Per Serving: Calories: 107;Fat: 2.1g;Protein: 3.2g;Carbs: 18.2g.

Fluffy Almond Flour Pancakes With Strawberries

Servings:4
Cooking Time: 15 Minutes

Ingredients:

- 1 cup plus 2 tablespoons unsweetened almond milk
- 1 cup almond flour
- 2 large eggs, whisked
- ⅓ cup honey
- 1 teaspoon baking soda
- ¼ teaspoon salt
- 2 tablespoons extra-virgin olive oil
- 1 cup sliced strawberries

Directions:

1. Combine the almond milk, almond flour, whisked eggs, honey, baking soda, and salt in a large bowl and whisk to incorporate.
2. Heat the olive oil in a large skillet over medium-high heat.
3. Make the pancakes: Pour ⅓ cup of batter into the hot skillet and swirl the pan so the batter covers the bottom evenly. Cook for 2 to 3 minutes until the pancake turns golden brown around the edges. Gently flip the pancake with a spatula and cook for 2 to 3 minutes until cooked through. Repeat with the remaining batter.
4. Serve the pancakes with the sliced strawberries on top.

Nutrition Info:

- Per Serving: Calories: 298;Fat: 11.7g;Protein: 11.8g;-Carbs: 34.8g.

Morning Zinger Smoothie

Servings:2
Cooking Time:5 Minutes

Ingredients:

- 1 green apple, chopped
- 2 cups spinach
- 1 avocado, peeled and diced
- 1 tsp honey
- 1 kiwi, peeled
- 2 cups almond milk

Directions:

1. Place spinach, apple, avocado, honey, kiwi, and almond milk in a food processor and blend until smooth. Serve chilled.

Nutrition Info:

- Per Serving: Calories: 170;Fat: 11g;Protein: 3g;Carbs: 22g.

Cheesy Kale & Egg Cupcakes

Servings:2
Cooking Time:30 Minutes

Ingredients:

- ¼ cup kale, chopped
- 3 eggs
- 1 leek, sliced
- 4 tbsp Parmesan, grated
- 2 tbsp almond milk
- 1 red bell pepper, chopped
- Salt and black pepper to taste
- 1 tomato, chopped
- 2 tbsp mozzarella, grated

Directions:

1. Preheat the oven to 360 F. Grease a muffin tin with cooking spray. Whisk the eggs in a bowl. Add in milk, kale, leek, Parmesan cheese, bell pepper, salt, black pepper, to-

mato, and mozzarella cheese and stir to combine. Divide the mixture between the cases and bake for 20-25 minutes. Let cool completely on a wire rack before serving.

Nutrition Info:

- Per Serving: Calories: 320;Fat: 20g;Protein: 26g;Carbs: 9g.

Quick Pumpkin Oatmeal

Servings:4
Cooking Time:15 Minutes

Ingredients:

- ¼ cup pumpkin seeds
- ½ cup milk
- 1 cup old-fashioned oats
- 1 cup pumpkin puree
- 2 tbsp superfine sugar
- ½ tsp ground cinnamon
- 1 ¾ cups water
- ¼ tsp sea salt

Directions:

1. Place milk, salt, and 1 ¾ cups of water in a pot over medium heat and bring to a boil. Mix in oats, then lower the heat and simmer for 5 minutes, stirring periodically.
2. Let sit covered for 5 minutes more. Combine with pumpkin puree, cinnamon, and sugar. Top with pumpkin seeds and serve.

Nutrition Info:

- Per Serving: Calories: 143;Fat: 5.4g;Protein: 5g;Carbs: 20.8g.

Creamy Peach Smoothie

Servings:2
Cooking Time: 0 Minutes

Ingredients:

- 2 cups packed frozen peaches, partially thawed
- ½ ripe avocado
- ½ cup plain or vanilla Greek yogurt
- 2 tablespoons flax meal
- 1 tablespoon honey
- 1 teaspoon orange extract
- 1 teaspoon vanilla extract

Directions:

1. Place all the ingredients in a blender and blend until completely mixed and smooth.
2. Divide the mixture into two bowls and serve immediately.

Nutrition Info:

- Per Serving: Calories: 212;Fat: 13.1g;Protein: 6.0g;-Carbs: 22.5g.

Avocado Bruschetta With Tomatoes

Servings:4

Cooking Time:5 Minutes

Ingredients:
- 1 tbsp olive oil
- 1 baguette, sliced
- 2 sun-dried tomatoes, chopped
- 1 avocado, chopped
- 2 tbsp lemon juice
- 8 cherry tomatoes, chopped
- ¼ cup red onion, chopped
- 1 tsp dried oregano
- 2 tbsp parsley, chopped
- 4 Kalamata olives, chopped
- Salt and black pepper to taste

Directions:
1. Preheat oven to 360 F. Arrange the bread slices on a greased baking tray and drizzle with olive oil. Bake until golden, about 6-8 minutes. Mash the avocado in a bowl with lemon juice, salt, and pepper. Stir in sun-dried tomatoes, onion, oregano, parsley, and olives. Spread the avocado mixture on toasted bread slices and top with cherry tomatoes to serve.

Nutrition Info:
- Per Serving: Calories: 120;Fat: 11g;Protein: 2g;Carbs: 7g.

Lime Watermelon Yogurt Smoothie

Servings:6
Cooking Time:5 Minutes

Ingredients:
- ½ cup almond milk
- 2 cups watermelon, cubed
- ½ cup Greek yogurt
- ½ tsp lime zest

Directions:
1. In a food processor, blend watermelon, almond milk, lime zest, and yogurt until smooth. Serve into glasses.

Nutrition Info:
- Per Serving: Calories: 260;Fat: 10g;Protein: 2g;Carbs: 6g.

Ricotta Toast With Strawberries

Servings:2
Cooking Time: 0 Minutes

Ingredients:
- ½ cup crumbled ricotta cheese
- 1 tablespoon honey, plus additional as needed
- Pinch of sea salt, plus additional as needed
- 4 slices of whole-grain bread, toasted
- 1 cup sliced fresh strawberries
- 4 large fresh basil leaves, sliced into thin shreds

Directions:

1. Mix together the cheese, honey, and salt in a small bowl until well incorporated.
2. Taste and add additional salt and honey if needed.
3. Spoon 2 tablespoons of the cheese mixture onto each slice of bread and spread it all over.
4. Sprinkle the sliced strawberry and basil leaves on top before serving.

Nutrition Info:
- Per Serving: Calories: 274;Fat: 7.9g;Protein: 15.1g;-Carbs: 39.8g.

Apple-tahini Toast

Servings:1
Cooking Time: 0 Minutes

Ingredients:
- 2 slices whole-wheat bread, toasted
- 2 tablespoons tahini
- 1 small apple of your choice, cored and thinly sliced
- 1 teaspoon honey

Directions:
1. Spread the tahini on the toasted bread.
2. Place the apple slices on the bread and drizzle with the honey. Serve immediately.

Nutrition Info:
- Per Serving: Calories: 458;Fat: 17.8g;Protein: 11.0g;-Carbs: 63.5g.

Spicy Tofu Tacos With Cherry Tomato Salsa

Servings:4
Cooking Time: 11 Minutes

Ingredients:
- Cherry Tomato Salsa:
- ¼ cup sliced cherry tomatoes
- ½ jalapeño, deseeded and sliced
- Juice of 1 lime
- 1 garlic clove, minced
- Sea salt and freshly ground black pepper, to taste
- 2 teaspoons extra-virgin olive oil
- Spicy Tofu Taco Filling:
- 4 tablespoons water, divided
- ½ cup canned black beans, rinsed and drained
- 2 teaspoons fresh chopped chives, divided
- ¾ teaspoon ground cumin, divided
- ¾ teaspoon smoked paprika, divided
- Dash cayenne pepper (optional)
- ¼ teaspoon sea salt
- ¼ teaspoon freshly ground black pepper
- 1 teaspoon extra-virgin olive oil
- 6 ounces firm tofu, drained, rinsed, and pressed
- 4 corn tortillas
- ¼ avocado, sliced

- ¼ cup fresh cilantro

Directions:

1. Make the Cherry Tomato Salsa:
2. Combine the ingredients for the salsa in a small bowl. Stir to mix well. Set aside until ready to use.
3. Make the Spicy Tofu Taco Filling:
4. Add 2 tablespoons of water into a saucepan, then add the black beans and sprinkle with 1 teaspoon of chives, ½ teaspoon of cumin, ¼ teaspoon of smoked paprika, and cayenne. Stir to mix well.
5. Cook for 5 minutes over medium heat until heated through, then mash the black beans with the back of a spoon. Turn off the heat and set aside.
6. Add remaining water into a bowl, then add the remaining chives, cumin, and paprika. Sprinkle with cayenne, salt, and black pepper. Stir to mix well. Set aside.
7. Heat the olive oil in a nonstick skillet over medium heat until shimmering.
8. Add the tofu and drizzle with taco sauce, then sauté for 5 minutes or until the seasoning is absorbed. Remove the tofu from the skillet and set aside.
9. Warm the tortillas in the skillet for 1 minutes or until heated through.
10. Transfer the tortillas onto a large plate and top with tofu, mashed black beans, avocado, cilantro, then drizzle the tomato salsa over. Serve immediately.

Nutrition Info:
- Per Serving: Calories: 240;Fat: 9.0g;Protein: 11.6g;-Carbs: 31.6g.

Carrot & Pecan Cupcakes

Servings:6
Cooking Time:30 Minutes

Ingredients:
- 2 tbsp olive oil
- 1 ½ cups grated carrots
- ¼ cup pecans, chopped
- 1 cup oat bran
- 1 cup wholewheat flour
- ½ cup all-purpose flour
- ½ cup old-fashioned oats
- 3 tbsp light brown sugar
- 1 tsp vanilla extract
- ½ lemon, zested
- 1 tsp baking powder
- 2 tsp ground cinnamon
- 2 tsp ground ginger
- ½ tsp ground nutmeg
- ¼ tsp salt
- 1¼ cups soy milk
- 2 tbsp honey
- 1 egg

Directions:

1. Preheat oven to 350 F. Mix whole-wheat flour, all-purpose flour, oat bran, oats, sugar, baking powder, cinnamon, nutmeg, ginger, and salt in a bowl; set aside.
2. Beat egg with soy milk, honey, vanilla, lemon zest, and olive oil in another bowl. Pour this mixture into the flour mixture and combine to blend, leaving some lumps. Stir in carrots and pecans. Spoon batter into greased muffin cups. Bake for about 20 minutes. Prick with a toothpick and if it comes out easily, the cakes are cooked done. Let cool and serve.

Nutrition Info:
- Per Serving: Calories: 346;Fat: 10g;Protein: 13g;Carbs: 59g.

Tomato & Spinach Egg Wraps

Servings:2
Cooking Time:15 Minutes

Ingredients:
- 1 tbsp parsley, chopped
- 1 tbsp olive oil
- ¼ onion, chopped
- 3 sun-dried tomatoes, chopped
- 3 large eggs, beaten
- 2 cups baby spinach, torn
- 1 oz feta cheese, crumbled
- Salt to taste
- 2 whole-wheat tortillas, warm

Directions:

1. Warm the olive oil in a pan over medium heat. Sauté the onion and tomatoes for about 3 minutes. Add the beaten eggs and stir to scramble them, about 4 minutes. Add the spinach and parsley stir to combine. Sprinkle the feta cheese over the eggs. Season with salt to taste. Divide the mixture between the tortillas. Roll them up and serve.

Nutrition Info:
- Per Serving: Calories: 435;Fat: 28g;Protein: 17g;Carbs: 31g.

Vegetable & Egg Sandwiches

Servings:2
Cooking Time:15 Minutes

Ingredients:
- 1 Iceberg lettuce, separated into leaves
- 1 tbsp olive oil
- 1 tbsp butter
- 2 fontina cheese slices, grated
- 3 eggs
- 4 slices multigrain bread
- 3 radishes, sliced
- ½ cucumber, sliced
- 2 pimiento peppers, chopped
- Salt and red pepper to taste

Directions:

1. Warm the oil in a skillet over medium heat. Crack in the eggs and cook until the whites are set. Season with salt and red pepper; remove to a plate. Brush the bread slices with butter and toast them in the same skillet for 2 minutes per side.

2. Arrange 2 bread slices on a flat surface and put themover the eggs. Add in the remaining ingredients and top with the remaining slices. Serve immediately.

Nutrition Info:

- Per Serving: Calories: 487;Fat: 13g;Protein: 24g;Carbs: 32g.

Pecan & Peach Parfait

Servings:2
Cooking Time:15 Minutes

Ingredients:

- 1 ½ cups Greek yogurt
- ½ cup pecans
- ½ cup whole-grain rolled oats
- 1 tsp honey
- 1 peeled and chopped peach
- Mint leaves for garnish

Directions:

1. Preheat oven to 310 F. Pour the oats and pecans into a baking sheet and spread evenly. Toast for 11-13 minutes; set aside. Microwave honey for 30 seconds. Stir in the peach.

2. Divide some peach mixture between 2 glasses, spread some yogurt on top, and sprinkle with the oat mixture. Repeat the layering process to exhaust the ingredients, finishing with the peach mixture. Serve with mint leaves.

Nutrition Info:

- Per Serving: Calories: 403;Fat: 19g;Protein: 22g;Carbs: 40g.

Couscous & Cucumber Bowl

Servings:4
Cooking Time:15 Minutes

Ingredients:

- 2 tbsp olive oil
- ¾ cup couscous
- 1 cup water
- 1 yellow onion, chopped
- 2 garlic cloves, minced
- 2 cups canned chickpeas
- Salt to taste
- 15 oz canned tomatoes, diced
- 1 cucumber, cut into ribbons
- ½ cup black olives, chopped
- 1 tbsp lemon juice
- 1 tbsp mint leaves, chopped

Directions:

1. Cover the couscous with salted boiling water, cover, and let it sit for about 5 minutes. Then fluff with a fork and set aside.

2. Warm the olive oil in a skillet over medium heat and sauté onion and garlic for 3 minutes until soft. Stir in chickpeas, salt, and tomatoes for 1-2 minutes. Turn off the heat and mix in olives, couscous, and lemon juice. Transfer to a bowl and top with cucumber ribbons and mint to serve.

Nutrition Info:

- Per Serving: Calories: 350;Fat: 11g;Protein: 12g;Carbs: 50g.

Berry And Nut Parfait

Servings:2
Cooking Time: 0 Minutes

Ingredients:

- 2 cups plain Greek yogurt
- 2 tablespoons honey
- 1 cup fresh raspberries
- 1 cup fresh blueberries
- ½ cup walnut pieces

Directions:

1. In a medium bowl, whisk the yogurt and honey. Spoon into 2 serving bowls.

2. Top each with ½ cup blueberries, ½ cup raspberries, and ¼ cup walnut pieces. Serve immediately.

Nutrition Info:

- Per Serving: Calories: 507;Fat: 23.0g;Protein: 24.1g;Carbs: 57.0g.

Grilled Caesar Salad Sandwiches

Servings:2
Cooking Time: 5 Minutes

Ingredients:

- ¾ cup olive oil, divided
- 2 romaine lettuce hearts, left intact
- 3 to 4 anchovy fillets
- Juice of 1 lemon
- 2 to 3 cloves garlic, peeled
- 1 teaspoon Dijon mustard
- ¼ teaspoon Worcestershire sauce
- Sea salt and freshly ground pepper, to taste
- 2 slices whole-wheat bread, toasted
- Freshly grated Parmesan cheese, for serving

Directions:

1. Preheat the grill to medium-high heat and oil the grates.

2. On a cutting board, drizzle the lettuce with 1 to 2 tablespoons of olive oil and place on the grates.

3. Grill for 5 minutes, turning until lettuce is slightly charred on all sides. Let lettuce cool enough to handle.

4. In a food processor, combine the remaining olive oil with the anchovies, lemon juice, garlic, mustard, and

Worcestershire sauce.

5. Pulse the ingredients until you have a smooth emulsion. Season with sea salt and freshly ground pepper to taste. Chop the lettuce in half and place on the bread.

6. Drizzle with the dressing and serve with a sprinkle of Parmesan cheese.

Nutrition Info:
- Per Serving: Calories: 949;Fat: 85.6g;Protein: 12.9g;-Carbs: 34.1g.

Lazy Blueberry Oatmeal

Servings:2
Cooking Time:10 Min + Chilling Time

Ingredients:
- ⅔ cup milk
- ⅓ cup quick rolled oats
- ¼ cup blueberries
- 1 tsp honey
- ½ tsp ground cinnamon
- ¼ tsp ground cloves

Directions:
1. Layer the oats, milk, blueberries, honey, cinnamon, and cloves into 2 mason jars. Cover and store in the refrigerator overnight. Serve cold and enjoy!

Nutrition Info:
- Per Serving: Calories: 82;Fat: 2.2g;Protein: 2g;Carbs: 14.1g.

Goat Cheese & Sweet Potato Tart

Servings:6
Cooking Time:1 Hour 20 Minutes

Ingredients:
- ¼ cup olive oil
- 2 eggs, whisked
- 2 lb sweet potatoes, cubed
- 7 oz goat cheese, crumbled
- 1 white onion, chopped
- ¼ cup milk
- Salt and black pepper to taste
- 6 phyllo sheets

Directions:
1. Preheat the oven to 380 F. Line a baking sheet with parchment paper. Place potatoes, half of the olive oil, salt, and pepper in a bowl and toss to combine. Arrange on the sheet and roast for 25 minutes.
2. In the meantime, warm half of the remaining oil in a skillet over medium heat and sauté onion for 3 minutes. Whisk eggs, milk, goat cheese, salt, pepper, onion, sweet potatoes, and remaining oil in a bowl.
3. Place phyllo sheets in a tart dish and rub with oil. Spoon sweet potato mixture, cover with foil and bake for 20 minutes. Remove the foil and bake another 20 minutes. Let cool

for a few minutes. Serve sliced.

Nutrition Info:
- Per Serving: Calories: 513;Fat: 23g;Protein: 17g;Carbs: 60g.

Egg Bake

Servings:2
Cooking Time: 30 Minutes

Ingredients:
- 1 tablespoon olive oil
- 1 slice whole-grain bread
- 4 large eggs
- 3 tablespoons unsweetened almond milk
- ½ teaspoon onion powder
- ¼ teaspoon garlic powder
- ¾ cup chopped cherry tomatoes
- ¼ teaspoon salt
- Pinch freshly ground black pepper

Directions:
1. Preheat the oven to 375ºF.
2. Coat two ramekins with the olive oil and transfer to a baking sheet. Line the bottom of each ramekin with ½ of bread slice.
3. In a medium bowl, whisk together the eggs, almond milk, onion powder, garlic powder, tomatoes, salt, and pepper until well combined.
4. Pour the mixture evenly into two ramekins. Bake in the preheated oven for 30 minutes, or until the eggs are completely set.
5. Cool for 5 minutes before serving.

Nutrition Info:
- Per Serving: Calories: 240;Fat: 17.4g;Protein: 9.0g;-Carbs: 12.2g.

Pecorino Bulgur & Spinach Cupcakes

Servings:6
Cooking Time:45 Minutes

Ingredients:
- 2 eggs, whisked
- 1 cup bulgur
- 3 cups water
- 1 cup spinach, torn
- 2 spring onions, chopped
- ¼ cup Pecorino cheese, grated
- ½ tsp garlic powder
- Sea salt and pepper to taste
- ½ tsp dried oregano

Directions:
1. Preheat the oven to 340 F. Grease a muffin tin with cooking spray. Warm 2 cups of salted water in a saucepan over medium heat and add in bulgur. Bring to a boil and cook for 10-15 minutes. Remove to a bowl and fluff with a fork.

Stir in spinach, spring onions, eggs, Pecorino cheese, garlic powder, salt, pepper, and oregano. Divide between muffin holes and bake for 25 minutes. Serve chilled.

Nutrition Info:

- Per Serving: Calories: 280;Fat: 12g;Protein: 5g;Carbs: 9g.

Maple-vanilla Yogurt With Walnuts

Servings:4

Cooking Time:10 Minutes

Ingredients:

- 2 cups Greek yogurt
- ¾ cup maple syrup
- 1 cup walnuts, chopped
- 1 tsp vanilla extract
- 2 tsp cinnamon powder

Directions:

1. Combine yogurt, walnuts, vanilla, maple syrup, and cinnamon powder in a bowl. Let sit in the fridge for 10 minutes.

Nutrition Info:

- Per Serving: Calories: 400;Fat: 25g;Protein: 11g;Carbs: 40g.

Cauliflower Breakfast Porridge

Servings:2

Cooking Time: 5 Minutes

Ingredients:

- 2 cups riced cauliflower
- ¾ cup unsweetened almond milk
- 4 tablespoons extra-virgin olive oil, divided
- 2 teaspoons grated fresh orange peel (from ½ orange)
- ½ teaspoon almond extract or vanilla extract
- ½ teaspoon ground cinnamon
- ⅛ teaspoon salt
- 4 tablespoons chopped walnuts, divided
- 1 to 2 teaspoons maple syrup (optional)

Directions:

1. Place the riced cauliflower, almond milk, 2 tablespoons of olive oil, orange peel, almond extract, cinnamon, and salt in a medium saucepan.
2. Stir to incorporate and bring the mixture to a boil over medium-high heat, stirring often.
3. Remove from the heat and add 2 tablespoons of chopped walnuts and maple syrup (if desired).
4. Stir again and divide the porridge into bowls. To serve, sprinkle each bowl evenly with remaining 2 tablespoons of walnuts and olive oil.

Nutrition Info:

- Per Serving: Calories: 381;Fat: 37.8g;Protein: 5.2g;-Carbs: 10.9g.

Breakfast Pancakes With Berry Sauce

Servings:4

Cooking Time: 10 Minutes

Ingredients:

- Pancakes:
- 1 cup almond flour
- 1 teaspoon baking powder
- ¼ teaspoon salt
- 6 tablespoon extra-virgin olive oil, divided
- 2 large eggs, beaten
- Zest and juice of 1 lemon
- ½ teaspoon vanilla extract
- Berry Sauce:
- 1 cup frozen mixed berries
- 1 tablespoon water, plus more as needed
- ½ teaspoon vanilla extract

Directions:

1. Make the Pancakes
2. In a large bowl, combine the almond flour, baking powder, and salt and stir to break up any clumps.
3. Add 4 tablespoons olive oil, beaten eggs, lemon zest and juice, and vanilla extract and stir until well mixed.
4. Heat 1 tablespoon of olive oil in a large skillet. Spoon about 2 tablespoons of batter for each pancake. Cook until bubbles begin to form, 4 to 5 minutes. Flip and cook for another 2 to 3 minutes. Repeat with the remaining 1 tablespoon of olive oil and batter.
5. Make the Berry Sauce
6. Combine the frozen berries, water, and vanilla extract in a small saucepan and heat over medium-high heat for 3 to 4 minutes until bubbly, adding more water as needed. Using the back of a spoon or fork, mash the berries and whisk until smooth.
7. Serve the pancakes with the berry sauce.

Nutrition Info:

- Per Serving: Calories: 275;Fat: 26.0g;Protein: 4.0g;-Carbs: 8.0g.

Cheesy Fig Pizzas With Garlic Oil

Servings:2

Cooking Time: 10 Minutes

Ingredients:

- Dough:
- 1 cup almond flour
- 1½ cups whole-wheat flour
- ¾ teaspoon instant or rapid-rise yeast
- 2 teaspoons raw honey
- 1¼ cups ice water
- 2 tablespoons extra-virgin olive oil
- 1¾ teaspoons sea salt
- Garlic Oil:
- 4 tablespoons extra-virgin olive oil, divided
- ½ teaspoon dried thyme

- 2 garlic cloves, minced
- ⅛ teaspoon sea salt
- ½ teaspoon freshly ground pepper
- Topping:
- 1 cup fresh basil leaves
- 1 cup crumbled feta cheese
- 8 ounces fresh figs, stemmed and quartered lengthwise
- 2 tablespoons raw honey

Directions:

1. Make the Dough:
2. Combine the flours, yeast, and honey in a food processor, pulse to combine well. Gently add water while pulsing. Let the dough sit for 10 minutes.
3. Mix the olive oil and salt in the dough and knead the dough until smooth. Wrap in plastic and refrigerate for at least 1 day.
4. Make the Garlic Oil:
5. Heat 2 tablespoons of olive oil in a nonstick skillet over medium-low heat until shimmering.
6. Add the thyme, garlic, salt, and pepper and sauté for 30 seconds or until fragrant. Set them aside until ready to use.
7. Make the pizzas:
8. Preheat the oven to 500ºF. Grease two baking sheets with 2 tablespoons of olive oil.
9. Divide the dough in half and shape into two balls. Press the balls into 13-inch rounds. Sprinkle the rounds with a tough of flour if they are sticky.
10. Top the rounds with the garlic oil and basil leaves, then arrange the rounds on the baking sheets. Scatter with feta cheese and figs.
11. Put the sheets in the preheated oven and bake for 9 minutes or until lightly browned. Rotate the pizza halfway through.
12. Remove the pizzas from the oven, then discard the bay leaves. Drizzle with honey. Let sit for 5 minutes and serve immediately.

Nutrition Info:
- Per Serving: Calories: 1350;Fat: 46.5g;Protein: 27.5g;-Carbs: 221.9g.

Lemon Cardamom Buckwheat Pancakes

Servings:2
Cooking Time:20 Minutes

Ingredients:
- ½ cup buckwheat flour
- ½ tsp cardamom
- ½ tsp baking powder
- ½ cup milk
- ¼ cup plain Greek yogurt
- 1 egg
- 1 tsp lemon zest
- 1 tbsp honey

Directions:

1. Mix the buckwheat flour, cardamom, and baking powder in a medium bowl. Whisk the milk, yogurt, egg, lemon zest, and honey in another bowl. Add the wet ingredients to the dry ingredients and stir until the batter is smooth.
2. Spray a frying pan with non-stick cooking oil and cook the pancakes over medium heat until the edges begin to brown. Flip and cook on the other side for 3 more minutes. Serve.

Nutrition Info:
- Per Serving: Calories: 196;Fat: 6g;Protein: 10g;Carbs: 27g.

Mediterranean Eggs (shakshuka)

Servings:4
Cooking Time: 20 Minutes

Ingredients:
- 2 tablespoons extra-virgin olive oil
- 1 cup chopped shallots
- 1 teaspoon garlic powder
- 1 cup finely diced potato
- 1 cup chopped red bell peppers
- 1 can diced tomatoes, drained
- ¼ teaspoon ground cardamom
- ¼ teaspoon paprika
- ¼ teaspoon turmeric
- 4 large eggs
- ¼ cup chopped fresh cilantro

Directions:

1. Preheat the oven to 350ºF.
2. Heat the olive oil in an ovenproof skillet over medium-high heat until it shimmers.
3. Add the shallots and sauté for about 3 minutes, stirring occasionally, until fragrant.
4. Fold in the garlic powder, potato, and bell peppers and stir to combine.
5. Cover and cook for 10 minutes, stirring frequently.
6. Add the tomatoes, cardamon, paprika, and turmeric and mix well.
7. When the mixture begins to bubble, remove from the heat and crack the eggs into the skillet.
8. Transfer the skillet to the preheated oven and bake for 5 to 10 minutes, or until the egg whites are set and the yolks are cooked to your liking.
9. Remove from the oven and garnish with the cilantro before serving.

Nutrition Info:
- Per Serving: Calories: 223;Fat: 11.8g;Protein: 9.1g;-Carbs: 19.5g.

Parsley Tomato Eggs

Servings:6
Cooking Time:25 Minutes

Ingredients:
- 2 tbsp olive oil
- 1 onion, chopped
- 2 garlic cloves, minced
- 2 cans tomatoes, diced
- 6 large eggs
- ½ cup fresh chives, chopped

Directions:
1. Warm the olive oil in a large skillet over medium heat. Add the onion and garlic and cook for 3 minutes, stirring occasionally. Pour in the tomatoes with their juices o and cook for 3 minutes until bubbling.
2. Crack one egg into a small custard cup. With a large spoon, make six indentations in the tomato mixture. Gently pour the first cracked egg into one indentation and repeat, cracking the remaining eggs, one at a time, into the custard cup and pouring one into each indentation. Cover the skillet and cook for 6-8 minutes. Top with chives and serve.

Nutrition Info:
- Per Serving: Calories: 123;Fat: 8g;Protein: 7g;Carbs: 4g.

Cinnamon Pistachio Smoothie

Servings:1
Cooking Time: 0 Minutes

Ingredients:
- ½ cup unsweetened almond milk, plus more as needed
- ½ cup plain Greek yogurt
- Zest and juice of ½ orange
- 1 tablespoon extra-virgin olive oil
- 1 tablespoon shelled pistachios, coarsely chopped
- ¼ to ½ teaspoon ground allspice
- ¼ teaspoon vanilla extract
- ¼ teaspoon ground cinnamon

Directions:
1. In a blender, combine ½ cup almond milk, yogurt, orange zest and juice, olive oil, pistachios, allspice, vanilla, and cinnamon. Blend until smooth and creamy, adding more almond milk to achieve your desired consistency.
2. Serve chilled.

Nutrition Info:
- Per Serving: Calories: 264;Fat: 22.0g;Protein: 6.0g;-Carbs: 12.0g.

Morning Pizza Frittata

Servings:4
Cooking Time:20 Minutes

Ingredients:
- 2 tbsp butter
- 8 oz pancetta, chopped
- ½ onion, finely chopped
- 1 cup mushrooms, sliced
- 8 large eggs, beaten
- ¼ cup heavy cream
- 1 tsp dried oregano
- ¼ tsp red pepper flakes
- ½ cup mozzarella, shredded
- 8 cherry tomatoes, halved
- 4 black olives, sliced

Directions:
1. Melt the butter in a large skillet over medium heat until. Add the pancetta and cook for 4 minutes until browned. Stir in the onion and mushrooms and cook for 3 more minutes, stirring occasionally, until the veggies are tender. In a bowl, beat the eggs, heavy cream, oregano, and red pepper flakes.
2. Pour over the veggies and pancetta. Cook for about 5-6 minutes until the eggs are set. Spread the mozzarella cheese all over and arrange the cherry tomatoes on top. Place under the preheated broiler for 4-5 minutes. Leave to cool slightly and cut into wedges. Top with sliced olives and serve warm.

Nutrition Info:
- Per Serving: Calories: 595;Fat: 43g;Protein: 38g;Carbs: 14g.

Maple Berry & Walnut Oatmeal

Servings:2
Cooking Time:10 Minutes

Ingredients:
- 1 cup mixed berries
- 1 ½ cups rolled oats
- 2 tbsp walnuts, chopped
- 2 tsp maple syrup

Directions:
1. Cook the oats according to the package instructions and share in 2 bowls. Microwave the maple syrup and berries for 30 seconds; stir well. Pour over each bowl. Top with walnuts.

Nutrition Info:
- Per Serving: Calories: 262;Fat: 10g;Protein: 15g;Carbs: 57g.

Salmon Salad Wraps

Servings:6
Cooking Time: 0 Minutes

Ingredients:
- 1 pound salmon fillets, cooked and flaked
- ½ cup diced carrots
- ½ cup diced celery
- 3 tablespoons diced red onion
- 3 tablespoons chopped fresh dill
- 2 tablespoons capers
- 1½ tablespoons extra-virgin olive oil
- 1 tablespoon aged balsamic vinegar
- ¼ teaspoon kosher or sea salt
- ½ teaspoon freshly ground black pepper
- 4 whole-wheat flatbread wraps or soft whole-wheat tortillas

Directions:
1. In a large bowl, stir together all the ingredients, except for the wraps.
2. On a clean work surface, lay the wraps. Divide the salmon mixture evenly among the wraps. Fold up the bottom of the wraps, then roll up the wrap.
3. Serve immediately.

Nutrition Info:
- Per Serving: Calories: 194;Fat: 8.0g;Protein: 18.0g;-Carbs: 13.0g.

Easy Zucchini & Egg Stuffed Tomatoes

Servings:4
Cooking Time:40 Minutes

Ingredients:
- 1 tbsp olive oil
- 1 small zucchini, grated
- 8 tomatoes, insides scooped
- 8 eggs
- Salt and black pepper to taste

Directions:
1. Preheat the oven to 360 F. Place tomatoes on a greased baking dish. Mix the zucchini with olive oil, salt, and pepper. Divide the mixture between the tomatoes and crack an egg on each one. Bake for 20-25 minutes. Serve warm.

Nutrition Info:
- Per Serving: Calories: 280;Fat: 22g;Protein: 14g;Carbs: 12g.

Savory Breakfast Oatmeal

Servings:2
Cooking Time: 15 Minutes

Ingredients:
- ½ cup steel-cut oats
- 1 cup water
- 1 medium cucumber, chopped
- 1 large tomato, chopped
- 1 tablespoon olive oil
- Pinch freshly grated Parmesan cheese
- Sea salt and freshly ground pepper, to taste
- Flat-leaf parsley or mint, chopped, for garnish

Directions:
1. Combine the oats and water in a medium saucepan and bring to a boil over high heat, stirring continuously, or until the water is absorbed, about 15 minutes.
2. Divide the oatmeal between 2 bowls and scatter the tomato and cucumber on top. Drizzle with the olive oil and sprinkle with the Parmesan cheese.
3. Season with salt and pepper to taste. Serve garnished with the parsley.

Nutrition Info:
- Per Serving: Calories: 197;Fat: 8.9g;Protein: 6.3g;Carbs: 23.1g.

Brown Rice Salad With Cheese

Servings:4
Cooking Time:10 Minutes

Ingredients:
- 2 tbsp olive oil
- ½ cup brown rice
- 1 lb watercress
- 1 Roma tomato, sliced
- 4 oz feta cheese, crumbled
- 2 tbsp fresh basil, chopped
- Salt and black pepper to taste
- 2 tbsp lemon juice
- ¼ tsp lemon zest

Directions:
1. Bring to a boil salted water in a pot over medium heat. Add in the rice and cook for 15-18 minutes. Drain and let cool completely. Whisk the olive oil, lemon zest, lemon juice, salt, and pepper in a salad bowl. Add in the watercress, cooled rice, and basil and toss to coat. Top with feta cheese and tomato. Serve immediately.

Nutrition Info:
- Per Serving: Calories: 480;Fat: 24g;Protein: 14g;Carbs: 55g.

Sides , Salads, And Soups Recipes

Spinach & Pea Salad With Rice

Servings:2
Cooking Time:30 Minutes

Ingredients:

- 1 tbsp olive oil
- Salt and black pepper to taste
- ½ cup baby spinach
- ½ cup green peas, blanched
- 1 garlic clove, minced
- ½ cup white rice, rinsed
- 6 cherry tomatoes, halved
- 1 tbsp parsley, chopped
- 2 tbsp Italian salad dressing

Directions:

1. Bring a large pot of salted water to a boil over medium heat. Pour in the rice, cover, and simmer on low heat for 15-18 minutes or until the rice is al dente. Drain and let cool.
2. In a bowl, whisk the olive oil, garlic, salt, and black pepper. Toss the green peas, baby spinach, and rice together. Pour the dressing all over and gently stir to combine. Decorate with cherry tomatoes and parsley and serve. Enjoy!

Nutrition Info:

- Per Serving: Calories: 160;Fat: 14g;Protein: 4g;Carbs: 9g.

Cucumber & Spelt Salad With Chicken

Servings:4
Cooking Time:35 Minutes

Ingredients:

- 4 tbsp olive oil
- ½ lb chicken breasts
- 1 tbsp dill, chopped
- 2 lemons, zested
- Juice of 2 lemons
- 3 tbsp parsley, chopped
- Salt and black pepper to taste
- 1 cup spelt grains
- 1 red leaf lettuce heads, torn
- 1 red onion, sliced
- 10 cherry tomatoes, halved
- 1 cucumber, sliced

Directions:

1. In a bowl, combine dill, lemon zest, lemon juice, 2 tbsp olive oil, parsley, salt, and pepper and mix well. Add in chicken breasts, toss to coat, cover, and refrigerate for 30 minutes. Place spelt grains in a pot and cover with water. Stir in salt and pepper. Put over medium heat and bring to a boil. Cook for 45 minutes and drain. Transfer to a bowl and let it cool.
2. Preheat the grill. Remove the chicken and grill for 12 minutes on all sides. Transfer to a bowl to cool before slicing. Once the spelt is cooled, add in the remaining olive oil, lettuce, onion, tomatoes, and cucumber and toss to coat. Top the salad with sliced chicken and serve.

Nutrition Info:

- Per Serving: Calories: 350;Fat: 18g;Protein: 27g;Carbs: 28g.

Cauliflower Soup With Pancetta Crisps

Servings:4
Cooking Time:50 Minutes

Ingredients:

- 2 tbsp olive oil
- 4 oz pancetta, cubed
- 5 oz cauliflower florets
- 1 yellow onion, chopped
- Salt and black pepper to taste
- 4 cups chicken stock
- 1 tsp mustard powder
- 2 garlic cloves, minced
- ½ cup mozzarella, shredded

Directions:

1. Place a saucepan over medium heat and add in the pancetta. Cook it until crispy, about 4 minutes, and set aside.
2. Add olive oil, onion, and garlic to the pot and cook for 3 minutes. Pour in chicken stock, cauliflower, mustard powder, salt, and pepper and cook for 20 minutes. Using an immersion blender, purée the soup and stir in the mozzarella cheese. Serve immediately topped with pancetta croutons.

Nutrition Info:

- Per Serving: Calories: 250;Fat: 18g;Protein: 14g;Carbs: 42g.

Seafood Fideuà

Servings:4
Cooking Time:35 Minutes

Ingredients:

- 2 tbsp olive oil
- ½ lb squid rings
- 1 lb mussels, cleaned
- ½ lb shrimp, deveined
- ½ tsp saffron
- 16 oz vermicelli pasta
- 1 yellow onion, chopped
- 1 tsp paprika
- 1 red bell pepper, chopped
- 3 garlic cloves, minced
- ½ cup tomatoes, crushed
- 4 cups fish stock
- 2 tbsp parsley, chopped
- 1 lemon cut into wedges
- Salt and black pepper to taste

Directions:

1. In a dry saucepan over medium heat, toast the vermicelli, shaking often until pale, 2 to 3 minutes; reserve. Warm the olive oil in the same saucepan and sauté onion, garlic, bell pepper for 5 minutes. Add in the squid and cook for 5 minutes. Stir in the tomatoes, paprika, and fish stock. Bring to a boil and add the saffron; stir. Lower the heat, cover, and simmer for 15 minutes. Add the vermicelli, shrimp, and mussels and simmer for 5 minutes. Discard any unopened mussels. Adjust the taste and sprinkle with parsley. Serve warm with lemon wedges.

Nutrition Info:

- Per Serving: Calories: 200;Fat: 9g;Protein: 27g;Carbs: 5g.

Turkey Egg Soup With Rice

Servings:4
Cooking Time:40 Minutes

Ingredients:

- 2 tbsp olive oil
- 1 lb turkey breasts, cubed
- ½ cup Arborio rice
- 1 onion, chopped
- 1 celery stalk, chopped
- 1 carrot, sliced
- 1 egg
- 2 tbsp yogurt
- 1 tsp dried tarragon
- 1 tsp lemon zest
- 2 tbsp fresh parsley, chopped
- Salt and black pepper to taste

Directions:

1. Heat olive oil in a pot over medium heat and sauté the onion, celery, turkey, and carrot for 6-7 minutes, stirring occasionally. Stir in the rice for 1-2 minutes, pour in 4 cups of water, and season with salt and pepper. Bring the soup to a boil. Lower the heat and simmer for 20 minutes.

2. In a bowl, beat the egg with yogurt until well combined. Remove 1 cup of the hot soup broth with a spoon and add slowly to the egg mixture, stirring constantly. Pour the whisked mixture into the pot and stir in salt, black pepper, tarragon, and lemon zest. Garnish with parsley and serve.

Nutrition Info:

- Per Serving: Calories: 303;Fat: 11g;Protein: 23g;Carbs: 28g.

Bell Pepper & Lentil Salad With Tomatoes

Servings:4
Cooking Time:10 Minutes

Ingredients:

- 2 tomatoes, chopped
- 1 green bell pepper, chopped
- 14 oz canned lentils, drained
- 2 spring onions, chopped
- 1 red bell pepper, chopped
- 2 tbsp cilantro, chopped
- 2 tsp balsamic vinegar

Directions:

1. Mix lentils, spring onions, tomatoes, bell peppers, cilantro, and vinegar in a bowl. Serve immediately.

Nutrition Info:

- Per Serving: Calories: 210;Fat: 3g;Protein: 7g;Carbs: 12g.

Moroccan Lamb Soup

Servings:4
Cooking Time:40 Minutes

Ingredients:

- 2 tbsp olive oil
- 2 carrots, chopped
- 1 red onion, chopped
- 2 celery stalks, chopped
- 2 garlic cloves, minced
- 1 tbsp thyme, chopped
- 4 cups vegetable stock
- 1 cup mushrooms, sliced
- 8 oz leftover lamb, shredded
- 14 oz canned chickpeas
- 2 tbsp cilantro, chopped

Directions:

1. Warm the olive oil in a pot over medium heat and cook onion, garlic, celery, mushrooms, carrots, and thyme for 5 minutes until tender. Stir in vegetable stock and lamb and bring to a boil. Reduce the heat to low and simmer for 20

minutes. Mix in chickpeas and cook for an additional 5 minutes. Ladle your soup into individual bowls. Top with cilantro.

Nutrition Info:
- Per Serving: Calories: 300;Fat: 12g;Protein: 15g;Carbs: 23g.

Brussels Sprout And Apple Slaw

Servings:4
Cooking Time: 0 Minutes

Ingredients:
- Salad:
- 1 pound Brussels sprouts, stem ends removed and sliced thinly
- 1 apple, cored and sliced thinly
- ½ red onion, sliced thinly
- Dressing:
- 1 teaspoon Dijon mustard
- 2 teaspoons apple cider vinegar
- 1 tablespoon raw honey
- 1 cup plain coconut yogurt
- 1 teaspoon sea salt
- For Garnish:
- ½ cup pomegranate seeds
- ½ cup chopped toasted hazelnuts

Directions:
1. Combine the ingredients for the salad in a large salad bowl, then toss to combine well.
2. Combine the ingredients for the dressing in a small bowl, then stir to mix well.
3. Dressing the salad. Let sit for 30 minutes, then serve with pomegranate seeds and toasted hazelnuts on top.

Nutrition Info:
- Per Serving: Calories: 248;Fat: 11.2g;Protein: 12.7g;-Carbs: 29.9g.

Cherry & Pine Nut Couscous

Servings:6
Cooking Time:10 Minutes

Ingredients:
- 2 tbsp olive oil
- 3 cups hot water
- 1 cup couscous
- ½ cup pine nuts, roasted
- ½ cup dry cherries, chopped
- ½ cup parsley, chopped
- Salt and black pepper to taste
- 1 tbsp lime juice

Directions:
1. Place couscous and hot water in a bowl and let sit for 10 minutes. Fluff with a fork and remove to a bowl. Stir in pine nuts, cherries, parsley, salt, pepper, lime juice, and olive oil.

Nutrition Info:
- Per Serving: Calories: 220;Fat: 8g;Protein: 6g;Carbs: 9g.

Simple Tuna Salad

Servings:2
Cooking Time:10 Minutes

Ingredients:
- 2 tbsp olive oil
- ½ iceberg lettuce, torn
- ¼ endive, chopped
- 1 tomato, cut into wedges
- 5 oz canned tuna, flaked
- 4 black olives, sliced
- 1 tbsp lemon juice
- Salt and black pepper to taste

Directions:
1. In a salad bowl, mix olive oil, lemon juice, salt, and pepper. Add in lettuce, endive, and tuna and toss to coat. Top with black olives and tomato wedges and serve.

Nutrition Info:
- Per Serving: Calories: 260;Fat: 18g;Protein: 11g;Carbs: 3g.

Cream Cheese Stuffed Cherry Tomatoes

Servings:6
Cooking Time:10 Minutes

Ingredients:
- 2 tbsp fresh dill, chopped
- 30 cherry tomatoes
- 3 oz cream cheese, softened
- ¼ cup mayonnaise
- 2 tbsp roasted garlic paste
- 3 tbsp grated Parmesan cheese

Directions:
1. Cut off the top of the cherry tomatoes. Discard the seeds and core with a small teaspoon. Drain upside down on paper towels. Beat the cream cheese in a small bowl until soft and fluffy. Add mayonnaise, roasted garlic paste, and Parmesan cheese; beat well. Divide the mixture between the cherry tomatoes and sprinkle with dill. Serve immediately.

Nutrition Info:
- Per Serving: Calories: 160;Fat: 11g;Protein: 7g;Carbs: 10g.

Green Bean And Halloumi Salad

Servings:2
Cooking Time: 5 Minutes

Ingredients:
- Dressing:
- ¼ cup unsweetened coconut milk
- 1 tablespoon olive oil
- 2 teaspoons freshly squeezed lemon juice
- ¼ teaspoon garlic powder
- ¼ teaspoon onion powder
- Pinch salt
- Pinch freshly ground black pepper
- Salad:
- ½ pound fresh green beans, trimmed
- 2 ounces Halloumi cheese, sliced into 2 (½-inch-thick) slices
- ½ cup halved cherry or grape tomatoes
- ¼ cup thinly sliced sweet onion

Directions:
1. Make the Dressing
2. Combine the coconut milk, olive oil, lemon juice, onion powder, garlic powder, salt, and pepper in a small bowl and whisk well. Set aside.
3. Make the Salad
4. Fill a medium-size pot with about 1 inch of water and add the green beans. Cover and steam them for about 3 to 4 minutes, or just until beans are tender. Do not overcook. Drain beans, rinse them immediately with cold water, and set them aside to cool.
5. Heat a nonstick skillet over medium-high heat and place the slices of Halloumi in the hot pan. After about 2 minutes, check to see if the cheese is golden on the bottom. If it is, flip the slices and cook for another minute or until the second side is golden.
6. Remove cheese from the pan and cut each piece into cubes.
7. Place the green beans, halloumi slices, tomatoes, and onion in a large bowl and toss to combine.
8. Drizzle the dressing over the salad and toss well to combine. Serve immediately.

Nutrition Info:
- Per Serving: Calories: 274;Fat: 18.1g;Protein: 8.0g;-Carbs: 16.8g.

Summer Gazpacho

Servings:6
Cooking Time:15 Minutes

Ingredients:
- ⅓ cup extra-virgin olive oil
- ½ cup of water
- 2 bread slices, torn
- 2 lb ripe tomatoes, seeded
- 1 cucumber, chopped

- 1 clove garlic, finely chopped
- ½ red onion, diced
- 2 tbsp red wine vinegar
- 1 tbsp fresh thyme, chopped
- Salt to taste

Directions:
1. Put the bread in 1 cup of water mixed with 1 tbsp of vinegar and salt to soak for 5 minutes. Then, blend the soaked bread, tomatoes, cucumber, garlic, red onion, olive oil, vinegar, thyme, and salt in your food processor until completely smooth. Pour the soup into a glass container and store in the fridge until chilled. Serve drizzled with olive oil.

Nutrition Info:
- Per Serving: Calories: 163;Fat: 13g;Protein: 2g;Carbs: 12.4g.

Fennel Salad With Olives & Hazelnuts

Servings:4
Cooking Time:5 Minutes

Ingredients:
- 2 tbsp olive oil
- 8 dates, pitted and sliced
- 2 fennel bulbs, sliced
- 2 tbsp chives, chopped
- ½ cup hazelnuts, chopped
- 2 tbsp lime juice
- Salt and black pepper to taste
- 40 green olives, chopped

Directions:
1. Place fennel, dates, chives, hazelnuts, lime juice, olives, olive oil, salt, and pepper in a bowl and toss to combine.

Nutrition Info:
- Per Serving: Calories: 210;Fat: 8g;Protein: 5g;Carbs: 15g.

Fruit Salad With Sesame Seeds & Nuts

Servings:4
Cooking Time:15 Minutes

Ingredients:
- ¼ cup extra-virgin olive oil
- 2 apples, peeled and sliced
- 1 tbsp lemon juice
- 1 orange, peeled and diced
- ½ cup sliced strawberries
- ½ cup shredded coleslaw mix
- ½ cup walnut halves
- ¼ cup slivered almonds
- ¼ cup balsamic vinegar
- 2 tbsp sesame seeds
- Salt and black pepper to taste

Directions:
1. Place the apples and lemon juice in a bowl and toss to

prevent browning. Add the orange, strawberries, coleslaw mix, walnuts, and almonds and toss well to mix. In a bowl, whisk together the balsamic vinegar and olive oil and season with salt and pepper. Pour the dressing over the salad and toss to coat. Top with sesame seeds and serve.

Nutrition Info:
- Per Serving: Calories: 299;Fat: 17g;Protein: 8g;Carbs: 44g.

Chorizo & Fire-roasted Tomato Soup

Servings:4
Cooking Time:25 Minutes

Ingredients:
- 28 oz fire-roasted diced tomatoes
- 1 tbsp olive oil
- 2 shallots, chopped
- 3 cloves garlic, minced
- Salt and black pepper to taste
- 4 cups beef broth
- ½ cup fresh ripe tomatoes
- 1 tbsp red wine vinegar
- 3 chorizo sausage, chopped
- ½ cup thinly chopped basil

Directions:
1. Warm the olive oil on Sauté in your Instant Pot. Cook the chorizo until crispy, stirring occasionally, about 5 minutes. Remove to a plate. Add the garlic and shallots to the pot and sauté for 3 minutes until soft. Season with salt and pepper.
2. Stir in red wine vinegar, broth, diced tomatoes, and ripe tomatoes. Seal the lid and cook on High Pressure for 8 minutes. Release the pressure quickly. Pour the soup into a blender and process until smooth. Divide into bowls, top with chorizo, and decorate with basil.

Nutrition Info:
- Per Serving: Calories: 771;Fat: 27g;Protein: 40g;Carbs: 117g.

Arugula & Caper Green Salad

Servings:4
Cooking Time:10 Minutes

Ingredients:
- 1 tbsp olive oil
- 10 green olives, sliced
- 4 cups baby arugula
- 1 tbsp capers, drained
- 1 tbsp balsamic vinegar
- 1 tsp lemon zest, grated
- 1 tbsp lemon juice
- 1 tsp parsley, chopped
- Salt and black pepper to taste

Directions:

1. Mix capers, olives, vinegar, lemon zest, lemon juice, oil, parsley, salt, pepper, and arugula in a bowl. Serve.

Nutrition Info:
- Per Serving: Calories: 160;Fat: 4g;Protein: 5g;Carbs: 4g.

Cucumber Salad With Mustard Dressing

Servings:4
Cooking Time:15 Minutes

Ingredients:
- 2 tbsp extra-virgin olive oil
- 2 cucumbers, chopped
- 1 red chili pepper, sliced
- 2 tbsp chives, chopped
- ¼ cup red wine vinegar
- 2 garlic cloves, minced
- 1 tsp yellow mustard
- ¼ tsp honey
- Salt and black pepper to taste

Directions:
1. Combine the cucumber, chili pepper, and chives in a bowl. Mix olive oil, honey, garlic, vinegar, mustard, salt, and pepper in another bowl. Pour over the salad and toss to combine.

Nutrition Info:
- Per Serving: Calories: 118;Fat: 7.5g;Protein: 2.5g;Carbs: 13g.

Party Summer Salad

Servings:4
Cooking Time:10 Minutes

Ingredients:
- ½ cup extra virgin olive oil
- 2 cucumbers, sliced
- 2 mixed bell peppers, sliced
- 2 tomatoes, sliced
- 2 green onions, thinly sliced
- 2 gem lettuces, sliced
- 1 cup arugula
- 2 tbsp parsley, chopped
- Salt to taste
- 1 cup feta cheese, crumbled
- 3 tbsp lemon juice

Directions:
1. In a bowl, mix the cucumbers, bell peppers, green onions, gem lettuce, and arugula. In a small bowl, whisk the olive oil, lemon juice, and salt. Pour over the salad and toss to coat. Scatter the feta over and top with tomato and parsley.

Nutrition Info:
- Per Serving: Calories: 398;Fat: 34g;Protein: 19g;Carbs: 20g.

Favorite Green Bean Stir-fry

Servings:4
Cooking Time:15 Minutes

Ingredients:
- 1 tbsp olive oil
- 1 tbsp butter
- 1 fennel bulb, sliced
- 1 red onion, sliced
- 4 cloves garlic, pressed
- 1 lb green beans, steamed
- ½ tsp dried oregano
- 2 tbsp balsamic vinegar
- Salt and black pepper to taste

Directions:
1. Heat the butter and olive oil a saucepan over medium heat. Add in the onion and garlic and sauté for 3 minutes. Stir in oregano, fennel, balsamic vinegar, salt, and pepper. Stir-fry for another 6-8 minutes and add in the green beans; cook for 2-3 minutes. Adjust the seasoning and serve.

Nutrition Info:
- Per Serving: Calories: 126;Fat: 6g;Protein: 3.3g;Carbs: 16.6g.

Easy Roasted Cauliflower

Servings:2
Cooking Time: 20 Minutes

Ingredients:
- ½ large head cauliflower, stemmed and broken into florets
- 1 tablespoon olive oil
- 2 tablespoons freshly squeezed lemon juice
- 2 tablespoons tahini
- 1 teaspoon harissa paste
- Pinch salt

Directions:
1. Preheat the oven to 400ºF. Line a sheet pan with parchment paper.
2. Toss the cauliflower florets with the olive oil in a large bowl and transfer to the sheet pan.
3. Roast in the preheated oven for 15 minutes, flipping the cauliflower once or twice, or until it starts to become golden.
4. Meanwhile, in a separate bowl, combine the lemon juice, tahini, harissa, and salt and stir to mix well.
5. Remove the pan from the oven and toss the cauliflower with the lemon tahini sauce. Return to the oven and roast for another 5 minutes. Serve hot.

Nutrition Info:
- Per Serving: Calories: 205;Fat: 15.0g;Protein: 4.0g;-Carbs: 15.0g.

Sautéed White Beans With Rosemary

Servings:2
Cooking Time: 12 Minutes

Ingredients:
- 1 tablespoon olive oil
- 2 garlic cloves, minced
- 1 can white cannellini beans, drained and rinsed
- 1 teaspoon minced fresh rosemary plus 1 whole fresh rosemary sprig
- ¼ teaspoon dried sage
- ½ cup low-sodium chicken stock
- Salt, to taste

Directions:
1. Heat the olive oil in a saucepan over medium-high heat.
2. Add the garlic and sauté for 30 seconds until fragrant.
3. Add the beans, minced and whole rosemary, sage, and chicken stock and bring the mixture to a boil.
4. Reduce the heat to medium and allow to simmer for 10 minutes, or until most of the liquid is evaporated. If desired, mash some of the beans with a fork to thicken them.
5. Season with salt to taste. Remove the rosemary sprig before serving.

Nutrition Info:
- Per Serving: Calories: 155;Fat: 7.0g;Protein: 6.0g;Carbs: 17.0g.

Corn & Cucumber Salad

Servings:4
Cooking Time:10 Minutes

Ingredients:
- 3 tbsp olive oil
- 3 tbsp pepitas, roasted
- 2 tbsp cilantro, chopped
- 1 cup corn
- 1 cup radishes, sliced
- 2 avocados, mashed
- 2 cucumbers, chopped
- 2 tbsp Greek yogurt
- 1 tsp balsamic vinegar
- 2 tbsp lime juice
- Salt and black pepper to taste

Directions:
1. In a bowl, whisk the olive oil, avocados, salt, pepper, lime juice, yogurt, and vinegar until smooth. Combine pepitas, cilantro, corn, radishes, and cucumbers in a salad bowl. Pour the avocado dressing over salad and toss to combine. Serve.

Nutrition Info:
- Per Serving: Calories: 410;Fat: 32g;Protein: 4g;Carbs: 25g.

Tuscan-style Panzanella Salad

Servings:4
Cooking Time:25 Minutes

Ingredients:
- 2 cups mixed cherry tomatoes, quartered
- 4 bread slices, crusts removed, cubed
- 4 tbsp extra-virgin olive oil
- 1 cucumber, sliced
- ½ red onion, thinly sliced
- ¼ cup chopped fresh basil
- ½ tsp dried oregano
- 1 tbsp capers
- 1 garlic clove, minced
- ¼ cup red wine vinegar
- 2 anchovy fillets, chopped
- Salt and black pepper to taste

Directions:
1. Preheat oven to 320 F. Pour the bread cubes into a baking dish and drizzle with 2 tbsp of olive oil. Bake for 6-8 minutes, shaking occasionally until browned and crisp. Let cool. Toss the cooled bread, cherry tomatoes, cucumber, red onion, basil, anchovies, and capers in a serving dish.
2. In another bowl, whisk the remaining olive oil, oregano, red wine vinegar, and garlic. Adjust the seasoning with salt and pepper. Drizzle the dressing over the salad and toss to coat.

Nutrition Info:
- Per Serving: Calories: 228;Fat: 21.6g;Protein: 2g;Carbs: 8.2g.

Authentic Marinara Sauce

Servings:6
Cooking Time:46 Minutes

Ingredients:
- 2 cans crushed tomatoes with their juices
- 1 tsp dried oregano
- 2 tbsp + ¼ cup olive oil
- 2 tbsp butter
- 1 small onion, diced
- 1 red bell pepper, chopped
- 4 garlic cloves, minced
- Salt and black pepper to taste
- ½ cup thinly sliced basil
- 2 tbsp chopped rosemary
- 1 tsp red pepper flakes

Directions:
1. Warm 2 tablespoons olive oil and butter in a large skillet over medium heat. Add the onion, garlic, and red pepper and sauté for about 5 minutes until tender. Season with salt and pepper. Reduce the heat to low and add the tomatoes and their juices, remaining olive oil, oregano, half of the basil, rosemary, and red pepper flakes. Bring to a simmer and cover. Cook for 50-60 minutes. Blitz the sauce with an immersion blender and sprinkle with the remaining basil.

Nutrition Info:
- Per Serving: Calories: 265;Fat: 19;Protein: 4.1g;Carbs: 18g.

Radicchio Salad With Sunflower Seeds

Servings:4
Cooking Time:10 Minutes

Ingredients:
- 3 tbsp olive oil
- 1 cup radicchio, shredded
- 1 lettuce head, torn
- 1 cup raisins
- 2 tbsp lemon juice
- ¼ cup chives, chopped
- Salt and black pepper to taste
- 1 tbsp sunflower seeds, toasted

Directions:
1. Mix olive oil, raisins, lemon juice, chives, radicchio, salt, pepper, lettuce, and sunflower seeds in a bowl. Serve.

Nutrition Info:
- Per Serving: Calories: 70;Fat: 3g;Protein: 1g;Carbs: 3g.

Asparagus & Red Onion Side Dish

Servings:6
Cooking Time:20 Minutes

Ingredients:
- 2 tbsp olive oil
- 1 ½ lb asparagus spears
- 1 tsp garlic powder
- 1 red onion, sliced
- Salt and black pepper to taste

Directions:
1. Preheat oven to 390 F. Brush the asparagus with olive oil. Toss with garlic powder, salt, and black pepper. Roast in the oven for about 15 minutes. Top the roasted asparagus with the red onion. Serve and enjoy!

Nutrition Info:
- Per Serving: Calories: 129;Fat: 3g;Protein: 3g;Carbs: 7g.

Chicken & Barley Soup

Servings: 4
Cooking Time: 40 Minutes

Ingredients:
- 2 tbsp olive oil
- 1 lb boneless chicken thighs
- ¼ cup pearl barley
- 1 red onion, chopped
- 2 cloves garlic, minced
- 4 cups chicken broth
- ¼ tsp oregano
- ½ lemon, juiced
- ¼ tsp parsley
- ¼ cup scallions, chopped
- Salt and black pepper to taste

Directions:
1. Heat the olive oil in a pot over medium heat and sweat the onion and garlic for 2-3 minutes until tender. Place in chicken thighs and cook for 5-6 minutes, stirring often.
2. Pour in chicken broth and barley and bring to a boil. Then lower the heat and simmer for 5 minutes. Remove the chicken and shred it with two forks. Return to the pot and add in lemon, oregano, and parsley. Simmer for 20-22 more minutes. Stir in shredded chicken and adjust the seasoning. Divide between 4 bowls and top with chopped scallions.

Nutrition Info:
- Per Serving: Calories: 373;Fat: 17g;Protein: 39g;Carbs: 14g.

Marinated Mushrooms And Olives

Servings: 8
Cooking Time: 0 Minutes

Ingredients:
- 1 pound white button mushrooms, rinsed and drained
- 1 pound fresh olives
- ½ tablespoon crushed fennel seeds
- 1 tablespoon white wine vinegar
- 2 tablespoons fresh thyme leaves
- Pinch chili flakes
- Sea salt and freshly ground pepper, to taste
- 2 tablespoons extra-virgin olive oil

Directions:
1. Combine all the ingredients in a large bowl. Toss to mix well.
2. Wrap the bowl in plastic and refrigerate for at least 1 hour to marinate.
3. Remove the bowl from the refrigerate and let sit under room temperature for 10 minutes, then serve.

Nutrition Info:
- Per Serving: Calories: 111;Fat: 9.7g;Protein: 2.4g;Carbs: 5.9g.

Cheesy Roasted Broccolini

Servings: 2
Cooking Time: 10 Minutes

Ingredients:
- 1 bunch broccolini
- 1 tablespoon olive oil
- ½ teaspoon garlic powder
- ¼ teaspoon salt
- 2 tablespoons grated Romano cheese

Directions:
1. Preheat the oven to 400ºF. Line a sheet pan with parchment paper.
2. Slice the tough ends off the broccolini and put in a medium bowl. Add the olive oil, garlic powder, and salt and toss to coat well. Arrange the broccolini on the prepared sheet pan.
3. Roast in the preheated oven for 7 minutes, flipping halfway through the cooking time.
4. Remove the pan from the oven and sprinkle the cheese over the broccolini. Using tongs, carefully flip the broccolini over to coat all sides.
5. Return to the oven and cook for an additional 2 to 3 minutes, or until the cheese melts and starts to turn golden. Serve warm.

Nutrition Info:
- Per Serving: Calories: 114;Fat: 9.0g;Protein: 4.0g;Carbs: 5.0g.

Homemade Lebanese Bulgur Salad

Servings: 4
Cooking Time: 20 Min + Cooling Time

Ingredients:
- ½ cup olive oil
- 2 cups fresh parsley, chopped
- ¼ cup mint leaves, chopped
- ½ cup bulgur
- 4 tomatoes, chopped
- 4 spring onions, chopped
- 1 tbsp lemon juice
- 2 tsp sumac
- Salt and black pepper to taste

Directions:
1. Place 1 cup of water in a pot over medium heat and bring to a boil. Add in the bulgur and cook for 10-12 minutes. Let chill in a bowl. When cooled, stir in tomatoes, spring onions, sumac, black pepper, and salt. Drizzle with lemon juice and olive oil and toss to coat. Top with mint and parsley to serve.

Nutrition Info:
- Per Serving: Calories: 451;Fat: 27g;Protein: 11g;Carbs: 48g.

Orange-honey Glazed Carrots

Servings: 2
Cooking Time: 15 To 20 Minutes

Ingredients:
- ½ pound rainbow carrots, peeled
- 2 tablespoons fresh orange juice
- 1 tablespoon honey
- ½ teaspoon coriander
- Pinch salt

Directions:
1. Preheat the oven to 400ºF.
2. Cut the carrots lengthwise into slices of even thickness and place in a large bowl.
3. Stir together the orange juice, honey, coriander, and salt in a small bowl. Pour the orange juice mixture over the carrots and toss until well coated.
4. Spread the carrots in a baking dish in a single layer. Roast for 15 to 20 minutes until fork-tender.
5. Let cool for 5 minutes before serving.

Nutrition Info:
- Per Serving: Calories: 85;Fat: 0g;Protein: 1.0g;Carbs: 21.0g.

Divine Fennel & Zucchini Salad

Servings: 4
Cooking Time: 10 Minutes

Ingredients:
- 2 tbsp olive oil
- 1 cup fennel bulb, sliced
- 1 red onion, sliced
- 2 zucchinis, cut into ribbons
- Salt and black pepper to taste
- 2 tsp white wine vinegar
- 1 tsp lemon juice

Directions:
1. In a large bowl, combine fennel, zucchini, red onion, salt, pepper, olive oil, vinegar, and lemon juice and toss to coat.

Nutrition Info:
- Per Serving: Calories: 200;Fat: 4g;Protein: 3g;Carbs: 4g.

Arugula And Fig Salad

Servings: 2
Cooking Time: 0 Minutes

Ingredients:
- 3 cups arugula
- 4 fresh, ripe figs, stemmed and sliced
- 2 tablespoons olive oil
- ¼ cup lightly toasted pecan halves
- 2 tablespoons crumbled blue cheese
- 1 to 2 tablespoons balsamic glaze

Directions:
1. Toss the arugula and figs with the olive oil in a large bowl until evenly coated.
2. Add the pecans and blue cheese to the bowl. Toss the salad lightly.
3. Drizzle with the balsamic glaze and serve immediately.

Nutrition Info:
- Per Serving: Calories: 517;Fat: 36.2g;Protein: 18.9g;-Carbs: 30.2g.

Garlic Wilted Greens

Servings: 2
Cooking Time: 5 Minutes

Ingredients:
- 1 tablespoon olive oil
- 2 garlic cloves, minced
- 3 cups sliced greens (spinach, chard, beet greens, dandelion greens, or a combination)
- Pinch salt
- Pinch red pepper flakes (or more to taste)

Directions:
1. Heat the olive oil in a skillet over medium-high heat.
2. Add garlic and sauté for 30 seconds, or just until fragrant.
3. Add the greens, salt, and pepper flakes and stir to combine. Let the greens wilt, but do not overcook.
4. Remove from the skillet and serve on a plate.

Nutrition Info:
- Per Serving: Calories: 93;Fat: 6.8g;Protein: 1.2g;Carbs: 7.3g.

Spanish Lentil Soup With Rice

Servings:4
Cooking Time:30 Minutes

Ingredients:

- 2 tbsp olive oil
- ½ cup red lentils, rinsed
- ½ cup Spanish rice
- 4 cups vegetable stock
- Salt to taste
- 1 onion, finely chopped
- 2 garlic cloves, sliced
- 1 carrot, finely diced
- 1 tsp turmeric
- 4 sage leaves, chopped

Directions:

1. Heat the olive oil in a stockpot over medium heat. Sauté the onion, carrot, and garlic for 5 minutes until the onion and garlic are golden brown. Stir in the turmeric for 1 minute. Pour in stock, lentils, rice, and salt. Simmer for 15-20 minutes, stirring occasionally. Serve the soup garnished with chopped sage leaves.

Nutrition Info:

- Per Serving: Calories: 230;Fat: 7.2g;Protein: 9g;Carbs: 36.8g.

Minty Bulgur With Fried Halloumi

Servings:4
Cooking Time:35 Minutes

Ingredients:

- 2 tbsp olive oil
- 4 halloumi cheese slices
- 1 cup bulgur
- 1 cup parsley, chopped
- ¼ cup mint, chopped
- 3 tbsp lemon juice
- 1 red onion, sliced
- Salt and black pepper to taste

Directions:

1. Bring to a boil a pot of water over medium heat. Add in bulgur and simmer for 15 minutes. Drain and let it cool in a bowl. Stir in parsley, mint, lemon juice, onion, salt, and pepper. Warm half of olive oil in a pan over medium heat. Cook the halloumi for 4-5 minutes on both sides until golden. Arrange the fried cheese on top of the bulgur and serve.

Nutrition Info:

- Per Serving: Calories: 330;Fat: 12g;Protein: 28g;Carbs: 31g.

Sun-dried Tomato & Spinach Pasta Salad

Servings:4
Cooking Time:45 Min + Cooling Time

Ingredients:

- 1 ½ cups farfalle
- 1 cup chopped baby spinach, rinsed and dried
- 8 sun-dried tomatoes, sliced
- 1 carrot, grated
- 2 scallions, thinly sliced
- 1 garlic clove, minced
- 1 dill pickle, diced
- ⅔ cup extra-virgin olive oil
- 1 tbsp red wine vinegar
- 1 tbsp lemon juice
- ½ cup Greek yogurt
- 1 tsp chopped fresh oregano
- Salt and black pepper to taste
- 1 cup feta cheese, crumbled

Directions:

1. Bring a large pot of salted water to a boil, add the farfalle, and cook for 7-9 minutes until al dente. Drain the pasta and set aside to cool. In a large bowl, combine spinach, sun-dried tomatoes, carrot, scallions, garlic, and pickle. Add pasta and toss to combine. In a medium bowl, whisk olive oil, vinegar, lemon juice, yogurt, oregano, pepper, and salt. Add dressing to pasta and toss to coat. Sprinkle with feta cheese and serve.

Nutrition Info:

- Per Serving: Calories: 239;Fat: 14g;Protein: 8g;Carbs: 20g.

Bell Pepper & Roasted Cabbage Salad

Servings:4
Cooking Time:35 Minutes

Ingredients:
- 1 head green cabbage, shredded
- 4 tbsp olive oil
- 1 carrot, julienned
- ½ red bell pepper, seeded and julienned
- ½ green bell pepper, julienned
- 1 cucumber, shredded
- 1 shallot, sliced
- 2 tbsp parsley, chopped
- 1 tsp Dijon mustard
- 1 lemon, juiced
- 1 tsp mayonnaise
- Salt to taste

Directions:
1. Preheat the oven to 380 F. Season the green cabbage with salt and drizzle with some olive oil. Transfer to a baking dish and roast for 20-25 minutes, stirring often. Remove to a bowl and let cool for a few minutes. Stir in carrot, bell peppers, shallot, cucumber, and parsley. In another bowl, add the remaining olive oil, lemon juice, mustard, mayonnaise, and salt and whisk until well mixed. Drizzle over the cabbage mixture and toss to coat. Serve.

Nutrition Info:
- Per Serving: Calories: 195;Fat: 15g;Protein: 3.2g;Carbs: 16g.

Creamy Roasted Red Pepper Soup With Feta

Servings:6
Cooking Time:30 Minutes

Ingredients:
- 8 roasted red peppers, chopped
- 2 roasted chili peppers, chopped
- 3 tbsp olive oil
- 2 shallots, chopped
- 4 garlic cloves, minced
- 2 tsp chopped fresh oregano
- 6 cups chicken broth
- Salt and black pepper to taste
- ¼ cup heavy cream
- 1 lemon, juiced
- ½ cup feta cheese, crumbled

Directions:
1. Puree all of the roasted peppers in your food processor until smooth. Warm the olive oil in a pot over medium heat and add the shallots and garlic. Cook until soft and translucent, about 5 minutes. Add the pepper mixture and oregano, followed by the broth. Bring to a boil on high heat and sprinkle with salt and pepper. Lower the heat to low and simmer for 15 minutes. Stir in the heavy cream and lemon juice. Ladle into individual bowls and garnish with feta. Serve immediately.

Nutrition Info:
- Per Serving: Calories: 223;Fat: 6g;Protein: 11g;Carbs: 31g.

Horiatiki Salad (greek Salad)

Servings:4
Cooking Time:10 Minutes

Ingredients:
- 1 green bell pepper, cut into chunks
- 1 head romaine lettuce, torn
- ½ red onion, cut into rings
- 2 tomatoes, cut into wedges
- 1 cucumber, thinly sliced
- 3 tbsp extra-virgin olive oil
- 2 tbsp lemon juice
- Garlic salt and pepper to taste
- ¼ tsp dried Greek oregano
- 1 cup feta cheese, cubed
- 1 handful of Kalamata olives

Directions:
1. In a salad bowl, whisk the olive oil, lemon juice, pepper, garlic salt, and oregano. Add in the lettuce, red onion, tomatoes, cucumber, and bell pepper and mix with your hands to coat. Top with feta and olives and serve immediately.

Nutrition Info:
- Per Serving: Calories: 226;Fat: 19g;Protein: 8g;Carbs: 9g.

Lamb & Spinach Soup

Servings:4
Cooking Time:60 Minutes

Ingredients:
- ½ lb lamb shoulder, cut into bite-sized pieces
- 2 tbsp olive oil
- 1 onion, chopped
- 2 garlic cloves, minced
- 10 oz spinach, chopped
- 4 cups vegetable broth
- Salt and black pepper to taste

Directions:
1. Warm the olive oil on Sauté in your Instant Pot. Sauté the lamb, onion, and garlic for 6-8 minutes, stirring often. Pour in the broth and adjust the seasoning with salt and pepper. Seal the lid, press Soup/Broth, and cook for 30 minutes on High Pressure. Do a natural pressure release for 10 minutes. Press Sauté and add the spinach. Cook for 5 minutes. Serve.

Nutrition Info:
- Per Serving: Calories: 188;Fat: 12g;Protein: 14g;Carbs: 9g.

Cucumber & Tomato Salad With Anchovies

Servings:4
Cooking Time:10 Minutes

Ingredients:
- 2 tbsp extra virgin olive oil
- 1 tbsp lemon juice
- 4 canned anchovy fillets
- 6 black olives
- ½ head Romaine lettuce, torn
- Salt and black pepper to taste
- 1 cucumber, cubed
- 3 tomatoes, cubed
- 2 spring onions, chopped

Directions:
1. Whisk the olive oil, lemon juice, salt, and pepper in a bowl. Add the cucumber, tomatoes, and spring onions and toss to coat. Top with anchovies and black olives and serve.

Nutrition Info:
- Per Serving: Calories: 113;Fat: 8.5g;Protein: 2.9g;Carbs: 9g.

Olive Tapenade Flatbread With Cheese

Servings:4
Cooking Time:35 Min + Chilling Time

Ingredients:
- For the flatbread
- 2 tbsp olive oil
- 2 ½ tsp dry yeast
- 1 ½ cups all-purpose flour
- ¾ tsp salt
- ½ cup lukewarm water
- ¼ tsp sugar
- For the tapenade
- 2 roasted red pepper slices, chopped
- ¼ cup extra-virgin olive oil
- 1 cup green olives, chopped
- 10 black olives, chopped
- 1 tbsp capers
- 1 garlic clove, minced
- 1 tbsp chopped basil leaves
- 1 tbsp chopped fresh oregano
- ¼ cup goat cheese, crumbled

Directions:
1. Combine lukewarm water, sugar, and yeast in a bowl. Set aside covered for 5 minutes. Mix the flour and salt in a bowl. Pour in the yeast mixture and mix. Knead until you obtain a ball. Place the dough onto a floured surface and knead for 5 minutes until soft. Leave the dough into an oiled bowl, covered to rise until it has doubled in size, about 40 minutes.
2. Preheat oven to 400 F. Cut the dough into 4 balls and roll each one out to a ½ inch thickness. Bake for 5 minutes. In a blender, mix black olives, roasted pepper, green olives, capers, garlic, oregano, basil, and olive oil for 20 seconds until coarsely chopped. Spread the olive tapenade on the flatbreads and top with goat cheese to serve.

Nutrition Info:
- Per Serving: Calories: 366;Fat: 19g;Protein: 7.3g;Carbs: 42g.

Three-bean Salad With Black Olives

Servings:6
Cooking Time:15 Minutes

Ingredients:
- 1 lb green beans, trimmed
- 1 red onion, thinly sliced
- 2 tbsp marjoram, chopped
- ¼ cup black olives, chopped
- ½ cup canned cannellini beans
- ½ cup canned chickpeas
- 2 tbsp extra-virgin olive oil
- ½ cup balsamic vinegar
- ½ tsp dried oregano
- Salt and black pepper to taste

Directions:
1. Steam the green beans for about 2 minutes or until just tender. Drain and place them in an ice-water bath. Drain thoroughly and pat them dry with paper towels. Put them in a large bowl and toss with the remaining ingredients. Serve.

Nutrition Info:
- Per Serving: Calories: 187;Fat: 6g;Protein: 7g;Carbs: 27g.

Simple Tahini Sauce

Servings:4
Cooking Time:5 Minutes

Ingredients:
- ¼ tsp ground cumin
- ½ cup tahini
- ¼ cup lemon juice
- 2 garlic cloves, minced
- Salt and black pepper to taste
- 1 tbsp parsley, chopped

Directions:
1. Place the tahini, lemon juice, and garlic, ½ cup of water in a bowl and whisk until combined. Season with salt and pepper to taste. Let sit for about 30 minutes until flavors meld. Refrigerate for up to 3 days. Serve topped with parsley.

Nutrition Info:
- Per Serving: Calories: 306;Fat: 13.3g;Protein: 2g;Carbs: 3.2g.

Parmesan Chicken Salad

Servings:4
Cooking Time:15 Minutes

Ingredients:

- 2 cups chopped cooked chicken breasts
- 1 cup canned artichoke hearts, chopped
- 2 tbsp extra-virgin olive oil
- 2 tomatoes, chopped
- 2 heads romaine lettuce, torn
- 2 cucumbers, chopped
- ½ red onion, finely chopped
- 3 oz Parmesan cheese, shaved
- 4 oz pesto
- 1 lemon, zested
- 2 garlic cloves, minced
- 2 tbsp chopped fresh basil
- 2 tbsp chopped scallions
- Salt and black pepper to taste

Directions:

1. Mix the lettuce, artichoke, chicken, tomatoes, cucumbers, and red onion in a bowl. In another bowl, mix pesto, olive oil, lemon zest, garlic, basil, salt, and pepper and stir to combine. Drizzle the pesto dressing over the salad and top with scallions and Parmesan cheese shavings to serve.

Nutrition Info:

- Per Serving: Calories: 461;Fat: 29g;Protein: 33g;Carbs: 19g.

Pork Chop & Arugula Salad

Servings:4
Cooking Time:50 Minutes

Ingredients:

- 1 lb pork chops
- 2 cups goat cheese, crumbled
- 2 garlic cloves, minced
- 2 tsp lemon zest
- ½ tsp thyme, chopped
- 2 cups arugula
- 1 tbsp lemon juice

Directions:

1. Preheat the oven to 390 F. Rub the pork chops with garlic, lemon zest, thyme, and lemon juice and arrange them on a greased baking pan. Roast for 30 minutes. Sprinkle with goat cheese and bake for another 10 minutes. Place the arugula on a platter and top with the pork chops to serve.

Nutrition Info:

- Per Serving: Calories: 670;Fat: 56g;Protein: 44g;Carbs: 5g.

Slow Cooker Lentil Soup

Servings:6
Cooking Time:8 Hours 10 Minutes

Ingredients:

- 1 cup dry lentils
- 2 carrots, sliced
- 1 yellow onion, chopped
- 2 celery stalks, chopped
- 2 garlic cloves, minced
- 14 oz canned tomatoes, diced
- 1 tbsp red pepper flakes
- 6 cups vegetable stock
- ½ tsp cumin
- Salt and black pepper to taste
- ¼ cup oregano, chopped
- 2 tbsp lime juice

Directions:

1. Place lentils, tomatoes, onion, celery, carrots, garlic, vegetable stock, cumin, red pepper flakes, salt, and pepper in your slow cooker. Place the lid cook on Low for 8 hours. Stir in oregano and lime juice and serve right away.

Nutrition Info:

- Per Serving: Calories: 280;Fat: 2g;Protein: 18g;Carbs: 49g.

Vegetable Mains And Meatless Recipes

Stir-fried Kale With Mushrooms

Servings:4
Cooking Time:10 Minutes

Ingredients:
- 1 cup cremini mushrooms, sliced
- 4 tbsp olive oil
- 1 small red onion, chopped
- 2 cloves garlic, thinly sliced
- 1 ½ lb curly kale
- 2 tomatoes, chopped
- 1 tsp dried oregano
- 1 tsp dried basil
- ½ tsp dried rosemary
- ½ tsp dried thyme
- Salt and black pepper to taste

Directions:
1. Warm the olive oil in a saucepan over medium heat. Sauté the onion and garlic for about 3 minutes or until they are softened. Add in the mushrooms, kale, and tomatoes, stirring to promote even cooking. Turn the heat to a simmer, add in the spices and cook for 5-6 minutes until the kale wilt.

Nutrition Info:
- Per Serving: Calories: 221;Fat: 16g;Protein: 9g;Carbs: 19g.

Roasted Asparagus With Hazelnuts

Servings:4
Cooking Time:25 Minutes

Ingredients:
- 2 tbsp olive oil
- 1 lb asparagus, trimmed
- ¼ cup hazelnuts, chopped
- 1 lemon, juiced and zested
- Salt and black pepper to taste
- ½ tsp red pepper flakes

Directions:
1. Preheat oven to 425 F. Arrange the asparagus on a baking sheet. Combine olive oil, lemon zest, lemon juice, salt, hazelnuts, and black pepper in a bowl and mix well. Pour the mixture over the asparagus. Place in the oven and roast for 15-20 minutes until tender and lightly charred. Serve topped with red pepper flakes.

Nutrition Info:
- Per Serving: Calories: 112;Fat: 10g;Protein: 3.2g;Carbs: 5.2g.

Sautéed Cabbage With Parsley

Servings:4
Cooking Time: 12 To 14 Minutes

Ingredients:
- 1 small head green cabbage, cored and sliced thin
- 2 tablespoons extra-virgin olive oil, divided
- 1 onion, halved and sliced thin
- ¾ teaspoon salt, divided
- ¼ teaspoon black pepper
- ¼ cup chopped fresh parsley
- 1½ teaspoons lemon juice

Directions:
1. Place the cabbage in a large bowl with cold water. Let sit for 3 minutes. Drain well.
2. Heat 1 tablespoon of the oil in a skillet over medium-high heat until shimmering. Add the onion and ¼ teaspoon of the salt and cook for 5 to 7 minutes, or until softened and lightly browned. Transfer to a bowl.
3. Heat the remaining 1 tablespoon of the oil in now-empty skillet over medium-high heat until shimmering. Add the cabbage and sprinkle with the remaining ½ teaspoon of the salt and black pepper. Cover and cook for about 3 minutes, without stirring, or until cabbage is wilted and lightly browned on bottom.
4. Stir and continue to cook for about 4 minutes, uncovered, or until the cabbage is crisp-tender and lightly browned in places, stirring once halfway through cooking. Off heat, stir in the cooked onion, parsley and lemon juice.
5. Transfer to a plate and serve.

Nutrition Info:
- Per Serving: Calories: 117;Fat: 7.0g;Protein: 2.7g;Carbs: 13.4g.

Creamy Cauliflower Chickpea Curry

Servings:4
Cooking Time: 15 Minutes

Ingredients:
- 3 cups fresh or frozen cauliflower florets
- 2 cups unsweetened almond milk
- 1 can low-sodium chickpeas, drained and rinsed
- 1 can coconut milk
- 1 tablespoon curry powder
- ¼ teaspoon garlic powder
- ¼ teaspoon ground ginger
- ⅛ teaspoon onion powder
- ¼ teaspoon salt

Directions:

1. Add the cauliflower florets, almond milk, chickpeas, coconut milk, curry powder, garlic powder, ginger, and onion powder to a large stockpot and stir to combine.
2. Cover and cook over medium-high heat for 10 minutes, stirring occasionally.
3. Reduce the heat to low and continue cooking uncovered for 5 minutes, or until the cauliflower is tender.
4. Sprinkle with the salt and stir well. Serve warm.

Nutrition Info:
- Per Serving: Calories: 409;Fat: 29.6g;Protein: 10.0g;-Carbs: 29.8g.

Baked Honey Acorn Squash

Servings:4
Cooking Time:35 Minutes

Ingredients:
- 1 acorn squash, cut into wedges
- 2 tbsp olive oil
- 2 tbsp honey
- 2 tbsp rosemary, chopped
- 2 tbsp walnuts, chopped

Directions:
1. Preheat oven to 400 F. In a bowl, mix honey, rosemary, and olive oil. Lay the squash wedges on a baking sheet and drizzle with the honey mixture. Bake for 30 minutes until squash is tender and slightly caramelized, turning each slice over halfway through. Serve cooled sprinkled with walnuts.

Nutrition Info:
- Per Serving: Calories: 136;Fat: 6g;Protein: 0.9g;Carbs: 20g.

Quick Steamed Broccoli

Servings:2
Cooking Time: 0 Minutes

Ingredients:
- ¼ cup water
- 3 cups broccoli florets
- Salt and ground black pepper, to taste

Directions:
1. Pour the water into the Instant Pot and insert a steamer basket. Place the broccoli florets in the basket.
2. Secure the lid. Select the Manual mode and set the cooking time for 0 minutes at High Pressure.
3. Once cooking is complete, do a quick pressure release. Carefully open the lid.
4. Transfer the broccoli florets to a bowl with cold water to keep bright green color.
5. Season the broccoli with salt and pepper to taste, then serve.

Nutrition Info:
- Per Serving: Calories: 16;Fat: 0.2g;Protein: 1.9g;Carbs: 1.7g.

Eggplant And Zucchini Gratin

Servings:6
Cooking Time: 19 Minutes

Ingredients:
- 2 large zucchinis, finely chopped
- 1 large eggplant, finely chopped
- ¼ teaspoon kosher salt
- ¼ teaspoon freshly ground black pepper
- 3 tablespoons extra-virgin olive oil, divided
- ¾ cup unsweetened almond milk
- 1 tablespoon all-purpose flour
- ⅓ cup plus 2 tablespoons grated Parmesan cheese, divided
- 1 cup chopped tomato
- 1 cup diced fresh Mozzarella
- ¼ cup fresh basil leaves

Directions:
1. Preheat the oven to 425°F.
2. In a large bowl, toss together the zucchini, eggplant, salt and pepper.
3. In a large skillet over medium-high heat, heat 1 tablespoon of the oil. Add half of the veggie mixture to the skillet. Stir a few times, then cover and cook for about 4 minutes, stirring occasionally. Pour the cooked veggies into a baking dish. Place the skillet back on the heat, add 1 tablespoon of the oil and repeat with the remaining veggies. Add the veggies to the baking dish.
4. Meanwhile, heat the milk in the microwave for 1 minute. Set aside.
5. Place a medium saucepan over medium heat. Add the remaining 1 tablespoon of the oil and flour to the saucepan. Whisk together until well blended.
6. Slowly pour the warm milk into the saucepan, whisking the entire time. Continue to whisk frequently until the mixture thickens a bit. Add ⅓ cup of the Parmesan cheese and whisk until melted. Pour the cheese sauce over the vegetables in the baking dish and mix well.
7. Fold in the tomatoes and Mozzarella cheese. Roast in the oven for 10 minutes, or until the gratin is almost set and not runny.
8. Top with the fresh basil leaves and the remaining 2 tablespoons of the Parmesan cheese before serving.

Nutrition Info:
- Per Serving: Calories: 122;Fat: 5.0g;Protein: 10.0g;-Carbs: 11.0g.

Moroccan Tagine With Vegetables

Servings:2
Cooking Time: 40 Minutes

Ingredients:
- 2 tablespoons olive oil
- ½ onion, diced
- 1 garlic clove, minced

- 2 cups cauliflower florets
- 1 medium carrot, cut into 1-inch pieces
- 1 cup diced eggplant
- 1 can whole tomatoes with their juices
- 1 can chickpeas, drained and rinsed
- 2 small red potatoes, cut into 1-inch pieces
- 1 cup water
- 1 teaspoon pure maple syrup
- ½ teaspoon cinnamon
- ½ teaspoon turmeric
- 1 teaspoon cumin
- ½ teaspoon salt
- 1 to 2 teaspoons harissa paste

Directions:

1. In a Dutch oven, heat the olive oil over medium-high heat. Sauté the onion for 5 minutes, stirring occasionally, or until the onion is translucent.
2. Stir in the garlic, cauliflower florets, carrot, eggplant, tomatoes, and potatoes. Using a wooden spoon or spatula to break up the tomatoes into smaller pieces.
3. Add the chickpeas, water, maple syrup, cinnamon, turmeric, cumin, and salt and stir to incorporate. Bring the mixture to a boil.
4. Once it starts to boil, reduce the heat to medium-low. Stir in the harissa paste, cover, allow to simmer for about 40 minutes, or until the vegetables are softened. Taste and adjust seasoning as needed.
5. Let the mixture cool for 5 minutes before serving.

Nutrition Info:

- Per Serving: Calories: 293;Fat: 9.9g;Protein: 11.2g;-Carbs: 45.5g.

Chargrilled Vegetable Kebabs

Servings:4
Cooking Time:26 Minutes

Ingredients:

- 2 red bell peppers, cut into squares
- 2 zucchinis, sliced into half-moons
- 6 portobello mushroom caps, quartered
- ¼ cup olive oil
- 1 tsp Dijon mustard
- 1 tsp fresh rosemary, chopped
- 1 garlic clove, minced
- Salt and black pepper to taste
- 2 red onions, cut into wedges

Directions:

1. Preheat your grill to High. Mix the olive oil, mustard, rosemary, garlic, salt, and pepper in a bowl. Reserve half of the oil mixture for serving. Thread the vegetables in alternating order onto metal skewers and brush them with the remaining oil mixture. Grill them for about 15 minutes until browned, turning occasionally. Transfer the kebabs to a serving platter and remove the skewers. Drizzle with re-

served oil mixture and serve.

Nutrition Info:

- Per Serving: Calories: 96;Fat: 9.2g;Protein: 1.1g;Carbs: 3.6g.

Potato Tortilla With Leeks And Mushrooms

Servings:2
Cooking Time: 50 Minutes

Ingredients:

- 1 tablespoon olive oil
- 1 cup thinly sliced leeks
- 4 ounces baby bella (cremini) mushrooms, stemmed and sliced
- 1 small potato, peeled and sliced ¼-inch thick
- 5 large eggs, beaten
- ½ cup unsweetened almond milk
- 1 teaspoon Dijon mustard
- ½ teaspoon dried thyme
- ½ teaspoon salt
- Pinch freshly ground black pepper
- 3 ounces Gruyère cheese, shredded

Directions:

1. Preheat the oven to 350ºF.
2. Heat the olive oil in a large sauté pan (nonstick is best) over medium-high heat. Add the leeks, mushrooms, and potato slices and sauté until the leeks are golden and the potatoes start to brown, about 10 minutes.
3. Reduce the heat to medium-low, cover, and let the vegetables cook for another 10 minutes, or until the potatoes begin to soften. If the potato slices stick to the bottom of the pan, add 1 to 2 tablespoons of water to the pan, but be careful because it may splatter.
4. Meanwhile, combine the beaten eggs, milk, mustard, thyme, salt, pepper, and cheese in a medium bowl and whisk everything together.
5. When the potatoes are soft enough to pierce with a fork or knife, turn off the heat.
6. Transfer the cooked vegetables to an oiled ovenproof pan (nonstick is best) and arrange them in a nice layer along the bottom and slightly up the sides of the pan.
7. Pour the egg mixture over the vegetables and give it a light shake or tap to distribute the eggs evenly through the vegetables.
8. Bake for 25 to 30 minutes, or until the eggs are set and the top is golden and puffed.
9. Remove from the oven and cool for 5 minutes before cutting and serving.

Nutrition Info:

- Per Serving: Calories: 541;Fat: 33.1g;Protein: 32.8g;-Carbs: 31.0g.

Brussels Sprouts Linguine

Servings:4
Cooking Time: 25 Minutes

Ingredients:

- 8 ounces whole-wheat linguine
- ⅓ cup plus 2 tablespoons extra-virgin olive oil, divided
- 1 medium sweet onion, diced
- 2 to 3 garlic cloves, smashed
- 8 ounces Brussels sprouts, chopped
- ½ cup chicken stock
- ⅓ cup dry white wine
- ½ cup shredded Parmesan cheese
- 1 lemon, quartered

Directions:

1. Bring a large pot of water to a boil and cook the pasta for about 5 minutes, or until al dente. Drain the pasta and reserve 1 cup of the pasta water. Mix the cooked pasta with 2 tablespoons of the olive oil. Set aside.
2. In a large skillet, heat the remaining ⅓ cup of the olive oil over medium heat. Add the onion to the skillet and sauté for about 4 minutes, or until tender. Add the smashed garlic cloves and sauté for 1 minute, or until fragrant.
3. Stir in the Brussels sprouts and cook covered for 10 minutes. Pour in the chicken stock to prevent burning. Once the Brussels sprouts have wilted and are fork-tender, add white wine and cook for about 5 minutes, or until reduced.
4. Add the pasta to the skillet and add the pasta water as needed.
5. Top with the Parmesan cheese and squeeze the lemon over the dish right before eating.

Nutrition Info:

- Per Serving: Calories: 502;Fat: 31.0g;Protein: 15.0g;-Carbs: 50.0g.

Spinach & Lentil Stew

Servings:4
Cooking Time:40 Minutes

Ingredients:

- 2 tbsp olive oil
- 1 cup dry red lentils, rinsed
- 1 carrot, chopped
- 1 celery stalk, chopped
- 1 red onion, chopped
- 4 garlic cloves, minced
- 3 tomatoes, puréed
- 3 cups vegetable broth
- 1 tsp cayenne pepper
- ½ tsp ground cumin
- ½ tsp thyme
- 1 tsp turmeric
- 1 tbsp sweet paprika
- 1 cup spinach, chopped
- 1 cup fresh cilantro, chopped

- Salt and black pepper to taste

Directions:

1. Heat the olive oil in a pot over medium heat and sauté the garlic, carrot, celery, and onion until tender, about 4-5 minutes. Stir in cayenne pepper, cumin, thyme, paprika, and turmeric for 1 minute and add tomatoes; cook for 3 more minutes. Pour in vegetable broth and lentils and bring to a boil. Reduce the heat and simmer covered for 15 minutes. Stir in spinach and cook for 5 minutes until wilted. Adjust the seasoning and divide between bowls. Top with cilantro.

Nutrition Info:

- Per Serving: Calories: 310;Fat: 9g;Protein: 18.3g;Carbs: 41g.

Sweet Mustard Cabbage Hash

Servings:4
Cooking Time:30 Minutes

Ingredients:

- 1 head Savoy cabbage, shredded
- 3 tbsp olive oil
- 1 onion, finely chopped
- 2 garlic cloves, minced
- ½ tsp fennel seeds
- ¼ cup red wine vinegar
- 1 tbsp mustard powder
- 1 tbsp honey
- Salt and black pepper to taste

Directions:

1. Warm olive oil in a pan over medium heat and sauté onion, fennel seeds, cabbage, salt, and pepper for 8-9 minutes.
2. In a bowl, mix vinegar, mustard, and honey; set aside. Sauté garlic in the pan for 30 seconds. Pour in vinegar mixture and cook for 10-15 minutes until the liquid reduces by half.

Nutrition Info:

- Per Serving: Calories: 181;Fat: 12g;Protein: 3.4g;Carbs: 19g.

Cauliflower Steaks With Arugula

Servings:4
Cooking Time: 20 Minutes

Ingredients:

- Cauliflower:
- 1 head cauliflower
- Cooking spray
- ½ teaspoon garlic powder
- 4 cups arugula
- Dressing:
- 1½ tablespoons extra-virgin olive oil
- 1½ tablespoons honey mustard
- 1 teaspoon freshly squeezed lemon juice

Directions:

1. Preheat the oven to 425°F.
2. Remove the leaves from the cauliflower head, and cut it in half lengthwise. Cut 1½-inch-thick steaks from each half.
3. Spritz both sides of each steak with cooking spray and season both sides with the garlic powder.
4. Place the cauliflower steaks on a baking sheet, cover with foil, and roast in the oven for 10 minutes.
5. Remove the baking sheet from the oven and gently pull back the foil to avoid the steam. Flip the steaks, then roast uncovered for 10 minutes more.
6. Meanwhile, make the dressing: Whisk together the olive oil, honey mustard and lemon juice in a small bowl.
7. When the cauliflower steaks are done, divide into four equal portions. Top each portion with one-quarter of the arugula and dressing.
8. Serve immediately.

Nutrition Info:
- Per Serving: Calories: 115;Fat: 6.0g;Protein: 5.0g;Carbs: 14.0g.

Chickpea Lettuce Wraps With Celery

Servings:4
Cooking Time: 0 Minutes

Ingredients:
- 1 can low-sodium chickpeas, drained and rinsed
- 1 celery stalk, thinly sliced
- 2 tablespoons finely chopped red onion
- 2 tablespoons unsalted tahini
- 3 tablespoons honey mustard
- 1 tablespoon capers, undrained
- 12 butter lettuce leaves

Directions:
1. In a bowl, mash the chickpeas with a potato masher or the back of a fork until mostly smooth.
2. Add the celery, red onion, tahini, honey mustard, and capers to the bowl and stir until well incorporated.
3. For each serving, place three overlapping lettuce leaves on a plate and top with ¼ of the mashed chickpea filling, then roll up. Repeat with the remaining lettuce leaves and chickpea mixture.

Nutrition Info:
- Per Serving: Calories: 182;Fat: 7.1g;Protein: 10.3g;-Carbs: 19.6g.

Tasty Lentil Burgers

Servings:4
Cooking Time:25 Minutes

Ingredients:
- 1 cup cremini mushrooms, finely chopped
- 1 cup cooked green lentils
- ½ cup Greek yogurt
- ½ lemon, zested and juiced
- ½ tsp garlic powder
- ½ tsp dried oregano
- 1 tbsp fresh cilantro, chopped
- Salt to taste
- 3 tbsp extra-virgin olive oil
- ¼ tsp tbsp white miso
- ¼ tsp smoked paprika
- ¼ cup flour

Directions:
1. Pour ½ cup of lentils in your blender and puree partially until somewhat smooth, but with many whole lentils still remaining. In a small bowl, mix the yogurt, lemon zest and juice, garlic powder, oregano, cilantro, and salt. Season and set aside. In a medium bowl, mix the mushrooms, 2 tablespoons of olive oil, miso, and paprika. Stir in all the lentils. Add in flour and stir until the mixture everything is well incorporated. Shape the mixture into patties about ¾-inch thick. Warm the remaining olive oil in a skillet over medium heat. Fry the patties until browned and crisp, about 3 minutes. Turn and fry on the second side. Serve with the reserved yogurt mixture.

Nutrition Info:
- Per Serving: Calories: 215;Fat: 13g;Protein: 10g;Carbs: 19g.

Zucchini Ribbons With Ricotta

Servings:4
Cooking Time:10 Minutes

Ingredients:
- 3 tbsp olive oil
- 1 garlic clove, minced
- 1 tsp lemon zest
- 1 tbsp lemon juice
- 4 zucchinis, cut into ribbons
- Salt and black pepper to taste
- 2 tbsp chopped fresh parsley
- ½ ricotta cheese, crumbled

Directions:
1. Whisk 2 tablespoons oil, garlic, salt, pepper, and lemon zest, and lemon juice in a bowl. Warm the remaining olive oil in a skillet over medium heat. Season the zucchini ribbons with salt and pepper and add them to the skillet; cook for 3-4 minutes per side. Transfer to a serving bowl and drizzle with the dressing, sprinkle with parsley and cheese and serve.

Nutrition Info:
- Per Serving: Calories: 134;Fat: 2g;Protein: 2g;Carbs: 4g.

Roasted Caramelized Root Vegetables

Servings:6
Cooking Time:40 Minutes

Ingredients:

- 1 sweet potato, peeled and cut into chunks
- 3 tbsp olive oil
- 2 carrots, peeled
- 2 beets, peeled
- 1 turnip, peeled
- 1 tsp cumin
- 1 tsp sweet paprika
- Salt and black pepper to taste
- 1 lemon, juiced
- 2 tbsp parsley, chopped

Directions:

1. Preheat oven to 400 F. Cut the vegetables into chunks and toss them with olive oil and seasonings in a sheet pan. Drizzle with lemon juice and roast them for 35-40 minutes until vegetables are tender and golden. Serve topped with parsley.

Nutrition Info:

- Per Serving: Calories: 80;Fat: 4.8g;Protein: 1.5g;Carbs: 8.9g.

Lentil And Tomato Collard Wraps

Servings:4
Cooking Time: 0 Minutes

Ingredients:

- 2 cups cooked lentils
- 5 Roma tomatoes, diced
- ½ cup crumbled feta cheese
- 10 large fresh basil leaves, thinly sliced
- ¼ cup extra-virgin olive oil
- 1 tablespoon balsamic vinegar
- 2 garlic cloves, minced
- ½ teaspoon raw honey
- ½ teaspoon salt
- ¼ teaspoon freshly ground black pepper
- 4 large collard leaves, stems removed

Directions:

1. Combine the lentils, tomatoes, cheese, basil leaves, olive oil, vinegar, garlic, honey, salt, and black pepper in a large bowl and stir until well blended.
2. Lay the collard leaves on a flat work surface. Spoon the equal-sized amounts of the lentil mixture onto the edges of the leaves. Roll them up and slice in half to serve.

Nutrition Info:

- Per Serving: Calories: 318;Fat: 17.6g;Protein: 13.2g;-Carbs: 27.5g.

Hot Turnip Chickpeas

Servings:4
Cooking Time:50 Minutes

Ingredients:

- 2 tbsp olive oil
- 2 onions, chopped
- 2 red bell peppers, chopped
- Salt and black pepper to taste
- ¼ cup tomato paste
- 1 jalapeño pepper, minced
- 5 garlic cloves, minced
- ¾ tsp ground cumin
- ¼ tsp cayenne pepper
- 2 cans chickpeas
- 12 oz potatoes, chopped
- ¼ cup chopped fresh parsley
- 1 lemon, juiced

Directions:

1. Warm the olive oil in a saucepan oven over medium heat. Sauté the onions, bell peppers, salt, and pepper for 6 minutes until softened and lightly browned. Stir in tomato paste, jalapeño pepper, garlic, cumin, and cayenne pepper and cook for about 30 seconds until fragrant. Stir in chickpeas and their liquid, potatoes, and 1 cup of water. Bring to simmer and cook for 25-35 minutes until potatoes are tender and the sauce has thickened. Stir in parsley and lemon juice.

Nutrition Info:

- Per Serving: Calories: 124;Fat: 5.3g;Protein: 3.7g;Carbs: 17g.

Grilled Eggplant "steaks" With Sauce

Servings:6
Cooking Time:20 Minutes

Ingredients:

- 2 lb eggplants, sliced lengthways
- 6 tbsp olive oil
- 5 garlic cloves, minced
- 1 tsp dried oregano
- ½ tsp red pepper flakes
- ½ cup Greek yogurt
- 3 tbsp chopped fresh parsley
- 1 tsp grated lemon zest
- 2 tsp lemon juice
- 1 tsp ground cumin
- Salt and black pepper to taste

Directions:

1. In a bowl, whisk half of the olive oil, yogurt, parsley, lemon zest and juice, cumin, and salt; set aside until ready to serve. Preheat your grill to High. Rub the eggplant steaks with the remaining olive oil, oregano, salt, and pepper. Grill them for 4-6 minutes per side until browned and tender;

transfer to a serving platter. Drizzle yogurt sauce over egg-plant.

Nutrition Info:
- Per Serving: Calories: 112;Fat: 7g;Protein: 2.6g;Carbs: 11.3g.

Minty Broccoli & Walnuts

Servings:2
Cooking Time:10 Minutes

Ingredients:
- 1 garlic clove, minced
- ½ cups walnuts, chopped
- 3 cups broccoli florets, steamed
- 1 tbsp mint, chopped
- ½ lemon, juiced
- Salt and black pepper to taste

Directions:
1. Mix walnuts, broccoli, garlic, mint, lemon juice, salt, and pepper in a bowl. Serve chilled.

Nutrition Info:
- Per Serving: Calories: 210;Fat: 7g;Protein: 4g;Carbs: 9g.

Paprika Cauliflower Steaks With Walnut Sauce

Servings:2
Cooking Time: 30 Minutes

Ingredients:
- Walnut Sauce:
- ½ cup raw walnut halves
- 2 tablespoons virgin olive oil, divided
- 1 clove garlic, chopped
- 1 small yellow onion, chopped
- ½ cup unsweetened almond milk
- 2 tablespoons fresh lemon juice
- Salt and pepper, to taste
- Paprika Cauliflower:
- 1 medium head cauliflower
- 1 teaspoon sweet paprika
- 1 teaspoon minced fresh thyme leaves

Directions:
1. Preheat the oven to 350ºF.
2. Make the walnut sauce: Toast the walnuts in a large, ovenproof skillet over medium heat until fragrant and slightly darkened, about 5 minutes. Transfer the walnuts to a blender.
3. Heat 1 tablespoon of olive oil in the skillet. Add the garlic and onion and sauté for about 2 minutes, or until slightly softened. Transfer the garlic and onion into the blender, along with the almond milk, lemon juice, salt, and pepper. Blend the ingredients until smooth and creamy. Keep the sauce warm while you prepare the cauliflower.
4. Make the paprika cauliflower: Cut two 1-inch-thick

"steaks" from the center of the cauliflower. Lightly moisten the steaks with water and season both sides with paprika, thyme, salt, and pepper.
5. Heat the remaining 1 tablespoon of olive oil in the skillet over medium-high heat. Add the cauliflower steaks and sear for about 3 minutes until evenly browned. Flip the cauliflower steaks and transfer the skillet to the oven.
6. Roast in the preheated oven for about 20 minutes until crisp-tender.
7. Serve the cauliflower steaks warm with the walnut sauce on the side.

Nutrition Info:
- Per Serving: Calories: 367;Fat: 27.9g;Protein: 7.0g;-Carbs: 22.7g.

Roasted Veggies And Brown Rice Bowl

Servings:4
Cooking Time: 20 Minutes

Ingredients:
- 2 cups cauliflower florets
- 2 cups broccoli florets
- 1 can chickpeas, drained and rinsed
- 1 cup carrot slices
- 2 to 3 tablespoons extra-virgin olive oil, divided
- Salt and freshly ground black pepper, to taste
- Nonstick cooking spray
- 2 cups cooked brown rice
- 2 to 3 tablespoons sesame seeds, for garnish
- Dressing:
- 3 to 4 tablespoons tahini
- 2 tablespoons honey
- 1 lemon, juiced
- 1 garlic clove, minced
- Salt and freshly ground black pepper, to taste

Directions:
1. Preheat the oven to 400ºF. Spritz two baking sheets with nonstick cooking spray.
2. Spread the cauliflower and broccoli on the first baking sheet and the second with the chickpeas and carrot slices.
3. Drizzle each sheet with half of the olive oil and sprinkle with salt and pepper. Toss to coat well.
4. Roast the chickpeas and carrot slices in the preheated oven for 10 minutes, leaving the carrots tender but crisp, and the cauliflower and broccoli for 20 minutes until fork-tender. Stir them once halfway through the cooking time.
5. Meanwhile, make the dressing: Whisk together the tahini, honey, lemon juice, garlic, salt, and pepper in a small bowl.
6. Divide the cooked brown rice among four bowls. Top each bowl evenly with roasted vegetables and dressing. Sprinkle the sesame seeds on top for garnish before serving.

Nutrition Info:

- Per Serving: Calories: 453;Fat: 17.8g;Protein: 12.1g;-Carbs: 61.8g.

Simple Zoodles

Servings:2
Cooking Time: 5 Minutes

Ingredients:
- 2 tablespoons avocado oil
- 2 medium zucchinis, spiralized
- ¼ teaspoon salt
- Freshly ground black pepper, to taste

Directions:
1. Heat the avocado oil in a large skillet over medium heat until it shimmers.
2. Add the zucchini noodles, salt, and black pepper to the skillet and toss to coat. Cook for 1 to 2 minutes, stirring constantly, until tender.
3. Serve warm.

Nutrition Info:
- Per Serving: Calories: 128;Fat: 14.0g;Protein: 0.3g;-Carbs: 0.3g.

Eggplant Rolls In Tomato Sauce

Servings:4
Cooking Time:60 Minutes

Ingredients:
- 2 tbsp olive oil
- 1 ½ cups ricotta cheese
- 2 cans diced tomatoes
- 1 shallot, finely chopped
- 2 garlic cloves, minced
- 1 tbsp Italian seasoning
- 1 tsp dried oregano
- 2 eggplants
- ½ cup grated mozzarella
- Salt to taste
- ¼ tsp red pepper flakes

Directions:
1. Preheat oven to 350 F. Warm olive oil in a pot over medium heat and sauté shallot and garlic for 3 minutes until tender and fragrant. Mix in tomatoes, oregano, Italian seasoning, salt, and red flakes and simmer for 6 minutes.
2. Cut the eggplants lengthwise into 1,5-inch slices and season with salt. Grill them for 2-3 minutes per side until softened. Place them on a plate and spoon 2 tbsp of ricotta cheese. Wrap them and arrange on a greased baking dish. Pour over the sauce and scatter with the mozzarella cheese. Bake for 15-20 minutes until golden-brown and bubbling.

Nutrition Info:
- Per Serving: Calories: 362;Fat: 17g;Protein: 19g;Carbs: 38g.

Mushroom & Cauliflower Roast

Servings:4
Cooking Time:35 Minutes

Ingredients:
- 2 tbsp olive oil
- 4 cups cauliflower florets
- 1 celery stalk, chopped
- 1 cup mushrooms, sliced
- 10 cherry tomatoes, halved
- 1 yellow onion, chopped
- 2 garlic cloves, minced
- 2 tbsp dill, chopped
- Salt and black pepper to taste

Directions:
1. Preheat the oven to 340 F. Line a baking sheet with parchment paper. Place in cauliflower florets, olive oil, mushrooms, celery, tomatoes, onion, garlic, salt, and pepper and mix to combine. Bake for 25 minutes. Serve topped with dill.

Nutrition Info:
- Per Serving: Calories: 380;Fat: 15g;Protein: 12g;Carbs: 17g.

Simple Braised Carrots

Servings:4
Cooking Time:20 Minutes

Ingredients:
- 2 tbsp butter
- 1 lb carrots, cut into sticks
- ¾ cup water
- ¼ cup orange juice
- 1 tbsp honey
- Salt and white pepper to taste
- 1 tsp rosemary leaves

Directions:
1. Combine all the ingredients, except for the carrots and rosemary, in a heavy saucepan over medium heat and bring to a boil. Add carrots and cover. Turn the heat to a simmer and continue to cook for 5–8 minutes until carrots are soft when pierced with a knife. Remove the carrots to a serving plate. Then, increase heat to high and bring the liquid to a boil. Boil until the liquid has reduced and syrupy, about 4 minutes. Drizzle the sauce over the carrots and sprinkle with rosemary. Serve warm.

Nutrition Info:
- Per Serving: Calories: 122;Fat: 6g;Protein: 1g;Carbs: 17g.

Asparagus & Mushroom Farro

Servings:2
Cooking Time:40 Minutes

Ingredients:
- ½ oz dried porcini mushrooms, soaked
- 2 tbsp olive oil
- 1 cup hot water
- 3 cups vegetable stock
- ½ large onion, minced
- 1 garlic clove
- 1 cup fresh mushrooms, sliced
- ½ cup farro
- ½ cup dry white wine
- ½ tsp dried thyme
- ½ tsp dried marjoram
- 4 oz asparagus, chopped
- 2 tbsp grated Parmesan cheese

Directions:
1. Drain the soaked mushrooms, reserving the liquid, and cut them into slices. Warm the olive oil in a saucepan oven over medium heat. Sauté the onion, garlic, and soaked and fresh mushrooms for 8 minutes. Stir in the farro for 1-2 minutes. Add the wine, thyme, marjoram, reserved mushroom liquid, and a ladleful of stock. Bring it to a boil.
2. Lower the heat and cook for about 20 minutes, stirring occasionally and adding another ladleful of stock, until the farro is cooked through but not overcooked. Stir in the asparagus and the remaining stock. Cook for 3-5 more minutes or until the asparagus is softened. Sprinkle with Parmesan cheese and serve warm.

Nutrition Info:
- Per Serving: Calories: 341;Fat: 16g;Protein: 13g;Carbs: 26g.

Stir-fry Baby Bok Choy

Servings:6
Cooking Time: 10 To 13 Minutes

Ingredients:
- 2 tablespoons coconut oil
- 1 large onion, finely diced
- 2 teaspoons ground cumin
- 1-inch piece fresh ginger, grated
- 1 teaspoon ground turmeric
- ½ teaspoon salt
- 12 baby bok choy heads, ends trimmed and sliced lengthwise
- Water, as needed
- 3 cups cooked brown rice

Directions:
1. Heat the coconut oil in a large pan over medium heat.
2. Sauté the onion for 5 minutes, stirring occasionally, or until the onion is translucent.
3. Fold in the cumin, ginger, turmeric, and salt and stir to coat well.
4. Add the bok choy and cook for 5 to 8 minutes, stirring occasionally, or until the bok choy is tender but crisp. You can add 1 tablespoon of water at a time, if the skillet gets dry until you finish sautéing.
5. Transfer the bok choy to a plate and serve over the cooked brown rice.

Nutrition Info:
- Per Serving: Calories: 443;Fat: 8.8g;Protein: 30.3g;-Carbs: 75.7g.

5-ingredient Zucchini Fritters

Servings:14
Cooking Time: 5 Minutes

Ingredients:
- 4 cups grated zucchini
- Salt, to taste
- 2 large eggs, lightly beaten
- ⅓ cup sliced scallions (green and white parts)
- ⅔ all-purpose flour
- ⅛ teaspoon black pepper
- 2 tablespoons olive oil

Directions:
1. Put the grated zucchini in a colander and lightly season with salt. Set aside to rest for 10 minutes. Squeeze out as much liquid from the grated zucchini as possible.
2. Pour the grated zucchini into a bowl. Fold in the beaten eggs, scallions, flour, salt, and pepper and stir until everything is well combined.
3. Heat the olive oil in a large skillet over medium heat until hot.
4. Drop 3 tablespoons mounds of the zucchini mixture onto the hot skillet to make each fritter, pressing them lightly into rounds and spacing them about 2 inches apart.
5. Cook for 2 to 3 minutes. Flip the zucchini fritters and cook for 2 minutes more, or until they are golden brown and cooked through.
6. Remove from the heat to a plate lined with paper towels. Repeat with the remaining zucchini mixture.
7. Serve hot.

Nutrition Info:
- Per Serving: Calories: 113;Fat: 6.1g;Protein: 4.0g;Carbs: 12.2g.

Authentic Mushroom Gratin

Servings:4
Cooking Time:25 Minutes

Ingredients:

- 2 lb Button mushrooms, cleaned
- 2 tbsp olive oil
- 2 tomatoes, sliced
- 2 tomato paste
- ½ cup Parmesan cheese, grated
- ½ cup dry white wine
- ¼ tsp sweet paprika
- ½ tsp dried basil
- ½ tsp dried thyme
- Salt and black pepper to taste

Directions:

1. Preheat oven to 360 F. Combine tomatoes, tomato paste, wine, oil, mushrooms, paprika, black pepper, salt, basil, and thyme in a baking dish. Bake for 15 minutes. Top with Parmesan and continue baking for 5 minutes until the cheese melts.

Nutrition Info:

- Per Serving: Calories: 162;Fat: 8.6g;Protein: 9g;Carbs: 12.3g.

Pea & Carrot Noodles

Servings:4
Cooking Time:25 Minutes

Ingredients:

- 2 tbsp olive oil
- 4 carrots, spiralized
- 1 sweet onion, chopped
- 2 cups peas
- 2 garlic cloves, minced
- ¼ cup chopped fresh parsley
- Salt and black pepper to taste

Directions:

1. Warm 2 tbsp of olive oil in a pot over medium heat and sauté the onion and garlic for 3 minutes until just tender and fragrant. Add in spiralized carrots and cook for 4 minutes. Mix in peas, salt, and pepper and cook for 4 minutes. Drizzle with the remaining olive oil and sprinkle with parsley.

Nutrition Info:

- Per Serving: Calories: 157;Fat: 7g;Protein: 4.8g;Carbs: 19.6g.

Balsamic Cherry Tomatoes

Servings:4
Cooking Time:10 Minutes

Ingredients:

- 2 tbsp olive oil
- 2 lb cherry tomatoes, halved
- 2 tbsp balsamic glaze
- Salt and black pepper to taste
- 1 garlic clove, minced
- 2 tbsp fresh basil, torn

Directions:

1. Warm the olive oil in a skillet over medium heat. Add the cherry tomatoes and cook for 1-2 minutes, stirring occasionally. Stir in garlic, salt, and pepper and cook until fragrant, about 30 seconds. Drizzle with balsamic glaze and decorate with basil. Serve and enjoy!

Nutrition Info:

- Per Serving: Calories: 45;Fat: 2.5g;Protein: 1.1g;Carbs: 5.6g.

Roasted Celery Root With Yogurt Sauce

Servings:6
Cooking Time:50 Minutes

Ingredients:

- 3 tbsp olive oil
- 3 celery roots, sliced
- Salt and black pepper to taste
- ¼ cup plain yogurt
- ¼ tsp grated lemon zest
- 1 tsp lemon juice
- 1 tsp sesame seeds, toasted
- 1 tsp coriander seeds, crushed
- ¼ tsp dried thyme
- ¼ tsp chili powder
- ¼ cup fresh cilantro, chopped

Directions:

1. Preheat oven to 425 F. Place the celery slices on a baking sheet. Sprinkle them with olive oil, salt, and pepper. Roast for 25-30 minutes. Flip each piece and continue to roast for 10-15 minutes until celery root is very tender and sides touching sheet are browned. Transfer celery to a serving platter.
2. Whisk yogurt, lemon zest and juice, and salt together in a bowl. In a separate bowl, combine sesame seeds, coriander seeds, thyme, chili powder, and salt. Drizzle celery root with yogurt sauce and sprinkle with seed mixture and cilantro.

Nutrition Info:

- Per Serving: Calories: 75;Fat: 7.5g;Protein: 0.7g;Carbs: 1.8g.

Steamed Beetroot With Nutty Yogurt

Servings:4
Cooking Time:30 Min + Chilling Time

Ingredients:

- ¼ cup extra virgin olive oil
- 1 lb beetroots, cut into wedges
- 1 cup Greek yogurt
- 3 spring onions, sliced
- 5 dill pickles, finely chopped
- 2 garlic cloves, minced
- 2 tbsp fresh parsley, chopped
- 1 oz mixed nuts, crushed
- Salt to taste

Directions:

1. In a pot over medium heat, insert a steamer basket and pour in 1 cup of water. Place in the beetroots and steam for 10-15 minutes until tender. Remove to a plate and let cool. In a bowl, combine the pickles, spring onions, garlic, salt, 3 tbsp of olive oil, Greek yogurt, and nuts and mix well. Spread the yogurt mixture on a serving plate and arrange the beetroot wedges on top. Drizzle with the remaining olive oil and top with parsley. Serve and enjoy!

Nutrition Info:

- Per Serving: Calories: 271;Fat: 18g;Protein: 9.6g;Carbs: 22g.

Cauliflower Cakes With Goat Cheese

Servings:4
Cooking Time:50 Minutes

Ingredients:

- ¼ cup olive oil
- 10 oz cauliflower florets
- 1 tsp ground turmeric
- 1 tsp ground coriander
- Salt and black pepper to taste
- ½ tsp ground mustard seeds
- 4 oz Goat cheese, softened
- 2 scallions, sliced thin
- 1 large egg, lightly beaten
- 2 garlic cloves, minced
- 1 tsp grated lemon zest
- 4 lemon wedges
- ¼ cup flour

Directions:

1. Preheat oven to 420 F. In a bowl, whisk 1 tablespoon oil, turmeric, coriander, salt, ground mustard, and pepper. Add in the cauliflower and toss to coat. Transfer to a greased baking sheet and spread it in a single layer. Roast for 20-25 minutes until cauliflower is well browned and tender. Transfer the cauliflower to a large bowl and mash it coarsely with a potato masher. Stir in Goat cheese, scallions, egg, garlic, and lemon zest until well combined. Sprinkle flour over

cauliflower mixture and stir to incorporate. Shape the mixture into 10-12 cakes and place them on a sheet pan. Chill to firm, about 30 minutes. Warm the remaining olive oil in a skillet over medium heat. Fry the cakes for 5-6 minutes on each side until deep golden brown and crisp. Serve with lemon wedges.

Nutrition Info:

- Per Serving: Calories: 320;Fat: 25g;Protein: 13g;Carbs: 12g.

Spicy Potato Wedges

Servings:4
Cooking Time:30 Minutes

Ingredients:

- 1 ½ lb potatoes, peeled and cut into wedges
- 3 tbsp olive oil
- 1 tbsp minced fresh rosemary
- 2 tsp chili powder
- 3 garlic cloves, minced
- Salt and black pepper to taste

Directions:

1. Preheat the oven to 370 F. Toss the wedges with olive oil, garlic, salt, and pepper. Spread out in a roasting sheet. Roast for 15-20 minutes until browned and crisp at the edges. Remove and sprinkle with chili powder and rosemary.

Nutrition Info:

- Per Serving: Calories: 152;Fat: 7g;Protein: 2.5g;Carbs: 21g.

Zoodles With Beet Pesto

Servings:2
Cooking Time: 50 Minutes

Ingredients:

- 1 medium red beet, peeled, chopped
- ½ cup walnut pieces
- ½ cup crumbled goat cheese
- 3 garlic cloves
- 2 tablespoons freshly squeezed lemon juice
- 2 tablespoons plus 2 teaspoons extra-virgin olive oil, divided
- ¼ teaspoon salt
- 4 small zucchinis, spiralized

Directions:

1. Preheat the oven to 375°F.
2. Wrap the chopped beet in a piece of aluminum foil and seal well.
3. Roast in the preheated oven for 30 to 40 minutes until tender.
4. Meanwhile, heat a skillet over medium-high heat until hot. Add the walnuts and toast for 5 to 7 minutes, or until fragrant and lightly browned.
5. Remove the cooked beets from the oven and place in a

food processor. Add the toasted walnuts, goat cheese, garlic, lemon juice, 2 tablespoons of olive oil, and salt. Pulse until smoothly blended. Set aside.

6. Heat the remaining 2 teaspoons of olive oil in a large skillet over medium heat. Add the zucchini and toss to coat in the oil. Cook for 2 to 3 minutes, stirring gently, or until the zucchini is softened.

7. Transfer the zucchini to a serving plate and toss with the beet pesto, then serve.

Nutrition Info:
• Per Serving: Calories: 423;Fat: 38.8g;Protein: 8.0g;-Carbs: 17.1g.

Vegetable And Red Lentil Stew

Servings:6
Cooking Time: 35 Minutes

Ingredients:
• 1 tablespoon extra-virgin olive oil
• 2 onions, peeled and finely diced
• 6½ cups water
• 2 zucchinis, finely diced
• 4 celery stalks, finely diced
• 3 cups red lentils
• 1 teaspoon dried oregano
• 1 teaspoon salt, plus more as needed

Directions:
1. Heat the olive oil in a large pot over medium heat.
2. Add the onions and sauté for about 5 minutes, stirring constantly, or until the onions are softened.
3. Stir in the water, zucchini, celery, lentils, oregano, and salt and bring the mixture to a boil.
4. Reduce the heat to low and let simmer covered for 30 minutes, stirring occasionally, or until the lentils are tender.
5. Taste and adjust the seasoning as needed.

Nutrition Info:
• Per Serving: Calories: 387;Fat: 4.4g;Protein: 24.0g;-Carbs: 63.7g.

Mushroom Filled Zucchini Boats

Servings:2
Cooking Time:50 Minutes

Ingredients:
• 2 zucchini, cut in half lengthwise
• 2 cups button mushrooms, chopped
• 2 tbsp olive oil
• 2 cloves garlic, minced
• 2 tbsp chicken broth
• ¼ tsp dried thyme
• 1 tbsp parsley, finely chopped
• 1 tbsp Italian seasoning
• Salt and black pepper to taste

Directions:

1. Preheat oven to 350 F. Warm the olive oil in a large skillet over medium heat and add the olive oil. Sauté the mushrooms and garlic for 4-5 minutes until tender. Pour in the chicken broth and cook for another 3–4 minutes. Add the parsley, oregano, and Italian seasoning and season with salt and pepper. Stir and remove from the heat. Spoon the mixture into the zucchini halves. Place them in a casserole dish and pour 2-3 tbsp of water or broth in the bottom. Cover with foil and bake for 30-40 minutes until zucchini is tender.

Nutrition Info:
• Per Serving: Calories: 165;Fat: 13.9g;Protein: 3.8g;-Carbs: 8g.

Italian Hot Green Beans

Servings:4
Cooking Time:25 Minutes

Ingredients:
• 2 tbsp olive oil
• 1 red bell pepper, diced
• 1 ½ lb green beans
• 4 garlic cloves, minced
• ½ tsp mustard seeds
• ½ tsp fennel seeds
• 1 tsp dried dill weed
• 2 tomatoes, chopped
• 1 cup cream of celery soup
• 1 tsp Italian herb mix
• 1 tsp chili powder
• Salt and black pepper to taste

Directions:
1. Warm the olive oil in a saucepan over medium heat. Add and fry the bell pepper and green beans for about 5 minutes, stirring periodically to promote even cooking. Add in the garlic, mustard seeds, fennel seeds, and dill and continue sautéing for an additional 1 minute or until fragrant. Add in the pureed tomatoes, cream of celery soup, Italian herb mix, chili powder, salt, and black pepper. Continue to simmer, covered, for 10-12 minutes until the green beans are tender.

Nutrition Info:
• Per Serving: Calories: 160;Fat: 9g;Protein: 5g;Carbs: 19g.

Garlicky Zucchini Cubes With Mint

Servings:4
Cooking Time: 10 Minutes

Ingredients:
• 3 large green zucchinis, cut into ½-inch cubes
• 3 tablespoons extra-virgin olive oil
• 1 large onion, chopped
• 3 cloves garlic, minced
• 1 teaspoon salt

- 1 teaspoon dried mint

Directions:

1. Heat the olive oil in a large skillet over medium heat.
2. Add the onion and garlic and sauté for 3 minutes, stirring constantly, or until softened.
3. Stir in the zucchini cubes and salt and cook for 5 minutes, or until the zucchini is browned and tender.
4. Add the mint to the skillet and toss to combine, then continue cooking for 2 minutes.
5. Serve warm.

Nutrition Info:

- Per Serving: Calories: 146;Fat: 10.6g;Protein: 4.2g;-Carbs: 11.8g.

Sweet Potato Chickpea Buddha Bowl

Servings:2
Cooking Time: 10 To 15 Minutes

Ingredients:

- Sauce:
- 1 tablespoon tahini
- 2 tablespoons plain Greek yogurt
- 2 tablespoons hemp seeds
- 1 garlic clove, minced
- Pinch salt
- Freshly ground black pepper, to taste
- Bowl:
- 1 small sweet potato, peeled and finely diced
- 1 teaspoon extra-virgin olive oil
- 1 cup from 1 can low-sodium chickpeas, drained and rinsed
- 2 cups baby kale

Directions:

1. Make the Sauce
2. Whisk together the tahini and yogurt in a small bowl.
3. Stir in the hemp seeds and minced garlic. Season with salt pepper. Add 2 to 3 tablespoons water to create a creamy yet pourable consistency and set aside.
4. Make the Bowl
5. Preheat the oven to 425°F. Line a baking sheet with parchment paper.
6. Place the sweet potato on the prepared baking sheet and drizzle with the olive oil. Toss well
7. Roast in the preheated oven for 10 to 15 minutes, stirring once during cooking, or until fork-tender and browned.
8. In each of 2 bowls, place ½ cup of chickpeas, 1 cup of baby kale, and half of the cooked sweet potato. Serve drizzled with half of the prepared sauce.

Nutrition Info:

- Per Serving: Calories: 323;Fat: 14.1g;Protein: 17.0g;-Carbs: 36.0g.

Zucchini Crisp

Servings:2
Cooking Time: 20 Minutes

Ingredients:

- 4 zucchinis, sliced into ½-inch rounds
- ½ cup unsweetened almond milk
- 1 teaspoon fresh lemon juice
- 1 teaspoon arrowroot powder
- ½ teaspoon salt, divided
- ½ cup whole wheat bread crumbs
- ¼ cup nutritional yeast
- ¼ cup hemp seeds
- ½ teaspoon garlic powder
- ¼ teaspoon crushed red pepper
- ¼ teaspoon black pepper

Directions:

1. Preheat the oven to 375°F. Line two baking sheets with parchment paper and set aside.
2. Put the zucchini in a medium bowl with the almond milk, lemon juice, arrowroot powder, and ¼ teaspoon of salt. Stir to mix well.
3. In a large bowl with a lid, thoroughly combine the bread crumbs, nutritional yeast, hemp seeds, garlic powder, crushed red pepper and black pepper. Add the zucchini in batches and shake until the slices are evenly coated.
4. Arrange the zucchini on the prepared baking sheets in a single layer.
5. Bake in the preheated oven for about 20 minutes, or until the zucchini slices are golden brown.
6. Season with the remaining ¼ teaspoon of salt before serving.

Nutrition Info:

- Per Serving: Calories: 255;Fat: 11.3g;Protein: 8.6g;-Carbs: 31.9g.

Mini Crustless Spinach Quiches

Servings:6
Cooking Time: 20 Minutes

Ingredients:

- 2 tablespoons extra-virgin olive oil
- 1 onion, finely chopped
- 2 cups baby spinach
- 2 garlic cloves, minced
- 8 large eggs, beaten
- ¼ cup unsweetened almond milk
- ½ teaspoon sea salt
- ¼ teaspoon freshly ground black pepper
- 1 cup shredded Swiss cheese
- Cooking spray

Directions:

1. Preheat the oven to 375°F. Spritz a 6-cup muffin tin with cooking spray. Set aside.

2. In a large skillet over medium-high heat, heat the olive oil until shimmering. Add the onion and cook for about 4 minutes, or until soft. Add the spinach and cook for about 1 minute, stirring constantly, or until the spinach softens. Add the garlic and sauté for 30 seconds. Remove from the heat and let cool.

3. In a medium bowl, whisk together the eggs, milk, salt and pepper.

4. Stir the cooled vegetables and the cheese into the egg mixture. Spoon the mixture into the prepared muffin tins. Bake for about 15 minutes, or until the eggs are set.

5. Let rest for 5 minutes before serving.

Nutrition Info:
- Per Serving: Calories: 218;Fat: 17.0g;Protein: 14.0g;-Carbs: 4.0g.

Simple Broccoli With Yogurt Sauce

Servings:4
Cooking Time:25 Minutes

Ingredients:
- 2 tbsp olive oil
- 1 head broccoli, cut into florets
- 2 garlic cloves, minced
- ½ cup Greek yogurt
- Salt and black pepper to taste
- 2 tsp fresh dill, chopped

Directions:
1. Warm olive oil in a pan over medium heat and sauté broccoli, salt, and pepper for 12 minutes. Mix Greek yogurt, dill, and garlic in a small bowl. Drizzle the broccoli with the sauce.

Nutrition Info:
- Per Serving: Calories: 104;Fat: 7.7g;Protein: 4.5g;Carbs: 6g.

Rainbow Vegetable Kebabs

Servings:4
Cooking Time:30 Minutes

Ingredients:
- 1 cup mushrooms, cut into quarters
- 6 mixed bell peppers, cut into squares
- 4 red onions, cut into 6 wedges
- 4 zucchini, cut into half-moons
- 2 tomatoes, cut into quarters
- 3 tbsp herbed oil

Directions:
1. Preheat your grill to medium-high. Alternate the vegetables onto bamboo skewers. Grill them for 5 minutes on each side until the vegetables begin to char. Remove them from heat and drizzle with herbed oil.

Nutrition Info:
- Per Serving: Calories: 238;Fat: 12g;Protein: 6g;Carbs: 34.2g.

Roasted Vegetables

Servings:2
Cooking Time: 35 Minutes

Ingredients:
- 6 teaspoons extra-virgin olive oil, divided
- 12 to 15 Brussels sprouts, halved
- 1 medium sweet potato, peeled and cut into 2-inch cubes
- 2 cups fresh cauliflower florets
- 1 medium zucchini, cut into 1-inch rounds
- 1 red bell pepper, cut into 1-inch slices
- Salt, to taste

Directions:
1. Preheat the oven to 425ºF.
2. Add 2 teaspoons of olive oil, Brussels sprouts, sweet potato, and salt to a large bowl and toss until they are completely coated.
3. Transfer them to a large roasting pan and roast for 10 minutes, or until the Brussels sprouts are lightly browned.
4. Meantime, combine the cauliflower florets with 2 teaspoons of olive oil and salt in a separate bowl.
5. Remove from the oven. Add the cauliflower florets to the roasting pan and roast for 10 minutes more.
6. Meanwhile, toss the zucchini and bell pepper with the remaining olive oil in a medium bowl until well coated. Season with salt.
7. Remove the roasting pan from the oven and stir in the zucchini and bell pepper. Continue roasting for 15 minutes, or until the vegetables are fork-tender.
8. Divide the roasted vegetables between two plates and serve warm.

Nutrition Info:
- Per Serving: Calories: 333;Fat: 16.8g;Protein: 12.2g;-Carbs: 37.6g.

Beans , Grains, And Pastas Recipes

Power Green Barley Pilaf

Servings:6
Cooking Time:25 Minutes

Ingredients:

- 3 tbsp olive oil
- 1 small onion, chopped fine
- Salt and black pepper to taste
- 1 ½ cups pearl barley, rinsed
- 2 garlic cloves, minced
- ½ tsp dried thyme
- 2 ½ cups water
- ¼ cup parsley, minced
- 2 tbsp cilantro, chopped
- 1 ½ tsp lemon juice

Directions:

1. Warm the olive oil in a saucepan over medium heat. Stir-fry onion for 5 minutes until soft. Stir in barley, garlic, and thyme and cook, stirring frequently, until barley is lightly toasted and fragrant, 3-4 minutes. Stir in water and bring to a simmer. Reduce heat to low, cover, and simmer until barley is tender and water is absorbed, 25-35 minutes. Lay clean dish towel underneath the lid and let pilaf sit for 10 minutes. Add parsley, cilantro, and lemon juice and fluff gently with a fork to mix. Season with salt and pepper and serve warm.

Nutrition Info:

- Per Serving: Calories: 275;Fat: 21g;Protein: 12g;Carbs: 32g.

Arugula & Cheese Pasta With Red Sauce

Servings:6
Cooking Time:60 Minutes

Ingredients:

- ¼ cup olive oil
- 1 shallot, sliced thin
- 2 lb cherry tomatoes, halved
- 3 large garlic cloves, sliced
- 1 tbsp red wine vinegar
- 3 oz ricotta cheese, crumbled
- 1 tsp sugar
- Salt and black pepper to taste
- ¼ tsp red pepper flakes
- 1 lb penne
- 4 oz baby arugula

Directions:

1. Preheat oven to 350 F. Toss shallot with 1 tsp of oil in a bowl. In a separate bowl, toss tomatoes with remaining oil, garlic, vinegar, sugar, salt, pepper, and flakes. Spread tomato mixture in even layer in rimmed baking sheet, scatter shallot over tomatoes, and roast until edges of shallot begin to brown and tomato skins are slightly charred, 35-40 minutes; do not stir. Let cool for 5 to 10 minutes.

2. Meanwhile, bring a pot filled with salted water to a boil and add pasta. Cook, stirring often until al dente. Reserve ½ cup cooking water, then drain pasta and return it to pot. Add arugula to pasta and toss until wilted. Using a spatula, scrape tomato mixture onto pasta and toss to combine. Season to taste and adjust consistency with reserved cooking water as needed. Serve, passing ricotta cheese separately.

Nutrition Info:

- Per Serving: Calories: 444;Fat: 19g;Protein: 18g;Carbs: 44g.

Leftover Pasta & Mushroom Frittata

Servings:4
Cooking Time:25 Minutes

Ingredients:

- 2 tbsp olive oil
- 4 oz leftover spaghetti, cooked
- 8 large eggs, beaten
- ¼ cup heavy cream
- ½ tsp Italian seasoning
- ½ tsp garlic salt
- 1/8 tsp garlic pepper
- 1 cup chopped mushrooms
- 1 cup Pecorino cheese, grated

Directions:

1. Preheat your broiler. Warm the olive oil in a large skillet over medium heat. Add mushrooms and cook for 3–4 minutes, until almost tender. In a large bowl, beat the eggs with cream, Italian seasoning, garlic salt, and garlic pepper. Stir in the leftover spaghetti. Pour the egg mixture over the mushrooms and level with a spatula. Cook for 5–7 minutes until the eggs are almost set. Sprinkle with cheese and place under broiler for 3–5 minutes, until the cheese melts. Serve.

Nutrition Info:

- Per Serving: Calories: 400;Fat: 30g;Protein: 23g;Carbs: 11g.

Thyme Spinach & Cannellini Bean Stew

Servings:4
Cooking Time:40 Minutes

Ingredients:

- 2 tbsp olive oil
- 1 onion, chopped
- 1 can diced tomatoes
- 2 cans cannellini beans
- 1 cup carrots, chopped
- 1 celery stalk, chopped
- 4 cups vegetable broth
- ½ tsp dried thyme
- 1 lb baby spinach
- Salt and black pepper to taste

Directions:

1. Warm the olive oil in a saucepan over medium heat. Sauté the onion, celery, and carrots for 5 minutes until tender. Add the tomatoes, beans, carrots, broth, thyme, pepper, and salt. Stir and cook for 20 minutes. Add the spinach and cook for 5 minutes until the spinach wilts. Serve warm.

Nutrition Info:

- Per Serving: Calories: 256;Fat: 12g;Protein: 15g;Carbs: 47g.

Spicy Bean Rolls

Servings:4
Cooking Time:25 Minutes

Ingredients:

- 1 tbsp olive oil
- 1 red onion, chopped
- 2 garlic cloves, minced
- 1 green bell pepper, sliced
- 2 cups canned cannellini beans
- 1 red chili pepper, chopped
- 1 tbsp cilantro, chopped
- 1 tsp cumin, ground
- Salt and black pepper to taste
- 4 whole-wheat tortillas
- 1 cup mozzarella, shredded

Directions:

1. Warm the olive oil in a skillet over medium heat and sauté onion for 3 minutes. Stir in garlic, bell pepper, cannellini beans, red chili pepper, cilantro, cumin, salt, and pepper and cook for 15 minutes. Spoon bean mixture on each tortilla and top with cheese. Roll up and serve right away.

Nutrition Info:

- Per Serving: Calories: 680;Fat: 15g;Protein: 38g;Carbs: 75g.

Bean And Veggie Pasta

Servings:2
Cooking Time: 15 Minutes

Ingredients:

- 16 ounces small whole wheat pasta, such as penne, farfalle, or macaroni
- 5 cups water
- 1 can cannellini beans, drained and rinsed
- 1 can diced (with juice) or crushed tomatoes
- 1 yellow onion, chopped
- 1 red or yellow bell pepper, chopped
- 2 tablespoons tomato paste
- 1 tablespoon olive oil
- 3 garlic cloves, minced
- ¼ teaspoon crushed red pepper (optional)
- 1 bunch kale, stemmed and chopped
- 1 cup sliced basil
- ½ cup pitted Kalamata olives, chopped

Directions:

1. Add the pasta, water, beans, tomatoes (with juice if using diced), onion, bell pepper, tomato paste, oil, garlic, and crushed red pepper (if desired), to a large stockpot or deep skillet with a lid. Bring to a boil over high heat, stirring often.
2. Reduce the heat to medium-high, add the kale, and cook, continuing to stir often, until the pasta is al dente, about 10 minutes.
3. Remove from the heat and let sit for 5 minutes. Garnish with the basil and olives and serve.

Nutrition Info:

- Per Serving: Calories: 565;Fat: 17.7g;Protein: 18.0g;Carbs: 85.5g.

Raspberry & Nut Quinoa

Servings:4
Cooking Time:5 Minutes

Ingredients:

- 1 tbsp honey
- 2 cups almond milk
- 2 cups quinoa, cooked
- ½ tsp cinnamon powder
- 1 cup raspberries
- ¼ cup walnuts, chopped

Directions:

1. Combine quinoa, milk, cinnamon powder, honey, raspberries, and walnuts in a bowl. Serve in individual bowls.

Nutrition Info:

- Per Serving: Calories: 300;Fat: 15g;Protein: 5g;Carbs: 15g.

Hearty Butternut Spinach, And Cheeses Lasagna

Servings:4
Cooking Time: 3 Hours 45 Minutes

Ingredients:
- 2 tablespoons extra-virgin olive oil, divided
- 1 butternut squash, halved lengthwise and deseeded
- ½ teaspoon sage
- ½ teaspoon sea salt
- ¼ teaspoon ground black pepper
- ¼ cup grated Parmesan cheese
- 2 cups ricotta cheese
- ½ cup unsweetened almond milk
- 5 layers whole-wheat lasagna noodles
- 4 ounces fresh spinach leaves, divided
- ½ cup shredded part skim Mozzarella, for garnish

Directions:
1. Preheat the oven to 400°F. Line a baking sheet with parchment paper.
2. Brush 1 tablespoon of olive oil on the cut side of the butternut squash, then place the squash on the baking sheet.
3. Bake in the preheated oven for 45 minutes or until the squash is tender.
4. Allow to cool until you can handle it, then scoop the flesh out and put the flesh in a food processor to purée.
5. Combine the puréed butternut squash flesh with sage, salt, and ground black pepper in a large bowl. Stir to mix well.
6. Combine the cheeses and milk in a separate bowl, then sprinkle with salt and pepper, to taste.
7. Grease the slow cooker with 1 tablespoon of olive oil, then add a layer of lasagna noodles to coat the bottom of the slow cooker.
8. Spread half of the squash mixture on top of the noodles, then top the squash mixture with another layer of lasagna noodles.
9. Spread half of the spinach over the noodles, then top the spinach with half of cheese mixture. Repeat with remaining 3 layers of lasagna noodles, squash mixture, spinach, and cheese mixture.
10. Top the cheese mixture with Mozzarella, then put the lid on and cook on low for 3 hours or until the lasagna noodles are al dente.
11. Serve immediately.

Nutrition Info:
- Per Serving: Calories: 657;Fat: 37.1g;Protein: 30.9g;-Carbs: 57.2g.

Rich Cauliflower Alfredo

Servings:4
Cooking Time: 30 Minutes

Ingredients:
- Cauliflower Alfredo Sauce:
- 1 tablespoon avocado oil
- ½ yellow onion, diced
- 2 cups cauliflower florets
- 2 garlic cloves, minced
- 1½ teaspoons miso
- 1 teaspoon Dijon mustard
- Pinch of ground nutmeg
- ½ cup unsweetened almond milk
- 1½ tablespoons fresh lemon juice
- 2 tablespoons nutritional yeast
- Sea salt and ground black pepper, to taste
- Fettuccine:
- 1 tablespoon avocado oil
- ½ yellow onion, diced
- 1 cup broccoli florets
- 1 zucchini, halved lengthwise and cut into ¼-inch-thick half-moons
- Sea salt and ground black pepper, to taste
- ½ cup sun-dried tomatoes, drained if packed in oil
- 8 ounces cooked whole-wheat fettuccine
- ½ cup fresh basil, cut into ribbons

Directions:
1. Make the Sauce:
2. Heat the avocado oil in a nonstick skillet over medium-high heat until shimmering.
3. Add half of the onion to the skillet and sauté for 5 minutes or until translucent.
4. Add the cauliflower and garlic to the skillet. Reduce the heat to low and cook for 8 minutes or until the cauliflower is tender.
5. Pour them in a food processor, add the remaining ingredients for the sauce and pulse to combine well. Set aside.
6. Make the Fettuccine:
7. Heat the avocado oil in a nonstick skillet over medium-high heat.
8. Add the remaining half of onion and sauté for 5 minutes or until translucent.
9. Add the broccoli and zucchini. Sprinkle with salt and ground black pepper, then sauté for 5 minutes or until tender.
10. Add the sun-dried tomatoes, reserved sauce, and fettuccine. Sauté for 3 minutes or until well-coated and heated through.
11. Serve the fettuccine on a large plate and spread with basil before serving.

Nutrition Info:
- Per Serving: Calories: 288;Fat: 15.9g;Protein: 10.1g;-Carbs: 32.5g.

Parsley Beef Fusilli

Servings:4
Cooking Time:30 Minutes

Ingredients:
- 1 cup grated Pecorino Romano cheese
- 1 lb thick-cut New York strip steaks, cut into 1-inch cubes
- 4 tbsp butter
- 16 oz fusilli pasta
- Salt and black pepper to taste
- 4 garlic cloves, minced
- 2 tbsp chopped fresh parsley

Directions:
1. In a pot of boiling water, cook the fusilli pasta for 8-10 minutes until al dente. Drain and set aside.
2. Melt the butter in a large skillet, season the steaks with salt, black pepper and cook in the butter until brown, and cooked through, 10 minutes. Stir in the garlic and cook until fragrant, 1 minute. Mix in the parsley and fusilli pasta; toss well and season with salt and black pepper. Dish the food, top with the Pecorino Romano cheese and serve immediately.

Nutrition Info:
- Per Serving: Calories: 422;Fat: 22g;Protein: 36g;Carbs: 17g.

Fofu Spaghetti Bolognese

Servings:4
Cooking Time:25 Minutes

Ingredients:
- 2 tbsp olive oil
- 16 oz spaghetti, broken in half
- 1 cup crumbled firm tofu
- 1 medium onion, chopped
- 2 celery stalks, chopped
- 1 garlic clove, minced
- 1 bay leaf
- 2 cups passata
- ¼ cup vegetable broth
- Salt and black pepper to taste
- 1 small bunch basil, chopped
- 1 cup grated Parmesan cheese

Directions:
1. In a pot of boiling water, cook the spaghetti pasta for 8-10 minutes until al dente. Drain and set aside.
2. Heat the olive oil in a large pot and cook the tofu until brown, 5 minutes. Stir in the onion, celery, and cook until softened, 5 minutes. Add garlic, bay leaf and cook until fragrant, 30 seconds. Mix in passata, broth and season with salt and pepper. Cook until the sauce thickens, 8-10 minutes. Open the lid, stir in the basil and adjust the taste with salt and pepper. Divide the spaghetti between plates and top with the sauce. Sprinkle the Parmesan cheese and serve.

Nutrition Info:
- Per Serving: Calories: 424;Fat: 19g;Protein: 22g;Carbs: 31g.

Classic Falafel

Servings:6
Cooking Time:20 Minutes

Ingredients:
- 2 cups olive oil
- Salt and black pepper to taste
- 1 cup chickpeas, soaked
- 5 scallions, chopped
- ¼ cup fresh parsley leaves
- ¼ cup fresh cilantro leaves
- ¼ cup fresh dill
- 6 garlic cloves, minced
- ½ tsp ground cumin
- ½ tsp ground coriander

Directions:
1. Pat dry chickpeas with paper towels and place them in your food processor. Add in scallions, parsley, cilantro, dill, garlic, salt, pepper, cumin, and ground coriander and pulse, scraping downsides of the bowl as needed. Shape the chickpea mixture into 2-tablespoon-size disks, about 1 ½ inches wide and 1 inch thick, and place on a parchment paper–lined baking sheet.
2. Warm the olive oil in a skillet over medium heat. Fry the falafel until deep golden brown, 2-3 minutes per side. With a slotted spoon, transfer falafel to a paper towel-lined plate to drain. Serve hot.

Nutrition Info:
- Per Serving: Calories: 349;Fat: 26.3g;Protein: 19g;Carbs: 9g.

Kale & Feta Couscous

Servings:4
Cooking Time:20 Minutes

Ingredients:
- 2 tbsp olive oil
- 1 cup couscous
- 1 cup kale, chopped
- 1 tbsp parsley, chopped
- 3 spring onions, chopped
- 1 cucumber, chopped
- 1 tsp allspice
- ½ lemon, juiced and zested
- 4 oz feta cheese, crumbled

Directions:

1. In a bowl, place couscous and cover with hot water. Let sit for 10 minutes and fluff. Warm the olive oil in a skillet over medium heat and sauté onions and allspice for 3 minutes. Stir in the remaining ingredients and cook for 5-6 minutes.

Nutrition Info:
- Per Serving: Calories: 210;Fat: 7g;Protein: 5g;Carbs: 16g.

Mediterranean Brown Rice

Servings:4
Cooking Time:20 Minutes

Ingredients:
- 1 lb asparagus, steamed and chopped
- 2 tbsp olive oil
- 3 tbsp balsamic vinegar
- 1 cup brown rice
- 2 tsp mustard
- Salt and black pepper to taste
- 5 oz baby spinach
- ½ cup parsley, chopped
- 1 tbsp tarragon, chopped

Directions:

1. Bring to a boil a pot of salted water over medium heat. Add in brown rice and cook for 7-9 minutes until al dente. Drain and place in a bowl. Add the asparagus to the same pot and blanch them for 4-5 minutes. Remove them to the rice bowl. Mix in spinach, olive oil, balsamic vinegar, mustard, salt, pepper, parsley, and tarragon. Serve.

Nutrition Info:
- Per Serving: Calories: 330;Fat: 12g;Protein: 11g;Carbs: 17g.

Israeli Couscous With Asparagus

Servings:6
Cooking Time: 25 Minutes

Ingredients:
- 1½ pounds asparagus spears, ends trimmed and stalks chopped into 1-inch pieces
- 1 garlic clove, minced
- 1 tablespoon extra-virgin olive oil
- ¼ teaspoon freshly ground black pepper
- 1¾ cups water
- 1 box uncooked whole-wheat or regular Israeli couscous
- ¼ teaspoon kosher salt
- 1 cup garlic-and-herb goat cheese, at room temperature

Directions:

1. Preheat the oven to 425ºF.
2. In a large bowl, stir together the asparagus, garlic, oil, and pepper. Spread the asparagus on a large, rimmed baking sheet and roast for 10 minutes, stirring a few times. Remove the pan from the oven, and spoon the asparagus into a large serving bowl. Set aside.
3. While the asparagus is roasting, bring the water to a boil in a medium saucepan. Add the couscous and season with salt, stirring well.
4. Reduce the heat to medium-low. Cover and cook for 12 minutes, or until the water is absorbed.
5. Pour the hot couscous into the bowl with the asparagus. Add the goat cheese and mix thoroughly until completely melted.
6. Serve immediately.

Nutrition Info:
- Per Serving: Calories: 103;Fat: 2.0g;Protein: 6.0g;Carbs: 18.0g.

Lush Moroccan Chickpea, Vegetable, And Fruit Stew

Servings:6
Cooking Time: 6 Hours 4 Minutes

Ingredients:

- 1 large bell pepper, any color, chopped
- 6 ounces green beans, trimmed and cut into bite-size pieces
- 3 cups canned chickpeas, rinsed and drained
- 1 can diced tomatoes, with the juice
- 1 large carrot, cut into ¼-inch rounds
- 2 large potatoes, peeled and cubed
- 1 large yellow onion, chopped
- 1 teaspoon grated fresh ginger
- 2 garlic cloves, minced
- 1¾ cups low-sodium vegetable soup
- 1 teaspoon ground cumin
- 1 tablespoon ground coriander
- ¼ teaspoon ground red pepper flakes
- Sea salt and ground black pepper, to taste
- 8 ounces fresh baby spinach
- ¼ cup diced dried figs
- ¼ cup diced dried apricots
- 1 cup plain Greek yogurt

Directions:

1. Place the bell peppers, green beans, chicken peas, tomatoes and juice, carrot, potatoes, onion, ginger, and garlic in the slow cooker.
2. Pour in the vegetable soup and sprinkle with cumin, coriander, red pepper flakes, salt, and ground black pepper. Stir to mix well.
3. Put the slow cooker lid on and cook on high for 6 hours or until the vegetables are soft. Stir periodically.
4. Open the lid and fold in the spinach, figs, apricots, and yogurt. Stir to mix well.
5. Cook for 4 minutes or until the spinach is wilted. Pour them in a large serving bowl. Allow to cool for at least 20 minutes, then serve warm.

Nutrition Info:

- Per Serving: Calories: 611;Fat: 9.0g;Protein: 30.7g;-Carbs: 107.4g.

Florentine Bean & Vegetable Gratin

Servings:4
Cooking Time:50 Minutes

Ingredients:

- ½ cup Parmigiano Reggiano cheese, grated
- 4 pancetta slices
- 2 tbsp olive oil
- 4 garlic cloves, minced
- 1 onion, chopped
- ½ fennel bulb, chopped
- 1 tbsp brown rice flour
- 2 cans white beans
- 1 can tomatoes, diced
- 1 medium zucchini, chopped
- 1 tsp porcini powder
- 1 tbsp fresh basil, chopped
- ½ tsp dried oregano
- 1 tsp red pepper flakes
- Salt to taste
- 2 tbsp butter, cubed

Directions:

1. Heat the olive in a skillet over medium heat. Fry the pancetta for 5 minutes until crispy. Drain on paper towels, chop, and reserve. Add garlic, onion, and fennel to the skillet and sauté for 5 minutes until softened. Stir in rice flour for 3 minutes.
2. Preheat oven to 350 F. Add the beans, tomatoes, and zucchini to a casserole dish and pour in the sautéed vegetable and chopped pancetta; mix well. Sprinkle with porcini powder, oregano, red pepper flakes, and salt. Top with Parmigiano Reggiano cheese and butter and bake for 25 minutes or until the cheese is lightly browned. Garnish with basil and serve.

Nutrition Info:

- Per Serving: Calories: 483;Fat: 28g;Protein: 19g;Carbs: 42g.

Papaya, Jicama, And Peas Rice Bowl

Servings:4
Cooking Time: 45 Minutes

Ingredients:

- Sauce:
- Juice of ¼ lemon
- 2 teaspoons chopped fresh basil
- 1 tablespoon raw honey
- 1 tablespoon extra-virgin olive oil
- Sea salt, to taste
- Rice:
- 1½ cups wild rice
- 2 papayas, peeled, seeded, and diced
- 1 jicama, peeled and shredded
- 1 cup snow peas, julienned
- 2 cups shredded cabbage

- 1 scallion, white and green parts, chopped

Directions:

1. Combine the ingredients for the sauce in a bowl. Stir to mix well. Set aside until ready to use.
2. Pour the wild rice in a saucepan, then pour in enough water to cover. Bring to a boil.
3. Reduce the heat to low, then simmer for 45 minutes or until the wild rice is soft and plump. Drain and transfer to a large serving bowl.
4. Top the rice with papayas, jicama, peas, cabbage, and scallion. Pour the sauce over and stir to mix well before serving.

Nutrition Info:
- Per Serving: Calories: 446;Fat: 7.9g;Protein: 13.1g;-Carbs: 85.8g.

Italian Tarragon Buckwheat

Servings:6
Cooking Time:55 Minutes

Ingredients:
- 3 tbsp olive oil
- 1 ½ cups buckwheat, soaked
- 3 cups vegetable broth
- ½ onion, finely chopped
- 1 garlic clove, minced
- 2 tsp fresh tarragon, minced
- Salt and black pepper to taste
- 2 oz Parmesan cheese, grated
- 2 tbsp parsley, minced
- 2 tsp lemon juice

Directions:

1. Pulse buckwheat in your blender until about half of the grains are broken into smaller pieces. Bring broth and 3 cups of water to a boil in a medium saucepan over high heat. Reduce heat to low, cover, and keep warm.
2. Warm 2 tablespoons oil in a pot over medium heat. Add onion and cook until softened, 5 minutes. Stir in garlic and cook until fragrant, about 30 seconds. Add farro and cook, stirring frequently, until grains are lightly toasted, 3 minutes.
3. Stir 5 cups warm broth mixture into farro mixture, reduce heat to low, cover, and cook until almost all liquid has been absorbed and farro is just al dente, about 25 minutes, stirring twice during cooking.
4. Add tarragon, salt, and pepper and keep stirring for 5 minutes. Remove from heat and stir in Parmesan cheese, parsley, lemon juice, and the remaining olive oil. Adjust the seasoning and serve.

Nutrition Info:
- Per Serving: Calories: 321;Fat: 21g;Protein: 15g;Carbs: 35g.

Home-style Beef Ragu Rigatoni

Servings:6
Cooking Time:2 Hours

Ingredients:
- 1 tbsp olive oil
- 1 ½ lb bone-in short ribs
- Salt and black pepper to taste
- 1 onion, finely chopped
- 3 garlic cloves, minced
- 1 tsp fresh thyme, minced
- ½ tsp ground cinnamon
- A pinch of ground cloves
- ½ cup dry red wine
- 1 can tomatoes, diced
- 1 lb rigatoni
- 2 tbsp fresh parsley, minced
- 2 tbsp Pecorino cheese, grated

Directions:

1. Season the ribs with salt and pepper. Heat oil in a large skillet and brown the ribs on all sides, 7-10 minutes; transfer to a plate. Remove all but 1 tsp fat from skillet, add onion, and stir-fry over medium heat for 5 minutes. Stir in garlic, thyme, cinnamon, and cloves and cook until fragrant, 40 seconds. Pour in the wine, scraping off any browned bits, and simmer until almost evaporated, 2 minutes. Stir in tomatoes and their juice.
2. Nestle ribs into the sauce along with any accumulated juices and bring to a simmer. Lower the heat, cover and let simmer, turning the ribs from time to time until the meat is very tender and falling off bones, 2 hours. Transfer the ribs to cutting board, let cool slightly, then shred it using 2 forks; discard excess fat and bones.
3. Skim excess fat from the surface of the sauce with a spoon. Stir shredded meat and any accumulated juices into the sauce and bring to a simmer over medium heat. Season to taste. Meanwhile, bring a large pot filled with salted water to a boil and cook pasta until al dente. Reserve ½ cup of the cooking water, drain pasta and return it to pot. Add sauce and parsley and toss to combine. Season to taste and adjust consistency with reserved cooking water as needed. Serve with freshly grated Pecorino cheese.

Nutrition Info:
- Per Serving: Calories: 415;Fat: 11g;Protein: 12g;Carbs: 42g.

Wild Rice, Celery, And Cauliflower Pilaf

Servings:4
Cooking Time: 45 Minutes

Ingredients:

- 1 tablespoon olive oil, plus more for greasing the baking dish
- 1 cup wild rice
- 2 cups low-sodium chicken broth
- 1 sweet onion, chopped
- 2 stalks celery, chopped
- 1 teaspoon minced garlic
- 2 carrots, peeled, halved lengthwise, and sliced
- ½ cauliflower head, cut into small florets
- 1 teaspoon chopped fresh thyme
- Sea salt, to taste

Directions:

1. Preheat the oven to 350°F. Line a baking sheet with parchment paper and grease with olive oil.
2. Put the wild rice in a saucepan, then pour in the chicken broth. Bring to a boil. Reduce the heat to low and simmer for 30 minutes or until the rice is plump.
3. Meanwhile, heat the remaining olive oil in an oven-proof skillet over medium-high heat until shimmering.
4. Add the onion, celery, and garlic to the skillet and sauté for 3 minutes or until the onion is translucent.
5. Add the carrots and cauliflower to the skillet and sauté for 5 minutes. Turn off the heat and set aside.
6. Pour the cooked rice in the skillet with the vegetables. Sprinkle with thyme and salt.
7. Set the skillet in the preheated oven and bake for 15 minutes or until the vegetables are soft.
8. Serve immediately.

Nutrition Info:

- Per Serving: Calories: 214;Fat: 3.9g;Protein: 7.2g;Carbs: 37.9g.

Carrot & Barley Risotto

Servings:6
Cooking Time:1 Hour 20 Minutes

Ingredients:

- 2 tbsp olive oil
- 4 cups vegetable broth
- 4 cups water
- 1 onion, chopped fine
- 1 carrot, chopped
- 1 ½ cups pearl barley
- 1 cup dry white wine
- ¼ tsp dried oregano
- 2 oz Parmesan cheese, grated
- Salt and black pepper to taste

Directions:

1. Bring broth and water to a simmer in a saucepan. Re-duce heat to low and cover to keep warm.
2. Heat 1 tbsp of oil in a pot over medium heat until sizzling. Stir-fry onion and carrot until softened, 6-7 minutes. Add barley and cook, stirring often, until lightly toasted and aromatic, 4 minutes. Add wine and cook, stirring frequently for 2 minutes. Stir in 3 cups of water and oregano, bring to a simmer, and cook, stirring occasionally until liquid is absorbed, 25 minutes. Stir in 2 cups of broth, bring to a simmer, and cook until the liquid is absorbed, 15 minutes.
3. Continue cooking, stirring often and adding warm broth as needed to prevent the pot bottom from becoming dry until barley is cooked through but still somewhat firm in the center, 15-20 minutes. Off heat, adjust consistency with the remaining warm broth as needed. Stir in Parmesan and the remaining oil and season with salt and pepper to taste. Serve.

Nutrition Info:

- Per Serving: Calories: 355;Fat: 21g;Protein: 16g;Carbs: 35g.

Mediterranean-style Beans And Greens

Servings:2
Cooking Time: 15 Minutes

Ingredients:

- 1 can diced tomatoes with juice
- 1 can cannellini beans, drained and rinsed
- 2 tablespoons chopped green olives, plus 1 or 2 sliced for garnish
- ¼ cup vegetable broth, plus more as needed
- 1 teaspoon extra-virgin olive oil
- 2 cloves garlic, minced
- 4 cups arugula
- ¼ cup freshly squeezed lemon juice

Directions:

1. In a medium saucepan, bring the tomatoes, beans and chopped olives to a low boil, adding just enough broth to make the ingredients saucy (you may need more than ¼ cup if your canned tomatoes don't have a lot of juice). Reduce heat to low and simmer for about 5 minutes.
2. Meanwhile, in a large skillet, heat the olive oil over medium-high heat. When the oil is hot and starts to shimmer, add garlic and sauté just until it starts to turn slightly tan, about 30 seconds. Add the arugula and lemon juice, stirring to coat leaves with the olive oil and juice. Cover and reduce heat to low. Simmer for 3 to 5 minutes.
3. Serve beans over the greens and garnish with olive slices.

Nutrition Info:

- Per Serving: Calories: 262;Fat: 5.9g;Protein: 13.2g;-Carbs: 40.4g.

Spicy Farfalle With Zucchini & Tomatoes

Servings:6
Cooking Time:30 Minutes

Ingredients:
- 2 lb zucchini, halved lengthwise cut into ½ inch
- 2 tbsp Pecorino-Romano cheese, grated
- 5 tbsp extra-virgin olive oil
- Salt and black pepper to taste
- 3 garlic cloves, minced
- ½ tsp red pepper flakes
- 1 lb farfalle
- 12 oz grape tomatoes, halved
- ½ cup fresh basil, chopped
- ¼ cup pine nuts, toasted
- 2 tbsp balsamic vinegar

Directions:
1. Sprinkle zucchini with 1 tablespoon salt and let drain in a colander for 30 minutes; pat dry. Heat 1 tbsp of oil in a large skillet. Add half of the zucchini and cook until golden brown and slightly charred, 5-7 minutes, reducing the heat if the skillet begins to scorch; transfer to plate. Repeat with 1 tbsp of oil and remaining zucchini; set aside. Heat 1 tbsp of oil in the same skillet and stir-fry garlic and pepper flakes for 30 seconds. Add in squash and stir-fry for 40 seconds.
2. Meanwhile, bring a large pot filled with water to a boil. Add pasta, a pinch of salt and cook until al dente. Reserve ½ cup of cooking liquid, drain pasta and return it to pot. Add the zucchini mixture, tomatoes, basil, pine nuts, vinegar, and remaining oil and toss to combine. Season to taste and adjust consistency with the reserved cooking liquid as needed. Serve with freshly grated Pecorino-Romano cheese.

Nutrition Info:
- Per Serving: Calories: 422;Fat: 13g;Protein: 14g;Carbs: 41g.

Moroccan-style Vegetable Bean Stew

Servings:6
Cooking Time:50 Minutes

Ingredients:
- 3 tbsp olive oil
- 1 onion, chopped
- 8 oz Swiss chard, torn
- 4 garlic cloves, minced
- 1 tsp ground cumin
- ½ tsp paprika
- ½ tsp ground coriander
- ¼ tsp ground cinnamon
- 2 tbsp tomato paste
- 2 tbsp cornstarch
- 4 cups vegetable broth
- 2 carrots, chopped
- 1 can chickpeas
- 1 can butter beans
- 3 tbsp minced fresh parsley
- 3 tbsp harissa sauce
- Salt and black pepper to taste

Directions:
1. Warm the olive oil in a saucepan over medium heat. Sauté the onion until softened, about 3 minutes. Stir in garlic, cumin, paprika, coriander, and cinnamon and cook until fragrant, about 30 seconds. Stir in tomato paste and cornstarch and cook for 1 minute. Pour in broth and carrots, scraping up any browned bits, smoothing out any lumps, and bringing to boil. Reduce to a gentle simmer and cook for 10 minutes. Stir in chard, chickpeas, beans, salt, and pepper and simmer until vegetables are tender, 10-15 minutes. Sprinkle with parsley and some harissa sauce. Serve with the remaining sauce harissa on the side.

Nutrition Info:
- Per Serving: Calories: 387;Fat: 3.2g;Protein: 7g;Carbs: 28.7g.

Roasted Pepper Brown Rice

Servings:6
Cooking Time:1 Hour 50 Minutes

Ingredients:
- 2 tbsp Pecorino-Romano cheese, grated
- ¾ cup roasted red peppers, chopped
- 4 tsp olive oil
- 2 onions, finely chopped
- Salt and black pepper to taste
- 1 ½ cups vegetable broth
- 1 ½ cups brown rice, rinsed
- 1 lemon, cut into wedges

Directions:
1. Preheat oven to 375 F. Heat oil in a pot over medium heat until sizzling. Stir-fry the onions for 10-12 minutes until soft. Season with salt. Stir in 2 cups of water and broth and bring to a boil. Add in rice, cover, and transfer the pot to the oven. Cook until the rice is tender and liquid absorbed, 50-65 minutes. Remove from the oven. Sprinkle with red peppers and let sit for 5 minutes. Season to taste and stir in Pecorino-Romano cheese. Serve with lemon wedges.

Nutrition Info:
- Per Serving: Calories: 308;Fat: 10g;Protein: 11g;Carbs: 52g.

Spicy Italian Bean Balls With Marinara

Servings:2
Cooking Time: 30 Minutes

Ingredients:

- Bean Balls:
- 1 tablespoon extra-virgin olive oil
- ½ yellow onion, minced
- 1 teaspoon fennel seeds
- 2 teaspoons dried oregano
- ½ teaspoon crushed red pepper flakes
- 1 teaspoon garlic powder
- 1 can white beans (cannellini or navy), drained and rinsed
- ½ cup whole-grain bread crumbs
- Sea salt and ground black pepper, to taste
- Marinara:
- 1 tablespoon extra-virgin olive oil
- 3 garlic cloves, minced
- Handful basil leaves
- 1 can chopped tomatoes with juice reserved
- Sea salt, to taste

Directions:

1. Make the Bean Balls
2. Preheat the oven to 350°F. Line a baking sheet with parchment paper.
3. Heat the olive oil in a nonstick skillet over medium heat until shimmering.
4. Add the onion and sauté for 5 minutes or until translucent.
5. Sprinkle with fennel seeds, oregano, red pepper flakes, and garlic powder, then cook for 1 minute or until aromatic.
6. Pour the sautéed mixture in a food processor and add the beans and bread crumbs. Sprinkle with salt and ground black pepper, then pulse to combine well and the mixture holds together.
7. Shape the mixture into balls with a 2-ounce cookie scoop, then arrange the balls on the baking sheet.
8. Bake in the preheated oven for 30 minutes or until lightly browned. Flip the balls halfway through the cooking time.
9. Make the Marinara
10. While baking the bean balls, heat the olive oil in a saucepan over medium-high heat until shimmering.
11. Add the garlic and basil and sauté for 2 minutes or until fragrant.
12. Fold in the tomatoes and juice. Bring to a boil. Reduce the heat to low. Put the lid on and simmer for 15 minutes. Sprinkle with salt.
13. Transfer the bean balls on a large plate and baste with marinara before serving.

Nutrition Info:

- Per Serving: Calories: 351;Fat: 16.4g;Protein: 11.5g;-Carbs: 42.9g.

Turkish-style Orzo

Servings:2
Cooking Time:10 Minutes

Ingredients:

- 1 cup dry orzo
- 1 cup halved grape tomatoes
- 1 bag baby spinach
- 2 tbsp extra-virgin olive oil
- Salt and black pepper to taste
- ¾ cup feta cheese, crumbled
- 1 lemon, juiced and zested
- 1 tbsp fresh dill, chopped

Directions:

1. In a pot of boiling water, cook the orzo for 8 minutes. Drain well and return to the pot. Add in the tomatoes and spinach and cook until the spinach is wilted, 4-5 minutes. Mix in the olive oil, salt, and pepper. Top the dish with feta, dill, lemon juice, and lemon zest, then toss to coat. Serve and enjoy!

Nutrition Info:

- Per Serving: Calories: 612;Fat: 27g;Protein: 22g;Carbs: 74g.

Spaghetti With Pine Nuts And Cheese

Servings:4
Cooking Time: 11 Minutes

Ingredients:

- 8 ounces spaghetti
- 4 tablespoons almond butter
- 1 teaspoon freshly ground black pepper
- ½ cup pine nuts
- 1 cup fresh grated Parmesan cheese, divided

Directions:

1. Bring a large pot of salted water to a boil. Add the pasta and cook for 8 minutes.
2. In a large saucepan over medium heat, combine the butter, black pepper, and pine nuts. Cook for 2 to 3 minutes, or until the pine nuts are lightly toasted.
3. Reserve ½ cup of the pasta water. Drain the pasta and place it into the pan with the pine nuts.
4. Add ¾ cup of the Parmesan cheese and the reserved pasta water to the pasta and toss everything together to evenly coat the pasta.
5. Transfer the pasta to a serving dish and top with the remaining ¼ cup of the Parmesan cheese. Serve immediately.

Nutrition Info:

- Per Serving: Calories: 542;Fat: 32.0g;Protein: 20.0g;-Carbs: 46.0g.

Citrusy & Minty Farro

Servings:6
Cooking Time:28 Minutes

Ingredients:

- 3 tbsp olive oil
- 1 ½ cups whole farro
- Salt and black pepper to taste
- 1 onion, chopped fine
- 1 garlic clove, minced
- ¼ cup chopped fresh cilantro
- ¼ cup chopped fresh mint
- 1 tbsp lemon juice

Directions:

1. Bring 4 quarts of water to boil in a pot. Add farro and season with salt and pepper, bring to a boil and cook until grains are tender with a slight chew, 20-25 minutes. Drain farro, return to the empty pot and cover to keep warm. Heat 2 tbsp of oil in a large skillet over medium heat. Stir-fry onion for 5 minutes. Stir in garlic and cook until fragrant, about 30 seconds. Add the remaining oil and farro and stir-fry for 2 minutes. Remove from heat, stir in cilantro, mint, and lemon juice. Season to taste and serve.

Nutrition Info:

- Per Serving: Calories: 322;Fat: 16g;Protein: 11g;Carbs: 24g.

Tomato-mushroom Spaghetti

Servings:4
Cooking Time:30 Minutes

Ingredients:

- ¼ cup olive oil
- 16 oz spaghetti, cut in half
- 2 cups mushrooms, chopped
- 1 bell pepper, chopped
- ½ cup yellow onion, chopped
- 3 garlic cloves, minced
- ½ tsp five-spice powder
- 2 tbsp fresh parsley, chopped
- 1 tbsp tomato paste
- 2 ripe tomatoes, chopped
- ½ cup Parmesan cheese, grated
- Salt and black pepper to taste

Directions:

1. Heat olive oil in a skillet over medium heat. Add in mushrooms, bell pepper, onion, and garlic and stir-fry for 4-5 minutes until tender. Mix in salt, black pepper, five-spice powder, tomato paste, and tomatoes; stir well and cook for 10-12 minutes. In a pot with salted boiling water, add the pasta and cook until al dente, about 8-10 minutes, stirring occasionally. Drain and stir in the vegetable mixture. Serve topped with Parmesan cheese and fresh parsley.

Nutrition Info:

- Per Serving: Calories: 566;Fat: 22g;Protein: 24g;Carbs: 72g.

Arrabbiata Penne Rigate

Servings:4
Cooking Time:30 Minutes

Ingredients:

- 2 tbsp olive oil
- 1 onion, chopped
- 6 cloves garlic, minced
- ½ red chili, chopped
- 2 cups canned tomatoes, diced
- ½ tsp sugar
- Salt and black pepper to taste
- 1 lb penne rigate
- 1 cup shredded mozzarella
- 1 cup fresh basil, chopped
- ½ cup grated Parmesan cheese

Directions:

1. Bring a large pot of salted water to a boil, add the penne, and cook for 7-9 minutes until al dente. Reserve ¼ cup pasta cooking water and drain pasta. Set aside.
2. Warm the oil in a saucepan over medium heat. Sauté the onion and garlic for 3-5 minutes or until softened. Add tomatoes with their liquid, black pepper, sugar, and salt. Cook 20 minutes or until the sauce thickens. Add the pasta and reserved cooking water and stir for 2-3 minutes. Add mozzarella cheese and red chili and cook until the cheese melts, 3-4 minutes. Top with Parmesan and basil and serve.

Nutrition Info:

- Per Serving: Calories: 454;Fat: 12g;Protein: 18g;Carbs: 70g.

Lemony Green Quinoa

Servings:4
Cooking Time:30 Minutes

Ingredients:

- 2 tbsp olive oil
- 1 onion, chopped
- 2 garlic cloves, minced
- 1 cup quinoa, rinsed
- 1 lb asparagus, chopped
- 2 tbsp fresh parsley, chopped
- 2 tbsp lemon juice
- 1 tsp lemon zest, grated
- ½ lb green beans, trimmed and halved
- Salt and black pepper to taste
- ½ lb cherry tomatoes, halved

Directions:

1. Heat olive oil in a pot over medium heat and sauté onion and garlic for 3 minutes until soft. Stir in quinoa for 1-2 minutes. Pour in 2 cups of water and season with salt and

pepper. Bring to a bowl and reduce the heat. Simmer for 5 minutes. Stir in green beans and asparagus and cook for another 10 minutes. Remove from the heat and mix in cherry tomatoes, lemon juice and lemon zest. Top with parsley and serve.

Nutrition Info:
- Per Serving: Calories: 430;Fat: 16g;Protein: 17g;Carbs: 60g.

Traditional Beef Lasagna

Servings:4
Cooking Time:70 Minutes

Ingredients:
- 2 tbsp olive oil
- 1 lb lasagne sheets
- 1 lb ground beef
- 1 white onion, chopped
- 1 tsp Italian seasoning
- Salt and black pepper to taste
- 1 cup marinara sauce
- ½ cup grated Parmesan cheese

Directions:
1. Preheat oven to 350 F. Warm olive oil in a skillet and add the beef and onion. Cook until the beef is brown, 7-8 minutes. Season with Italian seasoning, salt, and pepper. Cook for 1 minute and mix in the marinara sauce. Simmer for 3 minutes.
2. Spread a layer of the beef mixture in a lightly greased baking sheet and make a first single layer on the beef mixture. Top with a single layer of lasagna sheets. Repeat the layering two more times using the remaining ingredients in the same quantities. Sprinkle with Parmesan cheese. Bake in the oven until the cheese melts and is bubbly with the sauce, 20 minutes. Remove the lasagna, allow cooling for 2 minutes and dish onto serving plates. Serve warm.

Nutrition Info:
- Per Serving: Calories: 557;Fat: 29g;Protein: 60g;Carbs: 4g.

Lemon Couscous With Broccoli

Servings:4
Cooking Time:20 Minutes

Ingredients:
- 2 tsp olive oil
- Salt and black pepper to taste
- 1 small red onion, sliced
- 1 lemon, zested
- 1 head broccoli, cut into florets
- 1 cup couscous

Directions:
1. Heat a pot filled with salted water over medium heat; bring to a boil. Add in the broccoli and cook for 4-6 min-

utes until tender. Remove to a boil with a slotted spoon. In another bowl, place the couscous and cover with boiling broccoli water. Cover and let sit for 3-4 minutes until the water is absorbrd. Fluff the couscous with a fork and season with lemon zest, salt. and pepper. Stir in broccoli and top with red onion to serve.

Nutrition Info:
- Per Serving: Calories: 620;Fat: 45g;Protein: 11g;Carbs: 51g.

Roasted Butternut Squash And Zucchini With Penne

Servings:6
Cooking Time: 30 Minutes

Ingredients:
- 1 large zucchini, diced
- 1 large butternut squash, peeled and diced
- 1 large yellow onion, chopped
- 2 tablespoons extra-virgin olive oil
- 1 teaspoon paprika
- ½ teaspoon garlic powder
- ½ teaspoon sea salt
- ½ teaspoon freshly ground black pepper
- 1 pound whole-grain penne
- ½ cup dry white wine
- 2 tablespoons grated Parmesan cheese

Directions:
1. Preheat the oven to 400ºF. Line a baking sheet with aluminum foil.
2. Combine the zucchini, butternut squash, and onion in a large bowl. Drizzle with olive oil and sprinkle with paprika, garlic powder, salt, and ground black pepper. Toss to coat well.
3. Spread the vegetables in the single layer on the baking sheet, then roast in the preheated oven for 25 minutes or until the vegetables are tender.
4. Meanwhile, bring a pot of water to a boil, then add the penne and cook for 14 minutes or until al dente. Drain the penne through a colander.
5. Transfer ½ cup of roasted vegetables in a food processor, then pour in the dry white wine. Pulse until smooth.
6. Pour the puréed vegetables in a nonstick skillet and cook with penne over medium-high heat for a few minutes to heat through.
7. Transfer the penne with the purée on a large serving plate, then spread the remaining roasted vegetables and Parmesan on top before serving.

Nutrition Info:
- Per Serving: Calories: 340;Fat: 6.2g;Protein: 8.0g;Carbs: 66.8g.

Sun-dried Tomato & Basil Risotto

Servings:4
Cooking Time:35 Minutes

Ingredients:
- 10 oz sundried tomatoes in olive oil, drained and chopped
- 2 tbsp olive oil
- 2 cups chicken stock
- 1 onion, chopped
- 1 cup Arborio rice
- Salt and black pepper to taste
- 1 cup Pecorino cheese, grated
- ¼ cup basil leaves, chopped

Directions:
1. Warm the olive oil in a skillet over medium heat and cook onion and sundried tomatoes for 5 minutes. Stir in rice, chicken stock, salt, pepper, and basil and bring to a boil. Cook for 20 minutes. Mix in Pecorino cheese and serve.

Nutrition Info:
- Per Serving: Calories: 430;Fat: 9g;Protein: 8g;Carbs: 57g.

Tomato Sauce And Basil Pesto Fettuccine

Servings:4
Cooking Time: 15 Minutes

Ingredients:
- 4 Roma tomatoes, diced
- 2 teaspoons no-salt-added tomato paste
- 1 tablespoon chopped fresh oregano
- 2 garlic cloves, minced
- 1 cup low-sodium vegetable soup
- ½ teaspoon sea salt
- 1 packed cup fresh basil leaves
- ¼ cup pine nuts
- ¼ cup grated Parmesan cheese
- 2 tablespoons extra-virgin olive oil
- 1 pound cooked whole-grain fettuccine

Directions:
1. Put the tomatoes, tomato paste, oregano, garlic, vegetable soup, and salt in a skillet. Stir to mix well.
2. Cook over medium heat for 10 minutes or until lightly thickened.
3. Put the remaining ingredients, except for the fettuccine, in a food processor and pulse to combine until smooth.
4. Pour the puréed basil mixture into the tomato mixture, then add the fettuccine. Cook for a few minutes or until heated through and the fettuccine is well coated.
5. Serve immediately.

Nutrition Info:
- Per Serving: Calories: 389;Fat: 22.7g;Protein: 9.7g;Carbs: 40.2g.

Old-fashioned Pasta Primavera

Servings:4
Cooking Time:25 Minutes

Ingredients:
- ½ cup grated Pecorino Romano cheese
- 2 cups cauliflower florets, cut into matchsticks
- ¼ cup olive oil
- 16 oz tortiglioni
- ½ cup chopped green onions
- 1 red bell pepper, sliced
- 4 garlic cloves, minced
- 1 cup grape tomatoes, halved
- 2 tsp dried Italian seasoning
- ½ lemon, juiced

Directions:
1. In a pot of boiling water, cook the tortiglioni pasta for 8-10 minutes until al dente. Drain and set aside.
2. Heat olive oil in a skillet and sauté onion, cauliflower, and bell pepper for 7 minutes. Mix in garlic and cook until fragrant, 30 seconds. Stir in the tomatoes and Italian seasoning; cook until the tomatoes soften, 5 minutes. Mix in the lemon juice and tortiglioni. Garnish with cheese.

Nutrition Info:
- Per Serving: Calories: 283;Fat: 18g;Protein: 15g;Carbs: 5g.

Lemony Farro And Avocado Bowl

Servings:4
Cooking Time: 25 Minutes

Ingredients:
- 1 tablespoon plus 2 teaspoons extra-virgin olive oil, divided
- ½ medium onion, chopped
- 1 carrot, shredded
- 2 garlic cloves, minced
- 1 cup pearled farro
- 2 cups low-sodium vegetable soup
- 2 avocados, peeled, pitted, and sliced
- Zest and juice of 1 small lemon
- ¼ teaspoon sea salt

Directions:
1. Heat 1 tablespoon of olive oil in a saucepan over medium-high heat until shimmering.
2. Add the onion and sauté for 5 minutes or until translucent.
3. Add the carrot and garlic and sauté for 1 minute or until fragrant.
4. Add the farro and pour in the vegetable soup. Bring to a boil over high heat. Reduce the heat to low. Put the lid on and simmer for 20 minutes or until the farro is al dente.
5. Transfer the farro in a large serving bowl, then fold in the avocado slices. Sprinkle with lemon zest and salt, then

drizzle with lemon juice and 2 teaspoons of olive oil.
6. Stir to mix well and serve immediately.

Nutrition Info:
• Per Serving: Calories: 210;Fat: 11.1g;Protein: 4.2g;-Carbs: 27.9g.

Mustard Vegetable Millet

Servings:6
Cooking Time:35 Minutes

Ingredients:
• 6 oz okra, cut into 1-inch lengths
• 3 tbsp olive oil
• 6 oz asparagus, chopped
• Salt and black pepper to taste
• 1 ½ cups whole millet
• 2 tbsp lemon juice
• 2 tbsp minced shallot
• 1 tsp Dijon mustard
• 6 oz cherry tomatoes, halved
• 3 tbsp chopped fresh dill
• 2 oz goat cheese, crumbled

Directions:
1. In a large pot, bring 4 quarts of water to a boil. Add asparagus, snap peas, and salt and cook until crisp-tender, about 3 minutes. Using a slotted spoon, transfer vegetables to a large plate and let cool completely, about 15 minutes. Add millet to water, return to a boil, and cook until grains are tender, 15-20 minutes.
2. Drain millet, spread in rimmed baking sheet, and let cool completely, 15 minutes. Whisk oil, lemon juice, shallot, mustard, salt, and pepper in a large bowl. Add vegetables, millet, tomatoes, dill, and half of the goat cheese and toss gently to combine. Season with salt and pepper. Sprinkle with remaining goat cheese to serve.

Nutrition Info:
• Per Serving: Calories: 315;Fat: 19g;Protein: 13g;Carbs: 35g.

Autumn Vegetable & Rigatoni Bake

Servings:6
Cooking Time:45 Minutes

Ingredients:
• 2 tbsp grated Pecorino-Romano cheese
• 2 tbsp olive oil
• 1 lb pumpkin, chopped
• 1 zucchini, chopped
• 1 onion, chopped
• 1 lb rigatoni
• Salt and black pepper to taste
• ½ tsp garlic powder
• ½ cup dry white wine

Directions:

1. Preheat oven to 420 F. Combine zucchini, pumpkin, onion, and olive oil in a bowl. Arrange on a lined aluminum foil sheet and season with salt, pepper, and garlic powder. Bake for 30 minutes until tender. In a pot of boiling water, cook rigatoni for 8-10 minutes until al dente. Drain and set aside.
2. In a food processor, place ½ cup of the roasted veggies and wine and pulse until smooth. Transfer to a skillet over medium heat. Stir in rigatoni and cook until heated through. Top with the remaining vegetables and Pecorino cheese to serve.

Nutrition Info:
• Per Serving: Calories: 186;Fat: 11g;Protein: 10g;Carbs: 15g.

Greek Chicken & Fusilli Bake

Servings:4
Cooking Time:55 Minutes

Ingredients:
• 2 tbsp olive oil
• 1 cup Provolone cheese, grated
• 16 oz fusilli pasta
• 1 lb ground chicken
• 1 shallot, thinly sliced
• 2 bell peppers, chopped
• 2 tomatoes, pureed
• 1 bay leaf
• 1 tbsp tomato paste
• ½ cup Greek yogurt
• 1 tsp dried oregano, divided
• ½ tsp salt

Directions:
1. To a pot with salted boiling water, add the fusilli pasta and cook until al dente, 8-10 minutes. Reserve ½ cup of the cooking water and drain the pasta. Transfer to a bowl.
2. Preheat oven to 380 F. Warm the olive oil in a skillet over medium heat. Add in the chicken and brown for 3-4 minutes, stirring periodically. Add in shallot, bell peppers, oregano, and bay leaf and cook for 3-4 minutes. Remove the mixture to the pasta bowl and mix in the tomato puree and tomato paste. Sprinkle with the reserved cooking liquid and toss to coat. Transfer the pasta mixture to a baking dish. Spread the yogurt on top and sprinkle with the cheese. Cover with aluminum foil and bake for 20 minutes. Discard the foil and cook for another 5 minutes until the cheese is golden brown.

Nutrition Info:
• Per Serving: Calories: 772;Fat: 28g;Protein: 58g;Carbs: 71g.

Spinach & Olive Penne

Servings:4
Cooking Time:30 Minutes

Ingredients:
- 1 tbsp olive oil
- 8 oz uncooked penne
- 2 garlic cloves, minced
- ¼ tsp paprika
- 2 cups parsley, chopped
- 4 cups baby spinach
- ¼ tsp ground nutmeg
- Salt and black pepper to taste
- ⅓ cup green olives, sliced
- ⅓ cup Parmesan cheese, grated

Directions:

1. Cook the pasta according to the package directions in a large pot until almost al dente. Drain the pasta, and save ¼ cup of the cooking water. Meanwhile, heat the oil in a skillet over medium heat. Add the garlic and paprika, and cook for 30 seconds, stirring constantly. Stir in the parsley for 1 minute. Add the spinach, nutmeg, pepper, and salt, and keep stirring for 3 minutes until the spinach wilts. Add the pasta and the reserved water to the skillet. Stir in the olives, and cook for about 2 minutes until most of the pasta water has been absorbed. Sprinkle with Parmesan cheese and serve.

Nutrition Info:
- Per Serving: Calories: 273;Fat: 5g;Protein: 17g;Carbs: 48g.

Cherry, Apricot, And Pecan Brown Rice Bowl

Servings:2
Cooking Time: 1 Hour 1 Minutes

Ingredients:
- 2 tablespoons olive oil
- 2 green onions, sliced
- ½ cup brown rice
- 1 cup low -sodium chicken stock
- 2 tablespoons dried cherries
- 4 dried apricots, chopped
- 2 tablespoons pecans, toasted and chopped
- Sea salt and freshly ground pepper, to taste

Directions:

1. Heat the olive oil in a medium saucepan over medium-high heat until shimmering.
2. Add the green onions and sauté for 1 minutes or until fragrant.
3. Add the rice. Stir to mix well, then pour in the chicken stock.
4. Bring to a boil. Reduce the heat to low. Cover and simmer for 50 minutes or until the brown rice is soft.
5. Add the cherries, apricots, and pecans, and simmer for 10 more minutes or until the fruits are tender.
6. Pour them in a large serving bowl. Fluff with a fork. Sprinkle with sea salt and freshly ground pepper. Serve immediately.

Nutrition Info:
- Per Serving: Calories: 451;Fat: 25.9g;Protein: 8.2g;-Carbs: 50.4g.

Slow Cooked Turkey And Brown Rice

Servings:6
Cooking Time: 3 Hours 10 Minutes

Ingredients:
- 1 tablespoon extra-virgin olive oil
- 1½ pounds ground turkey
- 2 tablespoons chopped fresh sage, divided
- 2 tablespoons chopped fresh thyme, divided
- 1 teaspoon sea salt
- ½ teaspoon ground black pepper
- 2 cups brown rice
- 1 can stewed tomatoes, with the juice
- ¼ cup pitted and sliced Kalamata olives
- 3 medium zucchini, sliced thinly
- ¼ cup chopped fresh flat-leaf parsley
- 1 medium yellow onion, chopped
- 1 tablespoon plus 1 teaspoon balsamic vinegar
- 2 cups low-sodium chicken stock
- 2 garlic cloves, minced
- ½ cup grated Parmesan cheese, for serving

Directions:

1. Heat the olive oil in a nonstick skillet over medium-high heat until shimmering.
2. Add the ground turkey and sprinkle with 1 tablespoon of sage, 1 tablespoon of thyme, salt and ground black pepper.
3. Sauté for 10 minutes or until the ground turkey is lightly browned.
4. Pour them in the slow cooker, then pour in the remaining ingredients, except for the Parmesan. Stir to mix well.
5. Put the lid on and cook on high for 3 hours or until the rice and vegetables are tender.
6. Pour them in a large serving bowl, then spread with Parmesan cheese before serving.

Nutrition Info:
- Per Serving: Calories: 499;Fat: 16.4g;Protein: 32.4g;-Carbs: 56.5g.

Easy Walnut And Ricotta Spaghetti

Servings:6
Cooking Time: 10 Minutes

Ingredients:

- 1 pound cooked whole-wheat spaghetti
- 2 tablespoons extra-virgin olive oil
- 4 cloves garlic, minced
- ¾ cup walnuts, toasted and finely chopped
- 2 tablespoons ricotta cheese
- ¼ cup flat-leaf parsley, chopped
- ½ cup grated Parmesan cheese
- Sea salt and freshly ground pepper, to taste

Directions:

1. Reserve a cup of spaghetti water while cooking the spaghetti.
2. Heat the olive oil in a nonstick skillet over medium-low heat or until shimmering.
3. Add the garlic and sauté for a minute or until fragrant.
4. Pour the spaghetti water into the skillet and cook for 8 more minutes.
5. Turn off the heat and mix in the walnuts and ricotta cheese.
6. Put the cooked spaghetti on a large serving plate, then pour the walnut sauce over. Spread with parsley and Parmesan, then sprinkle with salt and ground pepper. Toss to serve.

Nutrition Info:

- Per Serving: Calories: 264;Fat: 16.8g;Protein: 8.6g;-Carbs: 22.8g.

Lemon-basil Spaghetti

Servings:6
Cooking Time:30 Minutes

Ingredients:

- ½ cup extra-virgin olive oil
- Zest and juice from 1 lemon
- 1 garlic clove, minced
- Salt and black pepper to taste
- 2 oz ricotta cheese, chopped
- 1 lb spaghetti
- 6 tbsp shredded fresh basil

Directions:

1. In a bowl, whisk oil, grated lemon zest, juice, garlic, salt, and pepper. Stir in ricotta cheese and mix well. Meanwhile, bring a pot filled with salted water to a boil. Cook the pasta until al dente. Reserve ½ cup of the cooking liquid, then drain pasta and return it to the pot. Add oil mixture and basil and toss to combine. Season to taste and adjust consistency with reserved cooking water as needed. Serve warm.

Nutrition Info:

- Per Serving: Calories: 395;Fat: 11g;Protein: 10g;Carbs: 37g.

Couscous With Carrots & Peas

Servings:6
Cooking Time:33 Minutes

Ingredients:

- ¼ cup olive oil
- 1 ½ cups couscous
- 2 carrots, chopped
- 1 onion, finely chopped
- Salt and black pepper to taste
- 3 garlic cloves, minced
- 1 tsp ground coriander
- ¼ tsp ground anise seed
- 1 can chickpeas
- 1 ½ cups frozen peas
- ½ cup chopped fresh cilantro
- 1 lemon, cut into wedges

Directions:

1. Warm 2 tablespoons of oil in a skillet. Stir in couscous until the grains are just starting to brown, 3-5 minutes. Transfer to bowl and wipe the skillet clean. Heat the remaining oil in the skillet and stir-fry carrots, onion, and salt until softened, 5 minutes. Stir in garlic, coriander, and anise and cook until fragrant, 30 seconds. Stir in 2 cups of water and chickpeas and bring to a simmer. Stir in peas and couscous.
2. Cover, remove the skillet from the heat, and let sit until couscous is tender, 7 minutes. Add the cilantro and fluff gently with a fork to mix well. Season to taste and drizzle with extra olive oil. Serve with lemon wedges.

Nutrition Info:

- Per Serving: Calories: 402;Fat: 11g;Protein: 9g;Carbs: 42g.

Poultry And Meats Recipes

Poultry And Meats Recipes

Cream Zucchini & Chicken Dish

Servings:4
Cooking Time:70 Minutes

Ingredients:
- 3 tbsp canola oil
- 1 lb turkey breast, sliced
- Salt and black pepper to taste
- 3 garlic cloves, minced
- 2 zucchinis, sliced
- 1 cup chicken stock
- ¼ cup heavy cream
- 2 tbsp parsley, chopped

Directions:
1. Warm the olive oil in a pot over medium heat. Cook the turkey for 10 minutes on both sides. Put in garlic and cook for 1 minute. Season with salt and pepper. Stir in zucchinis for 3-4 minutes and pour in the chicken stock. Bring to a boil and cook for 40 minutes. Stir in heavy cream and parsley.

Nutrition Info:
- Per Serving: Calories: 270;Fat: 11g;Protein: 16g;Carbs: 27g.

Asparagus & Chicken Skillet

Servings:4
Cooking Time:30 Minutes

Ingredients:
- 2 tbsp olive oil
- 1 lb chicken breasts, sliced
- Salt and black pepper to taste
- 1 lb asparagus, chopped
- 6 sundried tomatoes, diced
- 3 tbsp capers, drained
- 2 tbsp lemon juice

Directions:
1. Warm the olive oil in a skillet over medium heat. Cook asparagus, tomatoes, salt, pepper, capers, and lemon juice for 10 minutes. Remove to a bowl. Brown chicken in the same skillet for 8 minutes on both sides. Put veggies back to skillet and cook for another 2-3 minutes. Serve and enjoy!

Nutrition Info:
- Per Serving: Calories: 560;Fat: 29g;Protein: 45g;Carbs: 34g.

Pork Tenderloin With Caraway Seeds

Servings:4
Cooking Time:30 Minutes

Ingredients:
- 2 tbsp olive oil
- 1 lb pork tenderloin, sliced
- Salt and black pepper to taste
- 3 tbsp ground caraway seeds
- 1/3 cup half-and-half
- ½ cup dill, chopped

Directions:
1. Warm the olive oil in a skillet over medium heat and sear pork for 8 minutes on all sides. Stir in salt, pepper, ground caraway seeds, half-and-half, and dill and bring to a boil. Cook for another 12 minutes. Serve warm.

Nutrition Info:
- Per Serving: Calories: 330;Fat: 15g;Protein: 18g;Carbs: 15g.

Almond-crusted Chicken Tenders With Honey

Servings:4
Cooking Time: 20 Minutes

Ingredients:
- 1 tablespoon honey
- 1 tablespoon whole-grain or Dijon mustard
- ¼ teaspoon freshly ground black pepper
- ¼ teaspoon kosher or sea salt
- 1 pound boneless, skinless chicken breast tenders or tenderloins
- 1 cup almonds, roughly chopped
- Nonstick cooking spray

Directions:
1. Preheat the oven to 425ºF. Line a large, rimmed baking sheet with parchment paper. Place a wire cooling rack on the parchment-lined baking sheet, and spray the rack well with nonstick cooking spray.
2. In a large bowl, combine the honey, mustard, pepper, and salt. Add the chicken and toss gently to coat. Set aside.
3. Dump the almonds onto a large sheet of parchment paper and spread them out. Press the coated chicken tenders into the nuts until evenly coated on all sides. Place the chicken on the prepared wire rack.
4. Bake in the preheated oven for 15 to 20 minutes, or until the internal temperature of the chicken measures 165ºF on a meat thermometer and any juices run clear.
5. Cool for 5 minutes before serving.

Nutrition Info:
- Per Serving: Calories: 222;Fat: 7.0g;Protein: 11.0g;-

Carbs: 29.0g.

Greek-style Lamb Burgers

Servings:4
Cooking Time: 10 Minutes

Ingredients:
- 1 pound ground lamb
- ½ teaspoon salt
- ½ teaspoon freshly ground black pepper
- 4 tablespoons crumbled feta cheese
- Buns, toppings, and tzatziki, for serving (optional)

Directions:
1. Preheat the grill to high heat.
2. In a large bowl, using your hands, combine the lamb with the salt and pepper.
3. Divide the meat into 4 portions. Divide each portion in half to make a top and a bottom. Flatten each half into a 3-inch circle. Make a dent in the center of one of the halves and place 1 tablespoon of the feta cheese in the center. Place the second half of the patty on top of the feta cheese and press down to close the 2 halves together, making it resemble a round burger.
4. Grill each side for 3 minutes, for medium-well. Serve on a bun with your favorite toppings and tzatziki sauce, if desired.

Nutrition Info:
- Per Serving: Calories: 345;Fat: 29.0g;Protein: 20.0g;Carbs: 1.0g.

Provençal Flank Steak Au Pistou

Servings:4
Cooking Time:25 Minutes

Ingredients:
- 8 tbsp olive oil
- 1 lb flank steak
- Salt and black pepper to taste
- ½ cup parsley, chopped
- ¼ cup fresh basil, chopped
- 2 garlic cloves, minced
- ½ tsp celery seeds
- 1 orange, zested and juiced
- 1 tsp red pepper flakes
- 1 tbsp red wine vinegar

Directions:
1. Place the parsley, basil, garlic, orange zest and juice, celery seeds, salt, pepper, and red pepper flakes, and pulse until finely chopped in your food processor. With the processor running, stream in the red wine vinegar and 6 tbsp of olive oil until well combined. Set aside until ready to serve.
2. Preheat your grill. Rub the steak with the remaining olive oil, salt, and pepper. Place the steak on the grill and cook for 6-8 minutes on each side. Remove and leave to sit for 10 minutes. Slice the steak and drizzle with pistou. Serve.

Nutrition Info:
- Per Serving: Calories: 441;Fat: 36g;Protein: 25g;Carbs: 3g.

Rosemary Tomato Chicken

Servings:4
Cooking Time:50 Minutes

Ingredients:
- 2 tbsp olive oil
- 1 lb chicken breasts, sliced
- 1 onion, chopped
- 1 carrot, chopped
- 2 garlic cloves, minced
- ½ cup chicken stock
- 1 tsp oregano, dried
- 1 tsp tarragon, dried
- 1 tsp rosemary, dried
- 1 cup canned tomatoes, diced
- Salt and black pepper to taste

Directions:
1. Warm the olive oil in a pot over medium heat and cook the chicken for 8 minutes on both sides. Put in carrot, garlic, and onion and cook for an additional 3 minutes. Season with salt and pepper. Pour in stock, oregano, tarragon, rosemary, and tomatoes and bring to a boil; simmer for 25 minutes. Serve.

Nutrition Info:
- Per Serving: Calories: 260;Fat: 12g;Protein: 10g;Carbs: 16g.

Rich Beef Meal

Servings:4
Cooking Time:40 Minutes

Ingredients:
- 1 tbsp olive oil
- 1 lb beef meat, cubed
- 1 red onion, chopped
- 1 garlic clove, minced
- 1 celery stalk, chopped
- Salt and black pepper to taste
- 14 oz canned tomatoes, diced
- 1 cup vegetable stock
- ½ tsp ground nutmeg
- 2 tsp dill, chopped

Directions:
1. Warm the olive oil in a skillet over medium heat and cook onion and garlic for 5 minutes. Put in beef and cook for 5 more minutes. Stir in celery, salt, pepper, tomatoes, stock, nutmeg, and dill and bring to a boil. Cook for 20 minutes.

Nutrition Info:
- Per Serving: Calories: 300;Fat: 14g;Protein: 19g;Carbs: 16g.

Aromatic Beef Stew

Servings:4
Cooking Time:80 Minutes

Ingredients:
- 3 tbsp olive oil
- 2 lb beef shoulder, cubed
- Salt and black pepper to taste
- 1 onion, chopped
- 2 garlic cloves, minced
- 3 tomatoes, grated
- 1 tsp red chili flakes
- 2 cups chicken stock
- 1 cup couscous
- 10 green olives, sliced
- 1 tbsp cilantro, chopped

Directions:
1. Warm the olive oil in a pot over medium heat and cook beef for 5 minutes until brown, stirring often. Add in onion and garlic and cook for another 5 minutes. Stir in tomatoes, salt, pepper, chicken stock, olives, and red chili flakes. Bring to a boil and simmer for 1 hour. Cover the couscous with boiling water in a bowl, cover, and let sit for 4-5 minutes until the water has been absorbed. Fluff with a fork and season with salt and pepper. Pour the stew over and scatter with cilantro.

Nutrition Info:
- Per Serving: Calories: 420;Fat: 18g;Protein: 35g;Carbs: 26g.

Pork Loin With Cilantro-mustard Glaze

Servings:4
Cooking Time:35 Minutes

Ingredients:
- 2 tbsp olive oil
- 1 onion, chopped
- 2 lb pork loin, cut into strips
- ½ cup vegetable stock
- Salt and black pepper to taste
- 2 tsp mustard
- 1 tbsp cilantro, chopped

Directions:
1. Warm the olive oil in a skillet over medium heat and cook the onion for 5 minutes. Put in pork loin and cook for another 10 minutes, stirring often. Stir in vegetable stock, salt, pepper, mustard, and cilantro and cook for an additional 10 minutes.

Nutrition Info:
- Per Serving: Calories: 300;Fat: 13g;Protein: 24g;Carbs: 15g.

Thyme Chicken Roast

Servings:4
Cooking Time:65 Minutes

Ingredients:
- 1 tbsp butter, softened
- 1 lb chicken drumsticks
- 2 garlic cloves, minced
- 1 tsp paprika
- 1 lemon, zested
- 1 tbsp chopped fresh thyme
- Salt and black pepper to taste

Directions:
1. Preheat oven to 350 F. Mix butter, thyme, paprika, salt, garlic, pepper, and lemon zest in a bowl. Rub the mixture all over the chicken drumsticks and arrange them on a baking dish. Add in ½ cup of water and roast in the oven for 50-60 minutes. Remove the chicken from the oven and let it sit covered with foil for 10 minutes. Serve and enjoy!

Nutrition Info:
- Per Serving: Calories: 219;Fat: 9.4g;Protein: 31g;Carbs: 0.5g.

Baked Root Veggie & Chicken

Servings:6
Cooking Time:50 Minutes

Ingredients:
- 2 sweet potatoes, peeled and cubed
- ½ cup green olives, pitted and smashed
- ¼ cup olive oil
- 2 lb chicken breasts, sliced
- 2 tbsp harissa seasoning
- 1 lemon, zested and juiced
- Salt and black pepper to taste
- 2 carrots, chopped
- 1 onion, chopped
- ½ cup feta cheese, crumbled
- ½ cup parsley, chopped

Directions:
1. Preheat the oven to 390 F. Place chicken, harissa seasoning, lemon juice, lemon zest, olive oil, salt, pepper, carrots, sweet potatoes, and onion in a roasting pan and mix well. Bake for 40 minutes. Combine feta cheese and green olives in a bowl. Share chicken mixture into plates and top with olive mixture. Top with parsley and parsley and serve immediately.

Nutrition Info:
- Per Serving: Calories: 310;Fat: 10g;Protein: 15g;Carbs: 23g.

Quinoa & Chicken Bowl

Servings:4
Cooking Time:50 Minutes

Ingredients:

- 4 chicken things, skinless and boneless
- 2 tbsp olive oil
- Salt and black pepper to taste
- 1 celery stalk, chopped
- 2 leeks, chopped
- 2 cups chicken stock
- 2 tbsp cilantro, chopped
- 1 cup quinoa
- 1 tsp lemon zest

Directions:

1. Warm the olive oil in a pot over medium heat and cook the chicken for 6-8 minutes on all sides. Stir in leeks and celery and cook for another 5 minutes until tender. Season with salt and pepper. Stir in quinoa and lemon zest for 1 minute and pour in the chicken stock. Bring to a boil and simmer for 35 minutes. Serve topped with cilantro.

Nutrition Info:

- Per Serving: Calories: 250;Fat: 14g;Protein: 35g;Carbs: 17g.

Chicken With Halloumi Cheese

Servings:4
Cooking Time:40 Minutes

Ingredients:

- 2 tbsp butter
- 1 cup Halloumi cheese, cubed
- Salt and black pepper to taste
- 1 hard-boiled egg yolk
- ½ cup olive oil
- 6 black olives, halved
- 1 tbsp fresh cilantro, chopped
- 1 tbsp balsamic vinegar
- 1 tbsp garlic, finely minced
- 1 tbsp fresh lemon juice
- 1 ½ lb chicken wings

Directions:

1. Melt the butter in a saucepan over medium heat. Sear the chicken wings for 5 minutes per side. Season with salt and pepper to taste. Place the chicken wings on a parchment-lined baking pan. Mash the egg yolk with a fork and mix in the garlic, lemon juice, balsamic vinegar, olive oil, and salt until creamy, uniform, and smooth.
2. Preheat oven to 380 F. Spread the egg mixture over the chicken. Bake for 15-20 minutes. Top with the cheese and bake an additional 5 minutes until hot and bubbly. Scatter cilantro and olives on top of the chicken wings. Serve.

Nutrition Info:

- Per Serving: Calories: 560;Fat: 48g;Protein: 41g;Carbs: 2g.

Smooth Chicken Breasts With Nuts

Servings:4
Cooking Time:40 Minutes

Ingredients:

- 2 tbsp olive oil
- 1 ½ lb chicken breasts, cubed
- 4 spring onions, chopped
- 2 carrots, peeled and sliced
- ¼ cup mayonnaise
- ½ cup Greek yogurt
- 1 cup toasted cashews, chopped
- Salt and black pepper to taste

Directions:

1. Warm the olive oil in a skillet over medium heat and brown chicken for 8 minutes on all sides. Stir in spring onions, carrots, mayonnaise, yogurt, salt, and pepper and bring to a simmer. Cook for 20 minutes. Top with cashews to serve.

Nutrition Info:

- Per Serving: Calories: 310;Fat: 15g;Protein: 16g;Carbs: 20g.

Simple Chicken With Olive Tapenade

Servings:4
Cooking Time:35 Minutes

Ingredients:

- ½ cup olive oil
- 2 tbsp capers, canned
- 2 chicken breasts
- 1 cup black olives, pitted
- Salt and black pepper to taste
- ½ cup parsley, chopped
- ½ cup rosemary, chopped
- Salt and black pepper to taste
- 2 garlic cloves, minced
- ½ lemon, juiced and zested

Directions:

1. In a food processor, blend olives, capers, half of the oil, salt, pepper, parsley, rosemary, garlic, lemon zest, and lemon juice until smooth; set aside. Warm the remaining oil in a skillet over medium heat. Brown the chicken for 8-10 minutes on both sides. Top with tapenade. Serve and enjoy!

Nutrition Info:

- Per Serving: Calories: 300;Fat: 14g;Protein: 35g;Carbs: 17g.

Chicken With Chianti Sauce

Servings:4
Cooking Time:80 Min + Chilling Time

Ingredients:
- 4 tbsp olive oil
- 2 tbsp butter
- 3 garlic cloves, minced
- 1 tbsp lemon zest
- 2 tbsp fresh thyme, chopped
- 2 tbsp fresh parsley, chopped
- Salt and black pepper to taste
- 4 bone-in chicken legs
- 2 cups red grapes (in clusters)
- 1 red onion, sliced
- 1 cup Chianti red wine
- 1 cup chicken stock

Directions:

1. Toss the chicken with 2 tbsp of olive oil, garlic, thyme, parsley, lemon zest, salt, and pepper in a bowl. Refrigerate for 1 hour. Preheat oven to 400 F. Heat the remaining olive oil in a saucepan over medium heat. Sear the chicken for 3–4 minutes per side. Top chicken with the grapes. Transfer to the oven and bake for 20–30 minutes or until internal temperature registers 180 F on an instant-read thermometer.

2. Melt the butter in another saucepan and sauté the onion for 3–4 minutes. Add the wine and stock, stir, and simmer the sauce for about 30 minutes until it is thickened. Plate the chicken and grapes and pour the sauce over to serve.

Nutrition Info:
- Per Serving: Calories: 562;Fat: 31g;Protein: 52g;Carbs: 16g.

Chermoula Roasted Pork Tenderloin

Servings:2
Cooking Time: 20 Minutes

Ingredients:
- ½ cup fresh cilantro
- ½ cup fresh parsley
- 6 small garlic cloves
- 3 tablespoons olive oil, divided
- 3 tablespoons freshly squeezed lemon juice
- 2 teaspoons cumin
- 1 teaspoon smoked paprika
- ½ teaspoon salt, divided
- Pinch freshly ground black pepper
- 1 pork tenderloin

Directions:

1. Preheat the oven to 425ºF.
2. In a food processor, combine the cilantro, parsley, garlic, 2 tablespoons of olive oil, lemon juice, cumin, paprika, and ¼ teaspoon of salt. Pulse 15 to 20 times, or until the mixture is fairly smooth. Scrape the sides down as needed to incorporate all the ingredients. Transfer the sauce to a small bowl and set aside.
3. Season the pork tenderloin on all sides with the remaining ¼ teaspoon of salt and a generous pinch of black pepper.
4. Heat the remaining 1 tablespoon of olive oil in a sauté pan.
5. Sear the pork for 3 minutes, turning often, until golden brown on all sides.
6. Transfer the pork to a baking dish and roast in the preheated oven for 15 minutes, or until the internal temperature registers 145ºF.
7. Cool for 5 minutes before serving.

Nutrition Info:
- Per Serving: Calories: 169;Fat: 13.1g;Protein: 11.0g;-Carbs: 2.9g.

Mustardy Steak In Mushroom Sauce

Servings:4
Cooking Time:30 Min + Marinating Time

Ingredients:
- For the steak
- 2 tbsp olive oil
- 1 lb beef skirt steak
- 1 cup red wine
- 2 garlic cloves, minced
- 1 tbsp Worcestershire sauce
- 1 tbsp dried thyme
- 1 tsp yellow mustard
- For the mushroom sauce
- 1 lb mushrooms, sliced
- 1 tsp dried dill
- 2 garlic cloves, minced
- 1 cup dry red wine
- Salt and black pepper to taste

Directions:

1. Combine wine, garlic, Worcestershire sauce, 2 tbsp of olive oil, thyme, and mustard in a bowl. Place in the steak, cover with plastic wrap and let it marinate for at least 3 hours in the refrigerator. Remove the steak and pat dry with paper towels.

2. Warm olive oil in a pan over medium heat and sear steak for 8 minutes on all sides; set aside. In the same pan, sauté mushrooms, dill, salt, and pepper for 6 minutes, stirring periodically. Add in garlic and sauté for 30 seconds. Pour in the wine and scrape off any bits from the bottom. Simmer for 5 minutes until the liquid reduces. Slice the steak and top with the mushroom sauce. Serve hot.

Nutrition Info:
- Per Serving: Calories: 424;Fat: 24g;Protein: 29g;Carbs: 8g.

Chicken Thighs Al Orange

Servings:4
Cooking Time:40 Minutes

Ingredients:

- 2 tbsp olive oil
- 2 tbsp sweet chili sauce
- 2 lb chicken thighs, cubed
- Salt and black pepper to taste
- 1 ½ tsp orange extract
- ¼ cup orange juice
- 2 tbsp cilantro, chopped
- 1 cup chicken stock
- ¼ tsp red pepper flakes
- 2 cups cooked white rice

Directions:

1. Warm the olive oil in a skillet over medium heat and sear chicken for 8 minutes on all sides. Season with salt and pepper and stir in orange extract, orange juice, stock, sweet chili sauce, and red pepper flakes. Bring to a boil. Cook for 20 minutes. Top with cilantro and serve over cooked rice.

Nutrition Info:

- Per Serving: Calories: 310;Fat: 15g;Protein: 26g;Carbs: 23g.

Cannellini Bean & Chicken Cassoulet

Servings:4
Cooking Time:40 Minutes

Ingredients:

- 1 lb chicken thighs, boneless and skinless
- 2 tbsp olive oil
- 2 tbsp tomato paste
- 1 celery stalk, chopped
- 1 sweet onion, chopped
- 2 garlic cloves, chopped
- ½ cup chicken stock
- 14 oz canned cannellini beans
- Salt and black pepper to taste

Directions:

1. Warm the olive oil in a pot over medium heat. Cook onion, celery, and garlic for 3 minutes. Put in chicken and cook for 6 minutes on all sides. Stir in tomato paste, stock, beans, salt, and pepper and bring to a boil. Cook for 30 minutes.

Nutrition Info:

- Per Serving: Calories: 260;Fat: 11g;Protein: 25g;Carbs: 26g.

Spinach Pesto Chicken Breasts

Servings:4
Cooking Time:25 Minutes

Ingredients:

- ¼ cup + 1 tbsp olive oil
- 4 chicken breasts
- 1 cup spinach
- ¼ cup grated Pecorino cheese
- Salt and black pepper to taste
- ¼ cup pine nuts
- 1 garlic clove, minced

Directions:

1. Rub chicken with salt and black pepper. Grease a grill pan with 1 tbsp of olive oil and place over medium heat. Grill the chicken for 8-10 minutes, flipping once. Mix spinach, garlic, Pecorino cheese, and pine nuts in a food processor. Slowly, pour in the remaining oil; pulse until smooth. Spoon 1 tbsp of pesto on each breast and cook for an additional 5 minutes.

Nutrition Info:

- Per Serving: Calories: 493;Fat: 27g;Protein: 53g;Carbs: 4g.

Cilantro Turkey Penne With Asparagus

Servings:4
Cooking Time:40 Minutes

Ingredients:

- 3 tbsp olive oil
- 16 oz penne pasta
- 1 lb turkey breast strips
- 1 lb asparagus, chopped
- 1 tsp basil, chopped
- Salt and black pepper to taste
- ½ cup tomato sauce
- 2 tbsp cilantro, chopped

Directions:

1. Bring to a boil salted water in a pot over medium heat and cook penne until "al dente", 8-10 minutes. Drain and set aside; reserve 1 cup of the cooking water.
2. Warm the olive oil in a skillet over medium heat and sear turkey for 4 minutes, stirring periodically. Add in asparagus and sauté for 3-4 more minutes. Pour in the tomato sauce and reserved pasta liquid and bring to a boil; simmer for 20 minutes. Stir in cooked penne, season with salt and pepper, and top with the basil and cilantro to serve.

Nutrition Info:

- Per Serving: Calories: 350;Fat: 22g;Protein: 19g;Carbs: 23g.

Marsala Chicken With Mushrooms

Servings:4
Cooking Time:30 Minutes

Ingredients:

- 4 chicken breasts, pounded thin
- ¼ cup olive oil
- Salt and black pepper to taste
- ¼ cup whole-wheat flour
- ½ lb mushrooms, sliced
- 2 carrots, chopped
- 1 cup Marsala wine
- 1 cup chicken broth
- ¼ cup parsley, chopped

Directions:

1. Warm the olive oil in a saucepan on medium heat. Season the chicken with salt and pepper, then dredge them in the flour. Fry until golden brown on both sides, about 4-6 minutes; reserve. Sauté the mushrooms and carrots in the same pan. Add the wine and chicken broth and bring to a simmer. Cook for 10 minutes or until the sauce is reduced and thickened slightly. Return the chicken to the pan, and cook it in the sauce for 10 minutes. Top with parsley and serve.

Nutrition Info:

- Per Serving: Calories: 869;Fat: 36g;Protein: 89g;Carbs: 49g.

Rich Pork In Cilantro Sauce

Servings:4
Cooking Time:30 Minutes

Ingredients:

- ½ cup olive oil
- 1 lb pork stew meat, cubed
- 1 tbsp walnuts, chopped
- 2 tbsp cilantro, chopped
- 2 tbsp basil, chopped
- 2 garlic cloves, minced
- Salt and black pepper to taste
- 2 cups Greek yogurt

Directions:

1. In a food processor, blend cilantro, basil, garlic, walnuts, yogurt, salt, pepper, and half of the oil until smooth.
2. Warm the remaining oil in a skillet over medium heat. Brown pork meat for 5 minutes. Pour sauce over meat and bring to a boil. Cook for another 15 minutes. Serve.

Nutrition Info:

- Per Serving: Calories: 280;Fat: 12g;Protein: 19g;Carbs: 21g.

Marjoram Pork Loin With Ricotta Cheese

Servings:4
Cooking Time:70 Minutes

Ingredients:

- 2 tbsp olive oil
- 1 ½ lb pork loin, cubed
- 2 tbsp marjoram, chopped
- 1 garlic clove, minced
- 1 tbsp capers, drained
- 1 cup chicken stock
- Salt and black pepper to taste
- ½ cup ricotta cheese, crumbled

Directions:

1. Warm olive oil in a skillet over medium heat and sear pork for 5 minutes. Stir in marjoram, garlic, capers, stock, salt, and pepper and bring to a boil. Cook for 30 minutes. Mix in cheese.

Nutrition Info:

- Per Serving: Calories: 310;Fat: 15g;Protein: 34g;Carbs: 17g.

Picante Beef Stew

Servings:4
Cooking Time:35 Minutes

Ingredients:

- 2 tbsp olive oil
- 1 carrot, chopped
- 4 potatoes, diced
- 1 tsp ground nutmeg
- ½ tsp cinnamon
- 1 lb beef stew meat, cubed
- ½ cup sweet chili sauce
- ½ cup vegetable stock
- 1 tbsp cilantro, chopped
- Salt and black pepper to taste

Directions:

1. Warm the olive oil in a skillet over medium heat and sear beef for 5 minutes. Stir in chili sauce, carrot, potatoes, stock, nutmeg, cinnamon, cilantro, salt, and pepper and bring to a boil. Cook for another 20 minutes. Serve immediately.

Nutrition Info:

- Per Serving: Calories: 300;Fat: 22g;Protein: 20g;Carbs: 26g.

Lamb Tagine With Couscous And Almonds

Servings:6
Cooking Time: 7 Hours 7 Minutes

Ingredients:

- 2 tablespoons almond flour
- Juice and zest of 1 navel orange
- 2 tablespoons extra-virgin olive oil
- 2 pounds boneless lamb leg, fat trimmed and cut into 1½-inch cubes
- ½ cup low-sodium chicken stock
- 2 large white onions, chopped
- 1 teaspoon pumpkin pie spice
- ¼ teaspoon crushed saffron threads
- 1 teaspoon ground cumin
- ¼ teaspoon ground red pepper flakes
- ½ teaspoon sea salt
- 2 tablespoons raw honey
- 1 cup pitted dates
- 3 cups cooked couscous, for serving
- 2 tablespoons toasted slivered almonds, for serving

Directions:

1. Combine the almond flour with orange juice in a large bowl. Stir until smooth, then mix in the orange zest. Set aside.
2. Heat the olive oil in a nonstick skillet over medium-high heat until shimmering.
3. Add the lamb cubes and sauté for 7 minutes or until lightly browned.
4. Pour in the flour mixture and chicken stock, then add the onions, pumpkin pie spice, saffron, cumin, ground red pepper flakes, and salt. Stir to mix well.
5. Pour them in the slow cooker. Cover and cook on low for 6 hours or until the internal temperature of the lamb reaches at least 145°F.
6. When the cooking is complete, mix in the honey and dates, then cook for another an hour.
7. Put the couscous in a tagine bowl or a simple large bowl, then top with lamb mixture. Scatter with slivered almonds and serve immediately.

Nutrition Info:

- Per Serving: Calories: 447;Fat: 10.2g;Protein: 36.3g;-Carbs: 53.5g.

Chicken Breasts In White Sauce

Servings:4
Cooking Time:30 Minutes

Ingredients:

- 1 cup canned cream of onion soup
- 2 tbsp olive oil
- 1 lb chicken breasts, cubed
- ½ tsp dried basil
- ½ cup flour
- ½ cup white wine
- 1 cup heavy cream
- 4 garlic cloves, minced
- ¼ tsp chili flakes, crushed
- Salt and black pepper to taste
- 2 tbsp parsley, chopped

Directions:

1. In a bowl, combine salt, black pepper, chili flakes, basil, and flour. Add in chicken and toss to coat. Warm the olive oil in a skillet over medium heat. Add in the chicken and cook for 5 minutes, stirring occasionally. Pour in the white wine to scrape any bits from the bottom. Stir in garlic, onion soup, and ½ cup of water. Bring to a boil, then lower the heat, and simmer covered for 15-18 minutes. Stir in heavy cream, top with parsley and chili flakes, and serve.

Nutrition Info:

- Per Serving: Calories: 465;Fat: 27g;Protein: 35g;Carbs: 15g.

Parmesan Chicken Breasts

Servings:4
Cooking Time:35 Minutes

Ingredients:

- 1 tbsp olive oil
- 1 ½ lb chicken breasts, cubed
- 1 tsp ground coriander
- 1 tsp parsley flakes
- 2 garlic cloves, minced
- 1 cup heavy cream
- Salt and black pepper to taste
- ¼ cup Parmesan cheese, grated
- 1 tbsp basil, chopped

Directions:

1. Warm the olive oil in a skillet over medium heat and brown chicken, salt, and pepper for 6 minutes on all sides. Add in garlic and cook for another minute. Stir in coriander, parsley, and cream and cook for an additional 20 minutes. Serve scattered with basil and Parmesan cheese.

Nutrition Info:

- Per Serving: Calories: 260;Fat: 18g;Protein: 27g;Carbs: 26g.

Chicken Lentils With Artichokes

Servings:4
Cooking Time:50 Minutes

Ingredients:

- 2 tbsp olive oil
- 4 chicken breasts, halved
- 1 lemon, juiced and zested
- 2 garlic cloves, crushed
- 1 tbsp thyme, chopped
- 6 oz canned artichokes hearts
- 1 cup canned lentils, drained
- 1 cup chicken stock
- 1 tsp cayenne pepper
- Salt and black pepper to taste

Directions:

1. Warm the olive oil in a skillet over medium heat and cook chicken for 5-6 minutes until browned, flipping once. Mix in lemon zest, garlic, lemon juice, salt, pepper, thyme, artichokes, lentils, stock, and cayenne pepper and bring to a boil. Cook for 35 minutes. Serve immediately.

Nutrition Info:

- Per Serving: Calories: 300;Fat: 16g;Protein: 25g;Carbs: 25g.

Greek-style Veggie & Beef In Pita

Servings:2
Cooking Time:30 Minutes

Ingredients:

- Beef
- 1 tbsp olive oil
- ½ medium onion, minced
- 2 garlic cloves, minced
- 6 oz lean ground beef
- 1 tsp dried oregano
- Yogurt Sauce
- ⅓ cup plain Greek yogurt
- 1 oz crumbled feta cheese
- 1 tbsp minced fresh dill
- 1 tbsp minced scallions
- 1 tbsp lemon juice
- Garlic salt to taste
- Sandwiches
- 2 Greek-style pitas, warm
- 6 cherry tomatoes, halved
- 1 cucumber, sliced
- Salt and black pepper to taste

Directions:

1. Warm the 1 tbsp olive oil in a pan over medium heat. Sauté the onion, garlic, and ground for 5-7 minutes, breaking up the meat well. When the meat is no longer pink, drain off any fat and stir in oregano. Turn off the heat.
2. In a small bowl, combine the yogurt, feta, dill, scal-lions, lemon juice, and garlic salt. Divide the yogurt sauce between the warm pitas. Top with ground beef, cherry tomatoes, and diced cucumber. Season with salt and pepper. Serve.

Nutrition Info:

- Per Serving: Calories: 541;Fat: 21g;Protein: 29g;Carbs: 57g.

Slow Cooker Beef With Tomatoes

Servings:4
Cooking Time:8 Hours 10 Minutes

Ingredients:

- 1 ½ lb beef shoulder, cubed
- ½ cup chicken stock
- 2 tomatoes, chopped
- 2 garlic cloves, minced
- 1 tbsp cinnamon powder
- Salt and black pepper to taste
- 2 tbsp cilantro, chopped

Directions:

1. Place the beef, tomatoes, garlic, cinnamon, salt, pepper, chicken stock, and cilantro in your slow cooker. Cover with the lid and cook for 8 hours on Low. Serve immediately.

Nutrition Info:

- Per Serving: Calories: 360;Fat: 16g;Protein: 16g;Carbs: 19g.

French Chicken Cassoulet

Servings:4
Cooking Time:40 Minutes

Ingredients:

- 1 tbsp olive oil
- ½ cup heavy cream
- 4 chicken breasts, halved
- 1/3 cup yellow mustard
- Salt and black pepper to taste
- 1 onion, chopped
- 1 ½ cups chicken stock
- ¼ tsp dried oregano

Directions:

1. Warm stock in a saucepan over medium heat and stir in mustard, onion, salt, pepper, and oregano. Bring to a boil and cook for 8 minutes. Warm olive oil in a skillet over medium heat. Sear chicken for 6 minutes on both sides. Transfer to the saucepan and simmer for another 12 minutes. Stir in heavy cream for 2 minutes. Serve warm.

Nutrition Info:

- Per Serving: Calories: 260;Fat: 12g;Protein: 27g;Carbs: 18g.

Chicken Drumsticks With Peach Glaze

Servings:4
Cooking Time:35 Minutes

Ingredients:
- 2 tbsp olive oil
- 8 chicken drumsticks, skinless
- 3 peaches, peeled and chopped
- ¼ cup honey
- ¼ cup cider vinegar
- 1 sweet onion, chopped
- 1 tsp minced fresh rosemary
- Salt to taste

Directions:
1. Warm the olive oil in a large skillet over medium heat. Sprinkle chicken with salt and pepper and brown it for about 7 minutes per side. Remove to a plate. Add onion and rosemary to the skillet and sauté for 1 minute or until lightly golden. Add honey, vinegar, salt, and peaches and cook for 10-12 minutes or until peaches are softened. Add the chicken back to the skillet and heat just until warm, brushing with the sauce. Serve chicken thighs with peach sauce. Enjoy!

Nutrition Info:
- Per Serving: Calories: 1492;Fat: 26g;Protein: 54g;Carbs: 27g.

Creamy Beef Stew

Servings:4
Cooking Time:35 Minutes

Ingredients:
- 2 tbsp olive oil
- 2 pears, peeled and cubed
- 1 lb beef stew meat, cubed
- 2 tbsp dill, chopped
- 2 oz heavy cream
- Salt and black pepper to taste

Directions:
1. Warm the olive oil in a skillet over medium heat and sear beef for 5 minutes. Stir in pears, dill, heavy cream, salt, and pepper and bring to a boil. Simmer for 20 minutes.

Nutrition Info:
- Per Serving: Calories: 340;Fat: 18g;Protein: 16g;Carbs: 23g.

Pork Chops With Green Vegetables

Servings:4
Cooking Time:70 Minutes

Ingredients:
- 2 tbsp olive oil, divided
- ½ lb green beans, trimmed
- ½ lb asparagus spears
- ½ cup frozen peas, thawed
- 2 tomatoes, chopped
- 1 lb pork chops
- 1 tbsp tomato paste
- 1 onion, chopped
- Salt and black pepper to taste

Directions:
1. Warm olive oil in a saucepan over medium heat. Sprinkle the chops with salt and pepper. Place in the pan and brown for 8 minutes in total; set aside. In the same pan, sauté onion for 2 minutes until soft. In a bowl, whisk the tomato paste and 1 cup of water and pour in the saucepan. Bring to a simmer and scrape any bits from the bottom. Add the chops back and bring to a boil. Then lower the heat and simmer for 40 minutes. Add in green beans, asparagus, peas, tomatoes, salt, and pepper and cook for 10 minutes until the greens are soft.

Nutrition Info:
- Per Serving: Calories: 341;Fat: 16g;Protein: 36g;Carbs: 15g.

Greek Wraps

Servings:2
Cooking Time:10 Minutes

Ingredients:
- 2 cooked chicken breasts, shredded
- 2 tbsp roasted peppers, chopped
- 1 cup baby kale
- 2 whole-wheat tortillas
- 2 oz provolone cheese, grated
- 1 tomato, chopped
- 10 Kalamata olives, sliced
- 1 red onion, chopped

Directions:
1. In a bowl, mix all the ingredients except for the tortillas. Distribute the mixture across the tortillas and wrap them.

Nutrition Info:
- Per Serving: Calories: 200;Fat: 8g;Protein: 7g;Carbs: 16g.

Catalan Chicken In Romesco Sauce

Servings:6
Cooking Time:25 Minutes

Ingredients:

- 1 ½ lb chicken breasts, sliced
- 1 carrot, halved
- 1 celery stalk, halved
- 2 shallots, halved
- 2 garlic cloves, smashed
- 3 sprigs fresh thyme
- 1 cup romesco sauce
- 2 tbsp parsley, chopped
- ¼ tsp black pepper

Directions:

1. Place the chicken in a saucepan, cover well with water, and add the carrot, celery, onion, garlic, and thyme. Bring to the boil, then turn down to low and poach for 10-15 minutes until cooked through with no pink showing. Remove the chicken from the saucepan and leave to cool for 5 minutes. Spread some romesco sauce on the bottom of a serving plate. Arrange the chicken slices on top, and drizzle with the remaining romesco sauce. Sprinkle the tops with parsley and black pepper. Serve and enjoy!

Nutrition Info:

- Per Serving: Calories: 270;Fat: 11g;Protein: 13g;Carbs: 31g.

Saucy Turkey With Ricotta Cheese

Servings:4
Cooking Time:60 Minutes

Ingredients:

- 2 tbsp olive oil
- 1 turkey breast, cubed
- 1 ½ cups salsa verde
- Salt and black pepper to taste
- 4 oz ricotta cheese, crumbled
- 2 tbsp cilantro, chopped

Directions:

1. Preheat the oven to 380 F. Grease a roasting pan with oil. In a bowl, place turkey, salsa verde, salt, and pepper and toss to coat. Transfer to the roasting pan and bake for 50 minutes. Top with ricotta cheese and cilantro and serve.

Nutrition Info:

- Per Serving: Calories: 340;Fat: 16g;Protein: 35g;Carbs: 23g.

Quick Chicken Salad Wraps

Servings:2
Cooking Time: 0 Minutes

Ingredients:

- Tzatziki Sauce:
- ½ cup plain Greek yogurt
- 1 tablespoon freshly squeezed lemon juice
- Pinch garlic powder
- 1 teaspoon dried dill
- Salt and freshly ground black pepper, to taste
- Salad Wraps:
- 2 whole-grain pita bread
- 1 cup shredded chicken meat
- 2 cups mixed greens
- 2 roasted red bell peppers, thinly sliced
- ½ English cucumber, peeled if desired and thinly sliced
- ¼ cup pitted black olives
- 1 scallion, chopped

Directions:

1. Make the tzatziki sauce: In a bowl, whisk together the yogurt, lemon juice, garlic powder, dill, salt, and pepper until creamy and smooth.
2. Make the salad wraps: Place the pita bread on a clean work surface and spoon ¼ cup of the tzatziki sauce onto each piece of pita bread, spreading it all over. Top with the shredded chicken, mixed greens, red pepper slices, cucumber slices, black olives, finished by chopped scallion.
3. Roll the salad wraps and enjoy.

Nutrition Info:

- Per Serving: Calories: 428;Fat: 10.6g;Protein: 31.1g;-Carbs: 50.9g.

Milky Pork Stew

Servings:4
Cooking Time:50 Minutes

Ingredients:

- 1 tbsp avocado oil
- 1 ½ cups buttermilk
- 1 ½ lb pork meat, cubed
- 1 red onion, chopped
- 1 garlic clove, minced
- ½ cup chicken stock
- 2 tbsp hot paprika
- Salt and black pepper to taste
- 1 tbsp cilantro, chopped

Directions:

1. Warm the avocado oil in a pot over medium heat and sear pork for 5 minutes. Put in onion and garlic and cook for 5 minutes. Stir in stock, paprika, salt, pepper, and buttermilk and bring to a boil; cook for 30 minutes. Top with cilantro.

Nutrition Info:

- Per Serving: Calories: 310;Fat: 10g;Protein: 23g;Carbs: 16g.

Spanish Pork Shoulder

Servings:4
Cooking Time:35 Minutes

Ingredients:

- 3 tbsp olive oil
- 1 ½ lb pork shoulder, cubed
- 2 garlic cloves, minced
- Salt and black pepper to taste
- ½ cup vegetable stock
- ½ tsp saffron powder
- ¼ tsp cumin, ground
- 4 green onions, sliced

Directions:

1. Warm the olive oil in a skillet over medium heat and cook garlic, green onions, saffron, and cumin for 5 minutes. Put in pork and cook for another 5 minutes. Stir in salt, pepper, and stock and bring to a boil. Cook for an additional 15 minutes.

Nutrition Info:

- Per Serving: Calories: 300;Fat: 14g;Protein: 15g;Carbs: 14g.

Zesty Turkey Breast

Servings:4
Cooking Time:1 Hr 40 Min + Chilling Time

Ingredients:

- 2 tbsp olive oil
- 1 lb turkey breast
- 2 garlic cloves, minced
- ½ cup chicken broth
- 1 lemon, zested
- ¼ tsp dried thyme
- ¼ tsp dried tarragon
- ½ tsp red pepper flakes
- 2 tbsp chopped fresh parsley
- 1 tsp ground mustard
- Salt and black pepper to taste

Directions:

1. Preheat oven to 325 F. Mix the olive oil, garlic, lemon zest, thyme, tarragon, red pepper flakes, mustard, salt, and pepper in a bowl. Rub the breast with the mixture until well coated and transfer onto a roasting pan skin-side up. Pour in the chicken broth. Roast in the oven for 60-90 minutes. Allow to sit for 10 minutes covered with foil, then remove from the roasting tin and carve. Serve topped with parsley.

Nutrition Info:

- Per Serving: Calories: 286;Fat: 16g;Protein: 34g;Carbs: 0.9g.

Picante Green Pea & Chicken

Servings:4
Cooking Time:35 Minutes

Ingredients:

- 2 tbsp olive oil
- 1 lb chicken breasts, halved
- 1 tsp chili powder
- Salt and black pepper to taste
- 1 tsp garlic powder
- 1 tbsp smoked paprika
- ½ cup chicken stock
- 2 tsp sherry vinegar
- 3 tsp hot sauce
- 2 tsp cumin, ground
- 1 cup green peas
- 1 carrot, chopped

Directions:

1. Warm the olive oil in a skillet over medium heat and cook chicken for 6 minutes on both sides. Sprinkle with chili powder, salt, pepper, garlic powder, and paprika. Pour in the chicken stock, vinegar, hot sauce, cumin, carrot, and green peas and bring to a boil; cook for an additional 15 minutes.

Nutrition Info:

- Per Serving: Calories: 240;Fat: 19g;Protein: 14g;Carbs: 16g.

Sausage & Herb Eggs

Servings:2
Cooking Time:20 Minutes

Ingredients:

- 2 tbsp olive oil
- ½ cup leeks, chopped
- ½ lb pork sausage, crumbled
- 4 eggs, whisked
- 1 thyme sprig, chopped
- 1 tsp habanero pepper, minced
- ½ tsp dried marjoram
- 1 tsp garlic puree
- ½ cup green olives, sliced
- Salt and black pepper to taste

Directions:

1. Warm the olive oil in a skillet over medium heat. Sauté the leeks until they are just tender, about 4 minutes. Add the garlic, habanero pepper, salt, black pepper, and sausage; cook for 8 minutes, stirring frequently. Pour in the eggs and sprinkle with thyme and marjoram. Cook for an additional 4 minutes, stirring with a spoon. Garnish with olives. Serve.

Nutrition Info:

- Per Serving: Calories: 460;Fat: 41g;Protein: 16g;Carbs: 6g.

Baked Turkey With Veggies

Servings:4
Cooking Time:70 Minutes

Ingredients:
- 2 tbsp olive oil
- 1 lb turkey breasts, sliced
- ¼ cup chicken stock
- 1 carrot, chopped
- 1 red onion, chopped
- 2 mixed bell peppers, chopped
- Salt and black pepper to taste
- 1 tbsp cilantro, chopped

Directions:
1. Preheat oven to 380 F. Grease a roasting pan with olive oil. Combine turkey, stock, carrots, bell peppers, onion, salt, and pepper in the pan and bake for 1 hour. Top with cilantro.

Nutrition Info:
- Per Serving: Calories: 510;Fat: 15g;Protein: 11g;Carbs: 16g.

Citrus Chicken Wings

Servings:6
Cooking Time:50 Minutes

Ingredients:
- 2 tbsp canola oils
- 12 chicken wings, halved
- 2 garlic cloves, minced
- 1 lime, juiced and zested
- 1 cup raisins, soaked
- 1 tsp cumin, ground
- Salt and black pepper to taste
- ½ cup chicken stock
- 1 tbsp chives, chopped

Directions:
1. Preheat the oven to 340 F. Combine chicken wings, garlic, lime juice, lime zest, canola oil, raisins, cumin, salt, pepper, stock, and chives in a baking pan. Bake for 40 minutes.

Nutrition Info:
- Per Serving: Calories: 300;Fat: 20g;Protein: 19g;Carbs: 22g.

Chicken With Farro & Carrots

Servings:4
Cooking Time:50 Minutes

Ingredients:
- 2 tbsp olive oil
- 3 carrots, chopped
- 1 cup farro, soaked
- 1 lb chicken breasts, cubed
- 1 red onion, chopped
- 4 garlic cloves, minced
- 2 tbsp dill, chopped
- 2 tbsp tomato paste
- 2 cups vegetable stock
- Salt and black pepper to taste

Directions:
1. Warm olive oil in your pressure cooker on Sauté and sear the chicken for 10 minutes on all sides, stirring occasionally. Remove to a plate. Add onion, garlic, and carrots to the cooker and sauté for 3 minutes. Stir in tomato paste, farro, and vegetable stock and return the chicken. Seal the lid, select Pressure Cook, and cook for 30 minutes on High. Do a natural pressure release for 10 minutes. Adjust the taste with salt and pepper. Sprinkle with dill and serve.

Nutrition Info:
- Per Serving: Calories: 317;Fat: 13g;Protein: 8g;Carbs: 18g.

Fish And Sea-food Recipes

Herby Tuna Gratin

Servings:4
Cooking Time:20 Minutes

Ingredients:

- 10 oz canned tuna, flaked
- 4 eggs, whisked
- ½ cup mozzarella, shredded
- 1 tbsp chives, chopped
- 1 tbsp parsley, chopped
- Salt and black pepper to taste

Directions:

1. Preheat the oven to 360 F. Mix tuna, eggs, chives, parsley, salt, and pepper in a bowl. Transfer to a greased baking dish and bake for 15 minutes. Scatter cheese on top and let sit for 5 minutes. Cut before serving.

Nutrition Info:

- Per Serving: Calories: 300;Fat: 15g;Protein: 7g;Carbs: 13g.

Anchovy Spread With Avocado

Servings:2
Cooking Time:5 Minutes

Ingredients:

- 1 avocado, peeled and pitted
- 1 tsp lemon juice
- ¼ celery stalk, chopped
- ¼ cup chopped shallots
- 2 anchovy fillets in olive oil
- Salt and black pepper to taste

Directions:

1. Combine lemon juice, avocado, celery, shallots, and anchovy fillets (with their olive oil) in a food processor. Blitz until smooth. Season with salt and black pepper. Serve.

Nutrition Info:

- Per Serving: Calories: 271;Fat: 20g;Protein: 15g;Carbs: 12g.

Seafood Cakes With Radicchio Salad

Servings:4
Cooking Time:30 Minutes

Ingredients:

- 2 tbsp butter
- 2 tbsp extra-virgin olive oil
- 1 lb lump crabmeat
- 4 scallions, sliced
- 1 garlic clove, minced
- ¼ cup cooked shrimp
- 2 tbsp heavy cream
- ¼ head radicchio, thinly sliced
- 1 green apple, shredded
- 2 tbsp lemon juice
- Salt and black pepper to taste

Directions:

1. In a food processor, place the shrimp, heavy cream, salt, and pepper. Blend until smooth. Mix crab meat and scallions in a bowl. Add in shrimp mixture and toss to combine. Make 4 patties out of the mixture. Transfer to the fridge for 10 minutes. Warm butter in a skillet over medium heat and brown patties for 8 minutes on all sides. Remove to a serving plate. Mix radicchio and apple in a bowl. Combine olive oil, lemon juice, garlic, and salt in a small bowl and stir well. Pour over the salad and toss to combine. Serve and enjoy!

Nutrition Info:

- Per Serving: Calories: 238;Fat: 14.3g;Protein: 20g;Carbs: 8g.

Simple Salmon With Balsamic Haricots Vert

Servings:4
Cooking Time:25 Minutes

Ingredients:

- 2 tbsp olive oil
- 3 tbsp balsamic vinegar
- 1 garlic clove, minced
- ½ tsp red pepper flakes
- 1 ½ lb haricots vert, chopped
- Salt and black pepper to taste
- 1 red onion, sliced
- 4 salmon fillets, boneless

Directions:

1. Warm half of oil in a skillet over medium heat and sauté vinegar, onion, garlic, red pepper flakes, haricots vert, salt, and pepper for 6 minutes. Share into plates. Warm the remaining oil. Sprinkle salmon with salt and pepper and sear for 8 minutes on all sides. Serve with haricots vert.

Nutrition Info:

- Per Serving: Calories: 230;Fat: 16g;Protein: 17g;Carbs: 23g.

Lemon Grilled Shrimp

Servings:4
Cooking Time: 4 To 6 Minutes

Ingredients:

- 2 tablespoons garlic, minced
- 3 tablespoons fresh Italian parsley, finely chopped
- ¼ cup extra-virgin olive oil
- ½ cup lemon juice
- 1 teaspoon salt
- 2 pounds jumbo shrimp, peeled and deveined
- Special Equipment:
- 4 skewers, soaked in water for at least 30 minutes

Directions:

1. Whisk together the garlic, parsley, olive oil, lemon juice, and salt in a large bowl.
2. Add the shrimp to the bowl and toss well, making sure the shrimp are coated in the marinade. Set aside to sit for 15 minutes.
3. When ready, skewer the shrimps by piercing through the center. You can place about 5 to 6 shrimps on each skewer.
4. Preheat the grill to high heat.
5. Grill the shrimp for 4 to 6 minutes, flipping the shrimp halfway through, or until the shrimp are pink on the outside and opaque in the center.
6. Serve hot.

Nutrition Info:

- Per Serving: Calories: 401;Fat: 17.8g;Protein: 56.9g;-Carbs: 3.9g.

Shrimp & Salmon In Tomato Sauce

Servings:4
Cooking Time:30 Minutes

Ingredients:

- 1 lb shrimp, peeled and deveined
- 2 tbsp olive oil
- 1 lb salmon fillets
- Salt and black pepper to taste
- 1 cups tomatoes, chopped
- 1 onion, chopped
- 2 garlic cloves, minced
- ¼ tsp red pepper flakes
- 1 cup fish stock
- 1 tbsp cilantro, chopped

Directions:

1. Preheat the oven to 360F. Line a baking sheet with parchment paper. Season the salmon with salt and pepper, drizzle with some olive oil, and arrange them on the sheet. Bake for 15 minutes. Remove to a serving plate.
2. Warm the remaining olive oil in a skillet over medium heat and sauté onion and garlic for 3 minutes until tender. Pour in tomatoes, fish stock, salt, pepper, and red pepper flakes and bring to a boil. Simmer for 10 minutes. Stir in

shrimp and cook for another 8 minutes. Pour the sauce over the salmon and serve sprinkled with cilantro.

Nutrition Info:

- Per Serving: Calories: 240;Fat: 16g;Protein: 18g;Carbs: 22g.

Baked Salmon With Basil And Tomato

Servings:2
Cooking Time: 20 Minutes

Ingredients:

- 2 boneless salmon fillets
- 1 tablespoon dried basil
- 1 tomato, thinly sliced
- 1 tablespoon olive oil
- 2 tablespoons grated Parmesan cheese
- Nonstick cooking spray

Directions:

1. Preheat the oven to 375ºF. Line a baking sheet with a piece of aluminum foil and mist with nonstick cooking spray.
2. Arrange the salmon fillets onto the aluminum foil and scatter with basil. Place the tomato slices on top and drizzle with olive oil. Top with the grated Parmesan cheese.
3. Bake for about 20 minutes, or until the flesh is opaque and it flakes apart easily.
4. Remove from the oven and serve on a plate.

Nutrition Info:

- Per Serving: Calories: 403;Fat: 26.5g;Protein: 36.3g;-Carbs: 3.8g.

Dill Baked Sea Bass

Servings:6
Cooking Time: 10 To 15 Minutes

Ingredients:

- ¼ cup olive oil
- 2 pounds sea bass
- Sea salt and freshly ground pepper, to taste
- 1 garlic clove, minced
- ¼ cup dry white wine
- 3 teaspoons fresh dill
- 2 teaspoons fresh thyme

Directions:

1. Preheat the oven to 425ºF.
2. Brush the bottom of a roasting pan with the olive oil. Place the fish in the pan and brush the fish with oil.
3. Season the fish with sea salt and freshly ground pepper. Combine the remaining ingredients and pour over the fish.
4. Bake in the preheated oven for 10 to 15 minutes, depending on the size of the fish.
5. Serve hot.

Nutrition Info:

- Per Serving: Calories: 224;Fat: 12.1g;Protein: 28.1g;-

Carbs: 0.9g.

Parsley Littleneck Clams In Sherry Sauce

Servings:4
Cooking Time:20 Minutes

Ingredients:
- 2 tbsp olive oil
- 1 cup dry sherry
- 3 shallots, minced
- 4 garlic cloves, minced
- 4 lb littleneck clams, scrubbed
- 2 tbsp minced fresh parsley
- ½ tsp cayenne pepper
- 1 Lemon, cut into wedges

Directions:
1. Bring the sherry wine, shallots, and garlic to a simmer in a large saucepan and cook for 3 minutes. Add clams, cover, and cook, stirring twice, until clams open, about 7 minutes. With a slotted spoon, transfer clams to a serving bowl, discarding any that refuse to open. Stir in olive oil, parsley, and cayenne pepper. Pour sauce over clams and serve with lemon wedges.

Nutrition Info:
- Per Serving: Calories: 333;Fat: 9g;Protein: 44.9g;Carbs: 14g.

Mediterranean Braised Cod With Vegetables

Servings:2
Cooking Time: 18 Minutes

Ingredients:
- 1 tablespoon olive oil
- ½ medium onion, minced
- 2 garlic cloves, minced
- 1 teaspoon oregano
- 1 can artichoke hearts in water, drained and halved
- 1 can diced tomatoes with basil
- ¼ cup pitted Greek olives, drained
- 10 ounces wild cod
- Salt and freshly ground black pepper, to taste

Directions:
1. In a skillet, heat the olive oil over medium-high heat.
2. Sauté the onion for about 5 minutes, stirring occasionally, or until tender.
3. Stir in the garlic and oregano and cook for 30 seconds more until fragrant.
4. Add the artichoke hearts, tomatoes, and olives and stir to combine. Top with the cod.
5. Cover and cook for 10 minutes, or until the fish flakes easily with a fork and juices run clean.
6. Sprinkle with the salt and pepper. Serve warm.

Nutrition Info:
- Per Serving: Calories: 332;Fat: 10.5g;Protein: 29.2g;-Carbs: 30.7g.

Crispy Tilapia With Mango Salsa

Servings:2
Cooking Time: 10 Minutes

Ingredients:
- Salsa:
- 1 cup chopped mango
- 2 tablespoons chopped fresh cilantro
- 2 tablespoons chopped red onion
- 2 tablespoons freshly squeezed lime juice
- ½ jalapeño pepper, seeded and minced
- Pinch salt
- Tilapia:
- 1 tablespoon paprika
- 1 teaspoon onion powder
- ½ teaspoon dried thyme
- ½ teaspoon freshly ground black pepper
- ¼ teaspoon cayenne pepper
- ½ teaspoon garlic powder
- ¼ teaspoon salt
- ½ pound boneless tilapia fillets
- 2 teaspoons extra-virgin olive oil
- 1 lime, cut into wedges, for serving

Directions:
1. Make the salsa: Place the mango, cilantro, onion, lime juice, jalapeño, and salt in a medium bowl and toss to combine. Set aside.
2. Make the tilapia: Stir together the paprika, onion powder, thyme, black pepper, cayenne pepper, garlic powder, and salt in a small bowl until well mixed. Rub both sides of fillets generously with the mixture.
3. Heat the olive oil in a large skillet over medium heat.
4. Add the fish fillets and cook each side for 3 to 5 minutes until golden brown and cooked through.
5. Divide the fillets among two plates and spoon half of the prepared salsa onto each fillet. Serve the fish alongside the lime wedges.

Nutrition Info:
- Per Serving: Calories: 239;Fat: 7.8g;Protein: 25.0g;-Carbs: 21.9g.

Walnut-crusted Salmon

Servings:4
Cooking Time:25 Minutes

Ingredients:
- 2 tbsp olive oil
- 4 salmon fillets, boneless
- 2 tbsp mustard
- 5 tsp honey
- 1 cup walnuts, chopped

- 1 tbsp lemon juice
- 2 tsp parsley, chopped
- Salt and pepper to the taste

Directions:

1. Preheat the oven to 380F. Line a baking tray with parchment paper. In a bowl, whisk the olive oil, mustard, and honey. In a separate bowl, combine walnuts and parsley. Sprinkle salmon with salt and pepper and place them on the tray. Rub each fillet with mustard mixture and scatter with walnut mixture; bake for 15 minutes. Drizzle with lemon juice.

Nutrition Info:

- Per Serving: Calories: 300;Fat: 16g;Protein: 17g;Carbs: 22g.

Shrimp & Squid Medley

Servings:4
Cooking Time:25 Minutes

Ingredients:

- 2 tbsp butter
- ½ lb squid rings
- 1 lb shrimp, peeled, deveined
- Salt and black pepper to taste
- 2 garlic cloves, minced
- 1 tsp rosemary, dried
- 1 red onion, chopped
- 1 cup vegetable stock
- 1 lemon, juiced
- 1 tbsp parsley, chopped

Directions:

1. Melt butter in a skillet over medium heat and cook onion and garlic for 4 minutes. Stir in shrimp, salt, pepper, squid rings, rosemary, vegetable stock, and lemon juice and bring to a boil. Simmer for 8 minutes. Put in parsley and serve.

Nutrition Info:

- Per Serving: Calories: 300;Fat: 14g;Protein: 7g;Carbs: 23g.

Simple Fried Cod Fillets

Servings:4
Cooking Time: 10 Minutes

Ingredients:

- ½ cup all-purpose flour
- 1 teaspoon garlic powder
- 1 teaspoon salt
- 4 cod fillets
- 1 tablespoon extra-virgin olive oil

Directions:

1. Mix together the flour, garlic powder, and salt in a shallow dish.
2. Dredge each piece of fish in the seasoned flour until they are evenly coated.

3. Heat the olive oil in a medium skillet over medium-high heat.
4. Once hot, add the cod fillets and fry for 6 to 8 minutes, flipping the fish halfway through, or until the fish is opaque and flakes easily.
5. Remove from the heat and serve on plates.

Nutrition Info:

- Per Serving: Calories: 333;Fat: 18.8g;Protein: 21.2g;-Carbs: 20.0g.

Traditional Tuscan Scallops

Servings:4
Cooking Time:25 Minutes

Ingredients:

- 2 tbsp olive oil
- 1 lb sea scallops, rinsed
- 4 cups Tuscan kale
- 1 orange, juiced
- Salt and black pepper to taste
- ¼ tsp red pepper flakes

Directions:

1. Sprinkle scallops with salt and pepper.
2. Warm olive oil in a skillet over medium heat and brown scallops for 6-8 minutes on all sides. Remove to a plate and keep warm, covering with foil. In the same skillet, add the kale, red pepper flakes, orange juice, salt, and pepper and cook until the kale wilts, about 4-5 minutes. Share the kale mixture into 4 plates and top with the scallops. Serve warm.

Nutrition Info:

- Per Serving: Calories: 214;Fat: 8g;Protein: 21g;Carbs: 15.2g.

Parchment Orange & Dill Salmon

Servings:4
Cooking Time:25 Minutes

Ingredients:

- 2 tbsp butter, melted
- 4 salmon fillets
- Salt and black pepper to taste
- 1 orange, juiced and zested
- 4 tbsp fresh dill, chopped

Directions:

1. Preheat oven to 375 F. Coat the salmon fillets on both sides with butter. Season with salt and pepper and divide them between 4 pieces of parchment paper. Drizzle the orange juice over each piece of fish and top with orange zest and dill. Wrap the paper around the fish to make packets. Place on a baking sheet and bake for 15-20 minutes until the cod is cooked through. Serve and enjoy!

Nutrition Info:

- Per Serving: Calories: 481;Fat: 21g;Protein: 65g;Carbs: 4.2g.

North African Grilled Fish Fillets

Servings:4
Cooking Time:15 Minutes

Ingredients:

- 1 tbsp olive oil
- 1 tsp harissa seasoning
- 4 fish fillets
- 2 lemons, sliced
- 2 tbsp lemon juice
- Salt and black pepper to taste

Directions:

1. Preheat your grill to 400 F. In a bowl, whisk the lemon juice, olive oil, harissa seasoning, salt, and pepper. Coat both sides of the fish with the mixture. Carefully place the lemon slices on the grill, arranging 3-4 slices together in the shape of a fish fillet, and repeat with the remaining slices. Place the fish fillets directly on top of the lemon slices and grill with the lid closed. Turn the fish halfway through the cooking time only if the fillets are more than half an inch thick. The fish is done and ready to serve when it just begins to separate into chunks when pressed gently with a fork. Serve and enjoy!

Nutrition Info:

- Per Serving: Calories: 208;Fat: 12g;Protein: 21g;Carbs: 2g.

Farro & Trout Bowls With Avocado

Servings:4
Cooking Time:50 Minutes

Ingredients:

- 4 tbsp olive oil
- 8 trout fillets, boneless
- 1 cup farro
- Juice of 2 lemons
- Salt and black pepper to taste
- 1 avocado, chopped
- ¼ cup balsamic vinegar
- 1 garlic cloves, minced
- ¼ cup parsley, chopped
- ¼ cup mint, chopped
- 2 tbsp yellow mustard

Directions:

1. Boil salted water in a pot over medium heat and stir in farro. Simmer for 30 minutes and drain. Remove to a bowl and combine with lemon juice, mustard, garlic, salt, pepper, and half olive oil. Set aside. Mash the avocado with a fork in a bowl and mix with vinegar, salt, pepper, parsley, and mint.
2. Warm the remaining oil in a skillet over medium heat and brown trout fillets skin-side down for 10 minutes on both sides. Let cool and cut into pieces. Put over farro and stir in avocado dressing. Serve immediately.

Nutrition Info:

- Per Serving: Calories: 290;Fat: 13g;Protein: 37g;Carbs: 6g.

Steamed Trout With Lemon Herb Crust

Servings:2
Cooking Time: 15 Minutes

Ingredients:

- 3 tablespoons olive oil
- 3 garlic cloves, chopped
- 2 tablespoons fresh lemon juice
- 1 tablespoon chopped fresh mint
- 1 tablespoon chopped fresh parsley
- ¼ teaspoon dried ground thyme
- 1 teaspoon sea salt
- 1 pound fresh trout
- 2 cups fish stock

Directions:

1. Stir together the olive oil, garlic, lemon juice, mint, parsley, thyme, and salt in a small bowl. Brush the marinade onto the fish.
2. Insert a trivet in the Instant Pot. Pour in the fish stock and place the fish on the trivet.
3. Secure the lid. Select the Steam mode and set the cooking time for 15 minutes at High Pressure.
4. Once cooking is complete, do a quick pressure release. Carefully open the lid. Serve warm.

Nutrition Info:

- Per Serving: Calories: 477;Fat: 29.6g;Protein: 51.7g;Carbs: 3.6g.

Lemony Sea Bass

Servings:4
Cooking Time:25 Minutes

Ingredients:

- 1 tbsp butter, melted
- 4 skinless sea bass fillets
- Salt and black pepper to taste
- ½ tsp onion powder

Directions:

1. Preheat oven to 425 F. Rub the fish with salt, pepper, and onion powder and place on a greased baking dish. Drizzle the butter all over and bake for 20 minutes or until opaque.

Nutrition Info:

- Per Serving: Calories: 159;Fat: 6g;Protein: 23.8g;Carbs: 1.2g.

Trout Fillets With Horseradish Sauce

Servings:4
Cooking Time:35 Minutes

Ingredients:

- 3 tbsp olive oil
- 2 tbsp horseradish sauce
- 1 onion, sliced
- 2 tsp Italian seasoning
- 4 trout fillets, boneless
- ¼ cup panko breadcrumbs
- ½ cup green olives, pitted and chopped
- Salt and black pepper to taste
- 1 lemon, juiced

Directions:

1. Preheat the oven to 380F. Line a baking sheet with parchment paper. Sprinkle trout fillets with salt and pepper and dip in breadcrumbs. Arrange them along with the onion on the sheet. Sprinkle with olive oil, Italian seasoning, and lemon juice and bake for 15-18 minutes. Transfer to a serving plate and top with horseradish sauce and olives. Serve right away.

Nutrition Info:

- Per Serving: Calories: 310;Fat: 10g;Protein: 16g;Carbs: 25g.

Halibut Confit With Sautéed Leeks

Servings:4
Cooking Time:45 Minutes

Ingredients:

- 1 tsp fresh lemon zest
- ¼ cup olive oil
- 4 skinless halibut fillets
- Salt and black pepper to taste
- 1 lb leeks, sliced
- 1 tsp Dijon mustard
- ¾ cup dry white wine
- 1 tbsp fresh cilantro, chopped
- 4 lemon wedges

Directions:

1. Warm the olive oil in a skillet over medium heat. Season the halibut with salt and pepper. Sear in the skillet for 6-7 minutes until cooked all the way through. Carefully transfer the halibut to a large plate. Add leeks, mustard, salt, and pepper to the skillet and sauté for 10-12 minutes, stirring frequently, until softened. Pour in the wine and lemon zest and bring to a simmer. Top with halibut. Reduce the heat to low, cover, and simmer for 6-10 minutes. Carefully transfer halibut to a serving platter, tent loosely with aluminum foil, and let rest while finishing leeks. Increase the heat and cook the leeks for 2-4 minutes until the sauce is slightly thickened. Adjust the seasoning with salt and pepper. Pour the leek mixture around the halibut, sprinkle with cilantro, and

serve with lemon wedges.

Nutrition Info:

- Per Serving: Calories: 566;Fat: 19g;Protein: 78g;Carbs: 17g.

Salmon Packets

Servings:4
Cooking Time:25 Minutes

Ingredients:

- 2 tbsp olive oil
- ½ cup apple juice
- 4 salmon fillets
- 4 tsp lemon zest
- 4 tbsp chopped parsley
- Salt and black pepper to taste

Directions:

1. Preheat oven to 380F. Brush salmon with olive oil and season with salt and pepper. Cut four pieces of nonstick baking paper and divide the salmon between them. Top each one with apple juice, lemon zest, and parsley.
2. Wrap the paper to make packets and arrange them on a baking sheet. Cook for 15 minutes until the salmon is cooked through. Remove the packets to a serving plate, open them, and drizzle with cooking juices to serve.

Nutrition Info:

- Per Serving: Calories: 495;Fat: 21g;Protein: 55g;Carbs: 5g.

Grilled Sardines With Herby Sauce

Servings:4
Cooking Time:15 Min + Marinating Time

Ingredients:

- 12 sardines, gutted and cleaned
- 1 lemon, cut into wedges
- 2 garlic cloves, minced
- 2 tbsp capers, finely chopped
- 1 tbsp whole capers
- 1 shallot, diced
- 1 tsp anchovy paste
- 1 lemon, zested and juiced
- 2 tbsp olive oil
- 1 tbsp parsley, finely chopped
- 1 tbsp basil, finely chopped

Directions:

1. In a bowl, blend garlic, chopped capers, shallot, anchovy paste, lemon zest, and olive oil. Add the sardines and toss to coat; let them sit to marinate for about 30 minutes.
2. Preheat your grill to high. Place the sardines on the grill. Cook for 3-4 minutes per side until the skin is browned and beginning to blister. Pour the marinade in a saucepan over medium heat and add the whole capers, parsley, basil, and lemon juice. Cook for 2-3 minutes until thickens. Pour the

sauce over grilled sardines. Serve with lemon wedges.

Nutrition Info:
- Per Serving: Calories: 395;Fat: 21g;Protein: 46g;Carbs: 2.1g.

Lemon-garlic Sea Bass

Servings:2
Cooking Time:25 Minutes

Ingredients:
- 2 tbsp olive oil
- 2 sea bass fillets
- 1 lemon, juiced
- 4 garlic cloves, minced
- Salt and black pepper to taste

Directions:
1. Preheat the oven to 380F. Line a baking sheet with parchment paper. Brush sea bass fillets with lemon juice, olive oil, garlic, salt, and pepper and arrange them on the sheet. Bake for 15 minutes. Serve with salad.

Nutrition Info:
- Per Serving: Calories: 530;Fat: 30g;Protein: 54g;Carbs: 15g.

Tarragon Haddock With Capers

Servings:4
Cooking Time:25 Minutes

Ingredients:
- 2 tbsp olive oil
- 4 haddock fillets, boneless
- ¼ cup capers, drained
- 1 tbsp tarragon, chopped
- Salt and black pepper to taste
- 2 tbsp parsley, chopped
- 1 tbsp lemon juice

Directions:
1. Warm the olive oil in a skillet over medium heat and sear haddock for 6 minutes on both sides. Stir in capers, tarragon, salt, pepper, parsley, and lemon juice and cook for another 6-8 minutes. Serve right away.

Nutrition Info:
- Per Serving: Calories: 170;Fat: 10g;Protein: 18g;Carbs: 13g.

Parsley Halibut With Roasted Peppers

Servings:4
Cooking Time:45 Minutes

Ingredients:
- 3 tbsp olive oil
- 1 tsp butter
- 2 red peppers, cut into wedges
- 4 halibut fillets
- 2 shallots, cut into rings
- 2 garlic cloves, minced
- ¾ cup breadcrumbs
- 2 tbsp chopped fresh parsley
- Salt and black pepper to taste

Directions:
1. Preheat oven to 450 F. Combine red peppers, garlic, shallots, 1 tbsp of olive oil, salt, and pepper in a bowl. Spread on a baking sheet and bake for 40 minutes. Warm the remaining olive oil in a pan over medium heat and brown the breadcrumbs for 4-5 minutes, stirring constantly. Set aside.
2. Clean the pan and add in the butter to melt. Sprinkle the fish with salt and pepper. Add to the butter and cook for 8-10 minutes on both sides. Divide the pepper mixture between 4 plates and top with halibut fillets. Spread the crunchy breadcrumbs all over and top with parsley. Serve and enjoy!

Nutrition Info:
- Per Serving: Calories: 511;Fat: 19.4g;Protein: 64g;Carbs: 18g.

Salmon And Mushroom Hash With Pesto

Servings:6
Cooking Time: 20 Minutes

Ingredients:
- Pesto:
- ¼ cup extra-virgin olive oil
- 1 bunch fresh basil
- Juice and zest of 1 lemon
- ⅓ cup water
- ¼ teaspoon salt, plus additional as needed
- Hash:
- 2 tablespoons extra-virgin olive oil
- 6 cups mixed mushrooms (brown, white, shiitake, cremini, portobello, etc.), sliced
- 1 pound wild salmon, cubed

Directions:
1. Make the pesto: Pulse the olive oil, basil, juice and zest, water, and salt in a blender or food processor until smoothly blended. Set aside.
2. Heat the olive oil in a large skillet over medium heat.
3. Stir-fry the mushrooms for 6 to 8 minutes, or until they begin to exude their juices.
4. Add the salmon and cook each side for 5 to 6 minutes until cooked through.
5. Fold in the prepared pesto and stir well. Taste and add additional salt as needed. Serve warm.

Nutrition Info:
- Per Serving: Calories: 264;Fat: 14.7g;Protein: 7.0g;-Carbs: 30.9g.

Sole Piccata With Capers

Servings:4
Cooking Time: 17 Minutes

Ingredients:

- 1 teaspoon extra-virgin olive oil
- 4 sole fillets, patted dry
- 3 tablespoons almond butter
- 2 teaspoons minced garlic
- 2 tablespoons all-purpose flour
- 2 cups low-sodium chicken broth
- Juice and zest of ½ lemon
- 2 tablespoons capers

Directions:

1. Place a large skillet over medium-high heat and add the olive oil.
2. Sear the sole fillets until the fish flakes easily when tested with a fork, about 4 minutes on each side. Transfer the fish to a plate and set aside.
3. Return the skillet to the stove and add the butter.
4. Sauté the garlic until translucent, about 3 minutes.
5. Whisk in the flour to make a thick paste and cook, stirring constantly, until the mixture is golden brown, about 2 minutes.
6. Whisk in the chicken broth, lemon juice and zest.
7. Cook for about 4 minutes until the sauce is thickened.
8. Stir in the capers and serve the sauce over the fish.

Nutrition Info:

- Per Serving: Calories: 271;Fat: 13.0g;Protein: 30.0g;-Carbs: 7.0g.

Tomato Seafood Soup

Servings:4
Cooking Time:30 Minutes

Ingredients:

- ½ lb cod, skinless and cubed
- 2 tbsp olive oil
- ½ lb shrimp, deveined
- 1 yellow onion, chopped
- 1 carrot, finely chopped
- 1 celery stalk, finely chopped
- 1 small pepper, chopped
- 1 garlic clove, minced
- ½ cup tomatoes, crushed
- 4 cups fish stock
- ¼ tsp rosemary, dried
- Salt and black pepper to taste

Directions:

1. Warm the olive oil in a pot over medium heat. Cook onion, garlic, carrot, celery, and pepper for 5 minutes until soft, stirring occasionally. Stir in the tomatoes, stock, cod, shrimp, rosemary, salt, and pepper and simmer for 15 minutes.

Nutrition Info:

- Per Serving: Calories: 200;Fat: 9g;Protein: 27g;Carbs: 5g.

Roasted Cod With Cabbage

Servings:4
Cooking Time:30 Minutes

Ingredients:

- 2 tbsp olive oil
- 1 head white cabbage, shredded
- 1 tsp garlic powder
- 1 tsp smoked paprika
- 4 cod fillets, boneless
- ½ cup tomato sauce
- 1 tsp Italian seasoning
- 1 tbsp chives, chopped

Directions:

1. Preheat the oven to 390F. Mix cabbage, garlic powder, paprika, olive oil, tomato sauce, Italian seasoning, and chives in a roasting pan. Top with cod fillets and bake covered with foil for 20 minutes. Serve immediately.

Nutrition Info:

- Per Serving: Calories: 200;Fat: 14g;Protein: 18g;Carbs: 24g.

Rosemary Wine Poached Haddock

Servings:4
Cooking Time:40 Minutes

Ingredients:

- 4 haddock fillets
- Salt and black pepper to taste
- 2 garlic cloves, minced
- ½ cup dry white wine
- ½ cup seafood stock
- 4 rosemary sprigs for garnish

Directions:

1. Preheat oven to 380 F. Sprinkle haddock fillets with salt and black pepper and arrange them on a baking dish. Pour in the wine, garlic, and stock. Bake covered for 20 minutes until the fish is tender; remove to a serving plate. Pour the cooking liquid into a pot over high heat. Cook for 10 minutes until reduced by half. Place on serving dishes and top with the reduced poaching liquid. Serve garnished with rosemary.

Nutrition Info:

- Per Serving: Calories: 215;Fat: 4g;Protein: 35g;Carbs: 3g.

Roasted Trout Stuffed With Veggies

Servings:2
Cooking Time: 25 Minutes

Ingredients:

- 2 whole trout fillets, dressed (cleaned but with bones and skin intact)
- 1 tablespoon extra-virgin olive oil
- ¼ teaspoon salt
- ⅛ teaspoon freshly ground black pepper
- 1 small onion, thinly sliced
- ½ red bell pepper, seeded and thinly sliced
- 1 poblano pepper, seeded and thinly sliced
- 2 or 3 shiitake mushrooms, sliced
- 1 lemon, sliced
- Nonstick cooking spray

Directions:

1. Preheat the oven to 425ºF. Spray a baking sheet with nonstick cooking spray.
2. Rub both trout fillets, inside and out, with the olive oil. Season with salt and pepper.
3. Mix together the onion, bell pepper, poblano pepper, and mushrooms in a large bowl. Stuff half of this mixture into the cavity of each fillet. Top the mixture with 2 or 3 lemon slices inside each fillet.
4. Place the fish on the prepared baking sheet side by side. Roast in the preheated oven for 25 minutes, or until the fish is cooked through and the vegetables are tender.
5. Remove from the oven and serve on a plate.

Nutrition Info:

- Per Serving: Calories: 453;Fat: 22.1g;Protein: 49.0g;-Carbs: 13.8g.

Lemon-parsley Swordfish

Servings:4
Cooking Time: 17 To 20 Minutes

Ingredients:

- 1 cup fresh Italian parsley
- ¼ cup lemon juice
- ¼ cup extra-virgin olive oil
- ¼ cup fresh thyme
- 2 cloves garlic
- ½ teaspoon salt
- 4 swordfish steaks
- Olive oil spray

Directions:

1. Preheat the oven to 450ºF. Grease a large baking dish generously with olive oil spray.
2. Place the parsley, lemon juice, olive oil, thyme, garlic, and salt in a food processor and pulse until smoothly blended.
3. Arrange the swordfish steaks in the greased baking dish and spoon the parsley mixture over the top.

4. Bake in the preheated oven for 17 to 20 minutes until flaky.
5. Divide the fish among four plates and serve hot.

Nutrition Info:

- Per Serving: Calories: 396;Fat: 21.7g;Protein: 44.2g;-Carbs: 2.9g.

Cod Fillets In Mushroom Sauce

Servings:4
Cooking Time:45 Minutes

Ingredients:

- 2 cups cremini mushrooms, sliced
- ¼ cup olive oil
- 4 cod fillets
- ½ cup shallots, chopped
- 2 garlic cloves, minced
- 2 cups canned diced tomatoes
- ½ cup clam juice
- ¼ tsp chili flakes
- ¼ tsp sweet paprika
- 1 tbsp capers
- ¼ cup raisins, soaked
- 1 lemon, cut into wedges
- Salt to taste

Directions:

1. Heat the oil in a skillet over medium heat. Sauté shallots and garlic for 2-3 minutes. Add in mushrooms and cook for another 4 minutes. Stir in tomatoes, clam juice, chili flakes, paprika, capers, and salt. Bring to a boil and simmer for 15 minutes.
2. Preheat oven to 380 F. Arrange the cod fillets on a greased baking pan. Cover with the mushroom mixture and top with the soaked raisins. Bake for 18-20 minutes. Serve garnished with lemon wedges.

Nutrition Info:

- Per Serving: Calories: 317;Fat: 13g;Protein: 25g;Carbs: 26g.

Baked Haddock With Rosemary Gremolata

Servings:6
Cooking Time:35 Min + Marinating Time

Ingredients:

- 1 cup milk
- Salt and black pepper to taste
- 2 tbsp rosemary, chopped
- 1 garlic clove, minced
- 1 lemon, zested
- 1 ½ lb haddock fillets

Directions:

1. In a large bowl, coat the fish with milk, salt, pepper, and 1 tablespoon of rosemary. Refrigerate for 2 hours.

2. Preheat oven to 380 F. Carefully remove the haddock from the marinade, drain thoroughly, and place in a greased baking dish. Cover and bake 15–20 minutes until the fish is flaky. Remove fish from the oven and let it rest 5 minutes. To make the gremolata, mix the remaining rosemary, lemon zest, and garlic. Sprinkle the fish with gremolata and serve.

Nutrition Info:
- Per Serving: Calories: 112;Fat: 2g;Protein: 20g;Carbs: 3g.

Chili Flounder Parcels

Servings:4
Cooking Time:20 Minutes

Ingredients:
- 2 tbsp olive oil
- 4 flounder fillets
- ¼ tsp red pepper flakes
- 4 fresh rosemary sprigs
- 2 garlic cloves, thinly sliced
- 1 cup cherry tomatoes, halved
- ½ chopped onion
- 2 tbsp capers
- 8 black olives, sliced
- 2 tbsp dry white wine
- Salt and black pepper to taste

Directions:
1. Preheat oven to 420 F. Drizzle the flounder with olive oil and season with salt, pepper, and red pepper flakes. Divide fillets between 4 pieces of aluminium foil. Top each one with garlic, cherry tomatoes, capers, onion, and olives. Fold the edges to form packets with opened tops. Add in a rosemary sprig in each one and drizzle with the white wine. Seal the packets and arrange them on a baking sheet. Bake for 10 minutes or until the fish is cooked. Serve warm.

Nutrition Info:
- Per Serving: Calories: 242;Fat: 10g;Protein: 31.5g;Carbs: 4g.

Orange Flavored Scallops

Servings:4
Cooking Time: 10 Minutes

Ingredients:
- 2 pounds sea scallops, patted dry
- Sea salt and freshly ground black pepper, to taste
- 2 tablespoons extra-virgin olive oil
- 1 tablespoon minced garlic
- ¼ cup freshly squeezed orange juice
- 1 teaspoon orange zest
- 2 teaspoons chopped fresh thyme, for garnish

Directions:
1. In a bowl, lightly season the scallops with salt and pepper. Set aside.

2. Heat the olive oil in a large skillet over medium-high heat until it shimmers.
3. Add the garlic and sauté for about 3 minutes, or until fragrant.
4. Stir in the seasoned scallops and sear each side for about 4 minutes, or until the scallops are browned.
5. Remove the scallops from the heat to a plate and set aside.
6. Add the orange juice and zest to the skillet, scraping up brown bits from bottom of skillet.
7. Drizzle the sauce over the scallops and garnish with the thyme before serving.

Nutrition Info:
- Per Serving: Calories: 266;Fat: 7.6g;Protein: 38.1g;- Carbs: 7.9g.

Shrimp & Spinach A La Puttanesca

Servings:4
Cooking Time:20 Minutes

Ingredients:
- 1 lb fresh shrimp, shells and tails removed
- 1 cup baby spinach
- 16 oz cooked spaghetti
- 2 tbsp olive oil
- 3 anchovy fillets, chopped
- 3 garlic cloves, minced
- ½ tsp crushed red pepper
- 1 can tomatoes, diced
- 12 black olives, sliced
- 2 tbsp capers
- 1 tsp dried oregano

Directions:
1. Warm the olive oil in a large skillet over medium heat. Add in the anchovies, garlic, and crushed red peppers and cook for 3 minutes, stirring frequently and mashing up the anchovies with a wooden spoon until they have melted into the oil. Pour in the tomatoes with their juices, olives, capers, and oregano. Simmer until the sauce is lightly bubbling, about 3-4 minutes. Stir in the shrimp. Cook for 6-8 minutes or until they turn pink and white, stirring occasionally. Add the baby spinach and spaghetti and stir for 2 minutes until the spinach wilts. Serve and enjoy!

Nutrition Info:
- Per Serving: Calories: 362;Fat: 13g;Protein: 30g;Carbs: 31g.

Cioppino (seafood Tomato Stew)

Servings:2
Cooking Time: 20 Minutes

Ingredients:
- 2 tablespoons olive oil
- ½ small onion, diced
- ½ green pepper, diced
- 2 teaspoons dried basil
- 2 teaspoons dried oregano
- ½ cup dry white wine
- 1 can diced tomatoes with basil
- 1 can no-salt-added tomato sauce
- 1 can minced clams with their juice
- 8 ounces peeled, deveined raw shrimp
- 4 ounces any white fish (a thick piece works best)
- 3 tablespoons fresh parsley
- Salt and freshly ground black pepper, to taste

Directions:

1. In a Dutch oven, heat the olive oil over medium heat.
2. Sauté the onion and green pepper for 5 minutes, or until tender.
3. Stir in the basil, oregano, wine, diced tomatoes, and tomato sauce and bring to a boil.
4. Once boiling, reduce the heat to low and bring to a simmer for 5 minutes.
5. Add the clams, shrimp, and fish and cook for about 10 minutes, or until the shrimp are pink and cooked through.
6. Scatter with the parsley and add the salt and black pepper to taste.
7. Remove from the heat and serve warm.

Nutrition Info:
- Per Serving: Calories: 221;Fat: 7.7g;Protein: 23.1g;-Carbs: 10.9g.

Mushroom & Shrimp Rice

Servings:4
Cooking Time:40 Minutes

Ingredients:
- 2 tbsp olive oil
- 1 lb shrimp, peeled, deveined
- 1 cup white rice
- 4 garlic cloves, sliced
- ¼ tsp hot paprika
- 1 cup mushrooms, sliced
- ¼ cup green peas
- Juice of 1 lime
- Sea salt to taste
- ¼ cup chopped fresh chives

Directions:

1. Bring a pot of salted water to a boil. Cook the rice for 15-18 minutes, stirring occasionally. Drain and place in a bowl. Add in the green peas and mix to combine well. Taste

and adjust the seasoning. Remove to a serving plate.
2. Heat the olive oil in a saucepan over medium heat and sauté garlic and hot paprika for 30-40 seconds until garlic is light golden brown. Remove the garlic with a slotted spoon. Add the mushrooms to the saucepan and sauté them for 5 minutes until tender. Put in the shrimp, lime juice, and salt and stir for 4 minutes. Turn the heat off. Add the chives and reserved garlic to the shrimp and pour over the rice. Serve and enjoy!

Nutrition Info:
- Per Serving: Calories: 342;Fat: 12g;Protein: 24g;Carbs: 33g.

Salmon Baked In Foil

Servings:4
Cooking Time: 25 Minutes

Ingredients:
- 2 cups cherry tomatoes
- 3 tablespoons extra-virgin olive oil
- 3 tablespoons lemon juice
- 3 tablespoons almond butter
- 1 teaspoon oregano
- ½ teaspoon salt
- 4 salmon fillets

Directions:

1. Preheat the oven to 400ºF.
2. Cut the tomatoes in half and put them in a bowl.
3. Add the olive oil, lemon juice, butter, oregano, and salt to the tomatoes and gently toss to combine.
4. Cut 4 pieces of foil, about 12-by-12 inches each.
5. Place the salmon fillets in the middle of each piece of foil.
6. Divide the tomato mixture evenly over the 4 pieces of salmon. Bring the ends of the foil together and seal to form a closed pocket.
7. Place the 4 pockets on a baking sheet. Bake in the preheated oven for 25 minutes.
8. Remove from the oven and serve on a plate.

Nutrition Info:
- Per Serving: Calories: 410;Fat: 32.0g;Protein: 30.0g;-Carbs: 4.0g.

Pancetta-wrapped Scallops

Servings:6
Cooking Time:25 Minutes

Ingredients:
- 2 tsp olive oil
- 12 thin pancetta slices
- 12 medium scallops
- 2 tsp lemon juice
- 1 tsp chili powder

Directions:

1. Wrap pancetta around scallops and secure with toothpicks. Warm the olive oil in a skillet over medium heat and cook scallops for 6 minutes on all sides. Serve sprinkled with chili powder and lemon juice.

Nutrition Info:
- Per Serving: Calories: 310;Fat: 25g;Protein: 19g;Carbs: 24g.

Salmon & Celery Egg Bake

Servings:4
Cooking Time:40 Minutes

Ingredients:
- 2 tbsp olive oil
- 2 tbsp butter, melted
- 4 oz smoked salmon, flaked
- 1 cup cheddar cheese, grated
- 4 eggs, whisked
- ¼ cup plain yogurt
- 1 cup cream of celery soup
- 1 shallot, chopped
- 2 garlic cloves, minced
- ½ cup celery, chopped
- 8 slices fresh toast, cubed
- 1 tbsp mint leaves, chopped

Directions:

1. Preheat the oven to 360 F. In a bowl, mix eggs, yogurt, and celery soup. Warm olive oil in a skillet over medium heat and cook the shallot, garlic, and celery until tender. Place the toast cubes in a greased baking dish, top with cooked vegetables and salmon, and cover with egg mixture and butter. Bake for 22-25 minutes until it is cooked through. Scatter cheddar cheese on top and bake for another 5 minutes until the cheese melts. Serve garnished with mint leaves.

Nutrition Info:
- Per Serving: Calories: 392;Fat: 31g;Protein: 20g;Carbs: 9.6g.

Vegetable & Shrimp Roast

Servings:4
Cooking Time:30 Minutes

Ingredients:
- 2 lb shrimp, peeled and deveined
- 4 tbsp olive oil
- 2 bell peppers, cut into chunks
- 2 fennel bulbs, cut into wedges
- 2 red onions, cut into wedges
- 4 garlic cloves, unpeeled
- 8 Kalamata olives, halved
- 1 tsp lemon zest, grated
- 2 tsp oregano, dried
- 2 tbsp parsley, chopped
- Salt and black pepper to taste

Directions:

1. Preheat the oven to 390 F. Place bell peppers, garlic, fennel, red onions, and olives in a roasting tray. Add in the lemon zest, oregano, half of the olive oil, salt, and pepper and toss to coat; roast for 15 minutes. Coat the shrimp with the remaining olive oil and pour over the veggies; roast for another 7 minutes. Serve topped with parsley.

Nutrition Info:
- Per Serving: Calories: 350;Fat: 20g;Protein: 11g;Carbs: 35g.

Parsley Tomato Tilapia

Servings:4
Cooking Time:20 Minutes

Ingredients:
- 2 tbsp olive oil
- 4 tilapia fillets, boneless
- ½ cup tomato sauce
- 2 tbsp parsley, chopped
- Salt and black pepper to taste

Directions:

1. Warm olive oil in a skillet over medium heat. Sprinkle tilapia with salt and pepper and cook until golden brown, flipping once, about 6 minutes. Pour in the tomato sauce and parsley and cook for an additional 4 minutes. Serve immediately.

Nutrition Info:
- Per Serving: Calories: 308;Fat: 17g;Protein: 16g;Carbs: 3g.

Pan-fried Chili Sea Scallops

Servings:4
Cooking Time:25 Minutes

Ingredients:

- 1 ½ lb large sea scallops, tendons removed
- 3 tbsp olive oil
- 1 garlic clove, finely chopped
- ½ red pepper flakes
- 2 tbsp chili sauce
- ¼ cup tomato sauce
- 1 small shallot, minced
- 1 tbsp minced fresh cilantro
- Salt and black pepper to taste

Directions:

1. Warm the olive oil in a skillet over medium heat. Add the scallops and cook for 2 minutes without moving them. Flip them and continue to cook for 2 more minutes, without moving them, until golden browned. Set aside. Add the shallot and garlic to the skillet and sauté for 3-5 minutes until softened. Pour in the chili sauce, tomato sauce, and red pepper flakes and stir for 3-4 minutes. Add the scallops back and warm through. Adjust the taste and top with cilantro.

Nutrition Info:

- Per Serving: Calories: 204;Fat: 14.1g;Protein: 14g;Carbs: 5g.

Pesto Shrimp Over Zoodles

Servings:4
Cooking Time: 10 Minutes

Ingredients:

- 1 pound fresh shrimp, peeled and deveined
- Salt and freshly ground black pepper, to taste
- 2 tablespoons extra-virgin olive oil
- ½ small onion, slivered
- 8 ounces store-bought jarred pesto
- ¾ cup crumbled goat or feta cheese, plus additional for serving
- 2 large zucchini, spiralized, for serving
- ¼ cup chopped flat-leaf Italian parsley, for garnish

Directions:

1. In a bowl, season the shrimp with salt and pepper. Set aside.
2. In a large skillet, heat the olive oil over medium-high heat. Sauté the onion until just golden, 5 to 6 minutes.
3. Reduce the heat to low and add the pesto and cheese, whisking to combine and melt the cheese. Bring to a low simmer and add the shrimp. Reduce the heat back to low and cover. Cook until the shrimp is cooked through and pink, about 3 to 4 minutes.
4. Serve the shrimp warm over zoodles, garnishing with chopped parsley and additional crumbled cheese.

Nutrition Info:

- Per Serving: Calories: 491;Fat: 35.0g;Protein: 29.0g;-Carbs: 15.0g.

Caper & Squid Stew

Servings:4
Cooking Time:25 Minutes

Ingredients:

- 2 tbsp olive oil
- 1 onion, chopped
- 1 celery stalk, chopped
- 1 lb calamari rings
- 2 red chili peppers, chopped
- 2 garlic cloves, minced
- 14 oz canned tomatoes, diced
- 2 tbsp tomato paste
- Salt and black pepper to taste
- 2 tbsp capers, drained
- 12 black olives, pitted and halved

Directions:

1. Warm the olive oil in a skillet over medium heat and cook onion, celery, garlic, and chili peppers for 2 minutes. Stir in calamari rings, tomatoes, tomato paste, salt, and pepper and bring to a simmer. Cook for 20 minutes. Put in olives and capers and cook for another 5 minutes. Serve right away.

Nutrition Info:

- Per Serving: Calories: 280;Fat: 12g;Protein: 16g;Carbs: 14g.

Fruits, Desserts And Snacks Recipes

Country Pizza

Servings:4
Cooking Time:45 Minutes

Ingredients:
- For the crust
- 2 tbsp olive oil
- 2 cups flour
- 1 cup lukewarm water
- 1 pinch of sugar
- 1 tsp active dry yeast
- ¾ tsp salt
- For the ranch sauce
- 1 tbsp butter
- 2 garlic cloves, minced
- 1 tbsp cream cheese
- ¼ cup half and half
- 1 tbsp Ranch seasoning mix
- For the topping
- 3 bacon slices, chopped
- 2 chicken breasts
- Salt and black pepper to taste
- 1 cup grated mozzarella
- 6 fresh basil leaves

Directions:
1. Sift the flour and salt in a bowl and stir in yeast. Mix lukewarm water, olive oil, and sugar in another bowl. Add the wet mixture to the dry mixture and whisk until you obtain a soft dough. Place the dough on a lightly floured work surface and knead it thoroughly for 4-5 minutes until elastic. Transfer the dough to a greased bowl. Cover with cling film and leave to rise for 50-60 minutes in a warm place until doubled in size. Roll out the dough to a thickness of around 12 inches.
2. Preheat the oven to 400 F. Line a pizza pan with parchment paper. In a bowl, mix the sauce's ingredients butter, garlic, cream cheese, half and half, and ranch mix. Set aside. Heat a grill pan over medium heat and cook the bacon until crispy and brown, 5 minutes. Transfer to a plate and set aside.
3. Season the chicken with salt, pepper and grill in the pan on both sides until golden brown, 10 minutes. Remove to a plate, allow cooling and cut into thin slices. Spread the ranch sauce on the pizza crust, followed by the chicken and bacon, and then, mozzarella cheese and basil. Bake for 5 minutes or until the cheese melts. Slice and serve warm.

Nutrition Info:
- Per Serving: Calories: 528;Fat: 28g;Protein: 61g;Carbs: 5g.

Roasted Garlic & Spicy Lentil Dip

Servings:6
Cooking Time:40 Minutes

Ingredients:
- 1 roasted red bell pepper, chopped
- 4 tbsp olive oil
- 1 cup split red lentils
- ½ red onion
- 1 garlic bulb, top removed
- ½ tsp cumin seeds
- 1 tsp coriander seeds
- ¼ cup walnuts
- 2 tbsp tomato paste
- ½ tsp Cayenne powder
- Salt and black pepper to taste

Directions:
1. Preheat oven to 370 F. Drizzle the garlic with some olive oil and wrap it in a piece of aluminum foil. Roast for 35-40 minutes. Remove and allow to cool for a few minutes. Cover the lentils with salted water in a pot over medium heat and bring to a boil. Simmer for 15 minutes. Drain and set aside.
2. Squeeze out the garlic cloves and place them in a food processor. Add in the cooled lentils, cumin seeds, coriander seeds, roasted red bell pepper, onion, walnuts, tomato paste, Cayenne powder, remaining olive oil, salt, and black pepper. Pulse until smooth. Serve with crostiniif desire.

Nutrition Info:
- Per Serving: Calories: 234;Fat: 13g;Protein: 9g;Carbs: 21.7g.

Berry Sorbet

Servings:4
Cooking Time:10 Min + Freezing Time

Ingredients:
- 1 tsp lemon juice
- ¼ cup honey
- 1 cup fresh strawberries
- 1 cup fresh raspberries
- 1 cup fresh blueberries

Directions:
1. Bring 1 cup of water to a boil in a pot over high heat. Stir in honey until dissolved. Remove from the heat and mix in berries and lemon juice; let cool.
2. Once cooled, add the mixture to a food processor and pulse until smooth. Transfer to a shallow glass and freeze for 1 hour. Stir with a fork and freeze for 30 more minutes.

Repeat a couple of times. Serve in dessert dishes.

Nutrition Info:
- Per Serving: Calories: 115;Fat: 1g;Protein: 1g;Carbs: 29g.

Orange Pannacotta With Blackberries

Servings:2
Cooking Time:15 Min + Chilling Time

Ingredients:
- ¾ cup half-and-half
- 1 tsp powdered gelatin
- ½ cup heavy cream
- 3 tbsp sugar
- 1 tsp orange zest
- 1 tbsp orange juice
- 1 tsp orange extract
- ½ cup fresh blackberries
- 2 mint leaves

Directions:
1. Put ¼ cup of half-and-half in a bowl. Mix in gelatin powder and set it aside for 10 minutes to hydrate. In a saucepan over medium heat, combine the remaining half-and-half, heavy cream, sugar, orange zest, orange juice, and orange extract. Warm the mixture for 4 minutes. Don't let it come to a full boil. Remove from the heat. Let cool slightly.
2. Add the gelatin into the cream mixture and whisk until the gelatin melts. Pour the mixture into 2 dessert glasses and refrigerate for at least 2 hours. Serve with fresh berries and garnish with mint leaves.

Nutrition Info:
- Per Serving: Calories: 422;Fat: 33g;Protein: 6g;Carbs: 28g.

Citrus Cranberry And Quinoa Energy Bites

Servings:12
Cooking Time: 0 Minutes

Ingredients:
- 2 tablespoons almond butter
- 2 tablespoons maple syrup
- ¾ cup cooked quinoa
- 1 tablespoon dried cranberries
- 1 tablespoon chia seeds
- ¼ cup ground almonds
- ¼ cup sesame seeds, toasted
- Zest of 1 orange
- ½ teaspoon vanilla extract

Directions:
1. Line a baking sheet with parchment paper.
2. Combine the butter and maple syrup in a bowl. Stir to mix well.
3. Fold in the remaining ingredients and stir until the mix-

ture holds together and smooth.
4. Divide the mixture into 12 equal parts, then shape each part into a ball.
5. Arrange the balls on the baking sheet, then refrigerate for at least 15 minutes.
6. Serve chilled.

Nutrition Info:
- Per Serving: Calories: 110;Fat: 10.8g;Protein: 3.1g;-Carbs: 4.9g.

Crispy Potato Chips

Servings:4
Cooking Time:40 Minutes

Ingredients:
- 2 tbsp olive oil
- 4 potatoes, cut into wedges
- 2 tbsp grated Parmesan cheese
- Salt and black pepper to taste

Directions:
1. Preheat the oven to 340 F. In a bowl, combine the potatoes, olive oil, salt, and black pepper. Spread on a lined baking sheet and bake for 40 minutes until the edges are browned. Serve sprinkled with Parmesan cheese.

Nutrition Info:
- Per Serving: Calories: 359;Fat: 8g;Protein: 9g;Carbs: 66g.

Chocolate, Almond, And Cherry Clusters

Servings:10
Cooking Time: 3 Minutes

Ingredients:
- 1 cup dark chocolate, chopped
- 1 tablespoon coconut oil
- ½ cup dried cherries
- 1 cup roasted salted almonds

Directions:
1. Line a baking sheet with parchment paper.
2. Melt the chocolate and coconut oil in a saucepan for 3 minutes. Stir constantly.
3. Turn off the heat and mix in the cherries and almonds.
4. Drop the mixture on the baking sheet with a spoon. Place the sheet in the refrigerator and chill for at least 1 hour or until firm.
5. Serve chilled.

Nutrition Info:
- Per Serving: Calories: 197;Fat: 13.2g;Protein: 4.1g;-Carbs: 17.8g.

Honey Baked Cinnamon Apples

Servings:2
Cooking Time: 20 Minutes

Ingredients:
- 1 teaspoon extra-virgin olive oil
- 4 firm apples, peeled, cored, and sliced
- ½ teaspoon salt
- 1½ teaspoons ground cinnamon, divided
- 2 tablespoons unsweetened almond milk
- 2 tablespoons honey

Directions:
1. Preheat the oven to 375ºF. Coat a small casserole dish with the olive oil.
2. Toss the apple slices with the salt and ½ teaspoon of the cinnamon in a medium bowl. Spread the apples in the prepared casserole dish and bake in the preheated oven for 20 minutes.
3. Meanwhile, in a small saucepan, heat the milk, honey, and remaining 1 teaspoon of cinnamon over medium heat, stirring frequently.
4. When it reaches a simmer, remove the pan from the heat and cover to keep warm.
5. Divide the apple slices between 2 plates and pour the sauce over the apples. Serve warm.

Nutrition Info:
- Per Serving: Calories: 310;Fat: 3.4g;Protein: 1.7g;Carbs: 68.5g.

Amaretto Nut Bars

Servings:4
Cooking Time:10 Minutes

Ingredients:
- 2 tbsp olive oil
- ¼ cup shredded coconut
- 1 cup pistachios
- ½ tsp Amaretto liqueur
- 1 cup almonds
- 2 cups dates, pitted
- ¼ cup cocoa powder

Directions:
1. In a food processor, blend pistachios, dates, almonds, olive oil, Amaretto liqueur, and cocoa powder until well minced. Make tablespoon-size balls out of the mixture. Roll the balls in the shredded coconut to coat. Serve chilled.

Nutrition Info:
- Per Serving: Calories: 560;Fat: 28g;Protein: 11g;Carbs: 79g.

Pomegranate Blueberry Granita

Servings:2
Cooking Time:15 Min + Freezing Time

Ingredients:
- 1 cup blueberries
- 1 cup pomegranate juice
- ¼ cup sugar
- ¼ tsp lemon zest

Directions:
1. Place the blueberries, lemon zest, and pomegranate juice in a saucepan over medium heat and bring to a boil. Simmer for 5 minutes or until the blueberries start to break down. Stir the sugar in ¼ cup of water until the sugar is dissolved. Place the blueberry mixture and the sugar water in your blender and blitz for 1 minute or until the fruit is puréed.
2. Pour the mixture into a baking pan. The liquid should come about ½ inch up the sides. Let the mixture cool for 30 minutes, and then put it into the freezer. Every 30 minutes for the next 2 hours, scrape the granita with a fork to keep it from freezing solid. Serve it after 2 hours, or store it in a covered container in the freezer.

Nutrition Info:
- Per Serving: Calories: 214;Fat: 0g;Protein: 1g;Carbs: 54g.

Greek Yogurt Affogato With Pistachios

Servings:4
Cooking Time: 0 Minutes

Ingredients:
- 24 ounces vanilla Greek yogurt
- 2 teaspoons sugar
- 4 shots hot espresso
- 4 tablespoons chopped unsalted pistachios
- 4 tablespoons dark chocolate chips

Directions:
1. Spoon the yogurt into four bowls or tall glasses.
2. Mix ½ teaspoon of sugar into each of the espresso shots.
3. Pour one shot of the hot espresso over each bowl of yogurt.
4. Top each bowl with 1 tablespoon of the pistachios and 1 tablespoon of the chocolate chips and serve.

Nutrition Info:
- Per Serving: Calories: 190;Fat: 6.0g;Protein: 20.0g;Carbs: 14.0g.

Chili Grilled Eggplant Rounds

Servings:4
Cooking Time:25 Minutes

Ingredients:
- 1 cup roasted peppers, chopped
- 4 tbsp olive oil
- 2 eggplants, cut into rounds
- 12 Kalamata olives, chopped
- 1 tsp red chili flakes, crushed
- Salt and black pepper to taste
- 2 tbsp basil, chopped
- 2 tbsp Parmesan cheese, grated

Directions:
1. Combine roasted peppers, half of the olive oil, olives, red chili flakes, salt, and pepper in a bowl. Rub each eggplant slice with remaining olive oil and salt grill them on the preheated grill for 14 minutes on both sides. Remove to a platter. Distribute the pepper mixture across the eggplant rounds and top with basil and Parmesan cheese to serve.

Nutrition Info:
- Per Serving: Calories: 220;Fat: 11g;Protein: 6g;Carbs: 16g.

Hot Italian Sausage Pizza Wraps

Servings:2
Cooking Time:20 Minutes

Ingredients:
- 1 tbsp basil, chopped
- 1 tsp olive oil
- 6 oz spicy Italian sausage
- 1 shallot, chopped
- 1 tsp Italian seasoning
- 4 oz marinara sauce
- 2 flour tortillas
- ½ cup mozzarella, shredded
- 1/3 cup Parmesan, grated
- 1 tsp red pepper flakes

Directions:
1. Warm the olive oil in a skillet over medium heat. Add and cook the sausage for 5-6 minutes, stirring and breaking up larger pieces, until cooked through. Remove to a bowl. Sauté the shallot for 3 minutes until soft, stirring frequently. Stir in Italian seasoning, marinara sauce, and reserved sausage. Bring to a simmer and cook for about 2 minutes. Divide the mixture between the tortillas, top with the cheeses, add red pepper flakes and basil, and fold over. Serve immediately.

Nutrition Info:
- Per Serving: Calories: 744;Fat: 46g;Protein: 41g;Carbs: 40g.

Walnut And Date Balls

Servings:6
Cooking Time: 8 To 10 Minutes

Ingredients:
- 1 cup walnuts
- 1 cup unsweetened shredded coconut
- 14 medjool dates, pitted
- 8 tablespoons almond butter

Directions:
1. Preheat the oven to 350ºF.
2. Put the walnuts on a baking sheet and toast in the oven for 5 minutes.
3. Put the shredded coconut on a clean baking sheet. Toast for about 3 to 5 minutes, or until it turns golden brown. Once done, remove it from the oven and put it in a shallow bowl.
4. In a food processor, process the toasted walnuts until they have a medium chop. Transfer the chopped walnuts into a medium bowl.
5. Add the dates and butter to the food processor and blend until the dates become a thick paste. Pour the chopped walnuts into the food processor with the dates and pulse just until the mixture is combined, about 5 to 7 pulses.
6. Remove the mixture from the food processor and scrape it into a large bowl.
7. To make the balls, spoon 1 to 2 tablespoons of the date mixture into the palm of your hand and roll around between your hands until you form a ball. Put the ball on a clean, lined baking sheet. Repeat until all the mixture is formed into balls.
8. Roll each ball in the toasted coconut until the outside of the ball is coated. Put the ball back on the baking sheet and repeat.
9. Put all the balls into the refrigerator for 20 minutes before serving. Store any leftovers in the refrigerator in an airtight container.

Nutrition Info:
- Per Serving: Calories: 489;Fat: 35.0g;Protein: 5.0g;-Carbs: 48.0g.

Speedy Cucumber Canapes

Servings:4
Cooking Time:5 Minutes

Ingredients:
- 2 tbsp olive oil
- 2 cucumbers, sliced into rounds
- 12 cherry tomatoes, halved
- Salt and black pepper to taste
- 1 red chili pepper, dried
- 8 oz cream cheese, softened
- 1 tbsp balsamic vinegar
- 1 tsp chives, chopped

Directions:

1. In a bowl, mix cream cheese, balsamic vinegar, olive oil, chili pepper, and chives. Season with salt and pepper. Spread the mixture over the cucumber rounds and top with the cherry tomato halves. Serve.

Nutrition Info:
- Per Serving: Calories: 130;Fat: 3g;Protein: 3g;Carbs: 7g.

Chia Seed & Chocolate Pudding

Servings:4
Cooking Time:10 Min + Chilling Time

Ingredients:
- 2 cups heavy cream
- ¼ cup cocoa powder
- 1 tsp vanilla extract
- ½ ground cinnamon
- ½ cup chia seeds
- 2 tbsp chocolate shavings

Directions:

1. Warm the heavy cream in a saucepan over medium heat to just below a simmer. Remove from the heat and allow to cool slightly. In a large bowl, combine the warmed heavy cream, cocoa powder, vanilla extract, cinnamon, and salt and blend using an immersion blender until the cocoa is well incorporated. Stir in the chia seeds and let sit for 15 minutes. Divide the mixture evenly between small glass bowls and refrigerate for at least 2 hours or until set. Serve chilled.

Nutrition Info:
- Per Serving: Calories: 561;Fat: 53g;Protein: 8g;Carbs: 19g.

Fancy Baileys Ice Coffee

Servings:4
Cooking Time:5 Min + Chilling Time

Ingredients:
- 1 cup espresso
- 2 cups milk
- 4 tbsp Baileys
- ½ tsp ground cinnamon
- ½ tsp vanilla extract
- Ice cubes

Directions:

1. Fill four glasses with ice cubes. Mix milk, cinnamon, and vanilla in a food processor until nice and frothy. Pour into the glasses. Combine the Baileys with the espresso and mix well. Pour ¼ of the espresso mixture over the milk and serve.

Nutrition Info:
- Per Serving: Calories: 100;Fat: 5g;Protein: 4g;Carbs: 8g.

Frozen Mango Raspberry Delight

Servings:2
Cooking Time: 0 Minutes

Ingredients:
- 3 cups frozen raspberries
- 1 mango, peeled and pitted
- 1 peach, peeled and pitted
- 1 teaspoon honey

Directions:

1. Place all the ingredients into a blender and purée, adding some water as needed.
2. Put in the freezer for 10 minutes to firm up if desired. Serve chilled or at room temperature.

Nutrition Info:
- Per Serving: Calories: 276;Fat: 2.1g;Protein: 4.5g;Carbs: 60.3g.

Anchovy Stuffed Avocado Boats

Servings:4
Cooking Time:10 Minutes

Ingredients:
- 4 anchovy fillets, chopped
- 1 avocado, halved and pitted
- 2 tbsp sun-dried tomatoes, chopped
- 1 tbsp basil pesto
- 2 tbsp black olives, pitted and chopped
- Salt and black pepper to taste
- 2 tsp pine nuts, toasted
- 1 tbsp basil, chopped

Directions:

1. Toss anchovies, sun-dried tomatoes, basil pesto, olives, salt, pepper, pine nuts, and basil in a bowl. Fill each avocado half with the mixture and serve immediately.

Nutrition Info:
- Per Serving: Calories: 240;Fat: 10g;Protein: 6g;Carbs: 12g.

Cardamom Apple Slices

Servings:2
Cooking Time:30 Minutes

Ingredients:
- 1 ½ tsp cardamom
- ½ tsp salt
- 4 peeled, cored apples, sliced
- 2 tbsp honey
- 2 tbsp milk

Directions:

1. Preheat oven to 390 F. In a bowl, combine apple slices, salt, and ½ tsp of cardamom. Arrange them on a greased baking dish and cook for 20 minutes. Remove to a serving plate.

2. In the meantime, place milk, honey, and remaining cardamom in a pot over medium heat. Cook until simmer. Pour the sauce over the apples and serve immediately.

Nutrition Info:
- Per Serving: Calories: 287;Fat: 3g;Protein: 2g;Carbs: 69g.

Sicilian Sandwich Muffuletta

Servings:6
Cooking Time:10 Minutes

Ingredients:
- 1 focaccia bread
- 2 tbsp drained capers
- 2 tbsp black olive tapenade
- ½ lb fontina cheese, sliced
- ¼ lb smoked turkey, sliced
- ¼ lb salami, thinly sliced

Directions:
1. Slice the focaccia bread in half horizontally. Spread each piece with olive tapenade. Layer half of the fontina cheese, a layer of capers, smoked turkey, olive tapenade, salami, capers, and finish with fontina cheese. Top with the remaining focaccia half and press the sandwich together gently. Serve sliced into wedges.

Nutrition Info:
- Per Serving: Calories: 335;Fat: 27g;Protein: 18g;Carbs: 4g.

Avocado & Salmon Stuffed Cucumbers

Servings:4
Cooking Time:10 Minutes

Ingredients:
- 1 tbsp extra-virgin olive oil
- 2 large cucumbers, peeled
- 1 can red salmon
- 1 ripe avocado, mashed
- 2 tbsp chopped fresh dill
- Salt and black pepper to taste

Directions:
1. Cut the cucumber into 1-inch-thick segments, and using a spoon, scrape seeds out of the center of each piece and stand up on a plate. In a bowl, mix the salmon, avocado, olive oil, lime zest and juice, dill, salt, and pepper, and blend until creamy. Spoon the salmon mixture into the center of each cucumber segment and serve chilled.

Nutrition Info:
- Per Serving: Calories: 159;Fat: 11g;Protein: 9g;Carbs: 8g.

Baked Sweet Potatoes With Chickpeas

Servings:4
Cooking Time:30 Minutes

Ingredients:
- 4 sweet potatoes, halved lengthways
- 2 tbsp olive oil
- 1 tbsp butter
- 1 can chickpeas
- ¼ tsp dried thyme
- Salt and black pepper to taste
- 1 tsp paprika
- ½ tsp garlic powder
- 1 cup spinach
- 1 cup Greek-style yogurt
- 2 tsp hot sauce

Directions:
1. Preheat oven to 360 F. Drizzle the sweet potatoes with some oil. Place, cut-side down, in a lined baking tray and bake for 8-10 minutes. In a bowl, mix chickpeas with remaining olive oil, paprika, thyme, and garlic powder. Pour them onto the other end of the baking tray and roast for 20 minutes alongside the sweet potatoes, stirring the chickpeas once.
2. Melt the butter in a pan over medium heat and stir-fry the spinach and 1 tbsp of water for 3-4 minutes until the spinach wilts. Stir in the roasted chickpeas. Mix the yogurt with hot sauce in a small bowl. Top the sweet potato halves with chickpeas and spinach and serve with hot yogurt on the side.

Nutrition Info:
- Per Serving: Calories: 97;Fat: 3g;Protein: 5g;Carbs: 14g.

Fruit And Nut Chocolate Bark

Servings:2
Cooking Time: 2 Minutes

Ingredients:
- 2 tablespoons chopped nuts
- 3 ounces dark chocolate chips
- ¼ cup chopped dried fruit (blueberries, apricots, figs, prunes, or any combination of those)

Directions:
1. Line a sheet pan with parchment paper and set aside.
2. Add the nuts to a skillet over medium-high heat and toast for 60 seconds, or just fragrant. Set aside to cool.
3. Put the chocolate chips in a microwave-safe glass bowl and microwave on High for 1 minute.
4. Stir the chocolate and allow any unmelted chips to warm and melt. If desired, heat for an additional 20 to 30 seconds.
5. Transfer the chocolate to the prepared sheet pan. Scatter the dried fruit and toasted nuts over the chocolate evenly and gently pat in so they stick.
6. Place the sheet pan in the refrigerator for at least 1 hour

to let the chocolate harden.

7. When ready, break into pieces and serve.

Nutrition Info:

- Per Serving: Calories: 285;Fat: 16.1g;Protein: 4.0g;-Carbs: 38.7g.

5-minute Avocado Spread

Servings:4
Cooking Time:5 Minutes

Ingredients:

- 2 avocados, chopped
- ½ cup heavy cream
- 1 serrano pepper, chopped
- Salt and black pepper to taste
- 2 tbsp cilantro, chopped
- ¼ cup lime juice

Directions:

1. In a food processor, blitz heavy cream, serrano pepper, salt, pepper, avocados, cilantro, and lime juice until smooth. Refrigerate before serving.

Nutrition Info:

- Per Serving: Calories: 210;Fat: 15g;Protein: 8g;Carbs: 9g.

Prawn & Cucumber Bites

Servings:4
Cooking Time:5 Minutes

Ingredients:

- 1 lb prawns, cooked and chopped
- 1 cucumber, cubed
- 2 tbsp cream cheese
- Salt and black pepper to taste
- 12 whole-grain crackers

Directions:

1. Combine cucumber, prawns, cream cheese, salt, and pepper in a bowl. Place crackers on a plate and top them with the prawn mixture. Serve right away.

Nutrition Info:

- Per Serving: Calories: 160;Fat: 9g;Protein: 18g;Carbs: 12g.

Watermelon And Blueberry Salad

Servings:6
Cooking Time: 0 Minutes

Ingredients:

- 1 medium watermelon
- 1 cup fresh blueberries
- ⅓ cup honey
- 2 tablespoons lemon juice
- 2 tablespoons finely chopped fresh mint leaves

Directions:

1. Cut the watermelon into 1-inch cubes. Put them in a bowl.
2. Evenly distribute the blueberries over the watermelon.
3. In a separate bowl, whisk together the honey, lemon juice and mint.
4. Drizzle the mint dressing over the watermelon and blueberries.
5. Serve cold.

Nutrition Info:

- Per Serving: Calories: 238;Fat: 1.0g;Protein: 4.0g;Carbs: 61.0g.

Skillet Pesto Pizza

Servings:2
Cooking Time:10 Minutes

Ingredients:

- 1 tbsp butter
- 2 pieces of focaccia bread
- 2 tbsp pesto
- 1 medium tomato, sliced
- 2 large eggs

Directions:

1. Place a large skillet over medium heat. Place the focaccia in the skillet and let it warm for about 4 minutes on both sides until softened and just starting to turn golden. Remove to a platter. Spread 1 tablespoon of the pesto on one side of each slice. Cover with tomato slices. Melt the butter in the skillet over medium heat. Crack in the eggs, keeping them separated, and cook until the whites are no longer translucent and the yolk is cooked to desired doneness. Spoon one egg onto each pizza. Serve and enjoy!

Nutrition Info:

- Per Serving: Calories: 427;Fat: 17g;Protein: 17g;Carbs: 10g.

The Best Trail Mix

Servings:4
Cooking Time:20 Minutes

Ingredients:

- 1 tbsp olive oil
- 1 tbsp maple syrup
- 1 tsp vanilla
- ½ tsp paprika
- ½ tsp cardamom
- ½ tsp allspice
- 2 cups mixed, unsalted nuts
- ¼ cup sunflower seeds
- ½ cup dried apricots, diced
- ½ cup dried figs, diced
- Salt to taste

Directions:

1. Mix the olive oil, maple syrup, vanilla, cardamom, pa-

prika, and allspice in a pan over medium heat. Stir to combine. Add the nuts and seeds and stir well to coat. Let the nuts and seeds toast for about 10 minutes, stirring often. Remove from the heat, and add the dried apricots and figs. Stir everything well and season with salt. Store in an airtight container.

Nutrition Info:
- Per Serving: Calories: 261;Fat: 18g;Protein: 6g;Carbs: 23g.

Portuguese Orange Mug Cake

Servings:2
Cooking Time:12 Minutes

Ingredients:
- 2 tbsp butter, melted
- 6 tbsp flour
- 2 tbsp sugar
- ½ tsp baking powder
- ¼ tsp salt
- 1 tsp orange zest
- 1 egg
- 2 tbsp orange juice
- 2 tbsp milk
- ½ tsp orange extract
- ½ tsp vanilla extract
- Orange slices for garnish

Directions:
1. In a bowl, beat the egg, butter, orange juice, milk, orange extract, and vanilla extract. In another bowl, combine the flour, sugar, baking powder, salt, and orange zest. Pour the dry ingredients into the wet ingredients and stir to combine. Spoon the mixture into 2 mugs and microwave one at a time for 1-2 minutes. Garnish with orange slices.

Nutrition Info:
- Per Serving: Calories: 302;Fat: 17g;Protein: 6g;Carbs: 33g.

Savory Cauliflower Steaks

Servings:4
Cooking Time:35 Minutes

Ingredients:
- 1 head cauliflower, cut into steaks
- 2 tbsp olive oil
- Salt and paprika to taste

Directions:
1. Preheat oven to 360 F.Line a baking sheet with aluminum foil. Rub each cauliflower steak with olive oil, salt, and paprika. Arrange on the baking sheet and bake for 10-15 minutes, flip, and bake for another 15 minutes until crispy.

Nutrition Info:
- Per Serving: Calories: 78;Fat: 7g;Protein: 1g;Carbs: 4g.

Pesto Arugula Dip

Servings:4
Cooking Time:5 Minutes

Ingredients:
- 1 cup arugula, chopped
- 3 tbsp basil pesto
- 1 cup cream cheese, soft
- Salt and black pepper to taste
- 1 cup heavy cream
- 1 tbsp chives, chopped

Directions:
1. Combine arugula, basil pesto, salt, pepper, and heavy cream in a blender and pulse until smooth. Transfer to a bowl and mix in cream cheese. Serve topped with chives.

Nutrition Info:
- Per Serving: Calories: 240;Fat: 15g;Protein: 6g;Carbs: 7g.

Broccoli-pepper Pizza

Servings:4
Cooking Time:25 Minutes

Ingredients:
- For the crust
- 1 tbsp olive oil
- ½ cup almond flour
- ¼ tsp salt
- 2 tbsp ground psyllium husk
- 1 cup lukewarm water
- For the topping
- 1 tbsp olive oil
- 1 cup sliced fresh mushrooms
- 1 white onion, thinly sliced
- 3 cups broccoli florets
- 4 garlic cloves, minced
- ½ cup pizza sauce
- 4 tomatoes, sliced
- 1 ½ cup grated mozzarella
- ½ cup grated Parmesan cheese

Directions:
1. Preheat the oven to 400 F. Line a baking sheet with parchment paper. In a bowl, mix the almond flour, salt, psyllium powder, olive oil, and lukewarm water until dough forms. Spread the mixture on the pizza pan and bake in the oven until crusty, 10 minutes. Remove and allow cooling.
2. Heat olive oil in a skillet and sauté the mushrooms, onion, garlic, and broccoli until softened, 5 minutes. Spread the pizza sauce on the crust and top with the broccoli mixture, tomato, mozzarella and Parmesan. Bake for 5 minutes.

Nutrition Info:
- Per Serving: Calories: 180;Fat: 9g;Protein: 17g;Carbs: 3.6g.

Pesto & Egg Avocado Boats

Servings:2
Cooking Time:15 Minutes

Ingredients:
- 1 halved avocado, pitted
- 2 large eggs
- Salt and black pepper to taste
- 2 tbsp jarred pesto
- 2 sundried tomatoes, chopped

Directions:
1. Preheat oven to 420 F. Scoop out the middle of each avocado half. Arrange them on a baking sheet, cut-side up. Crack an egg into each avocado half and season to taste. Bake until the eggs are set and cooked to your desired level of doneness, 10-12 minutes. Remove from the oven and top with pesto and sundried tomatoes. Serve and enjoy!

Nutrition Info:
- Per Serving: Calories: 302;Fat: 26g;Protein: 8g;Carbs: 10g.

Easy Blueberry And Oat Crisp

Servings:4
Cooking Time: 20 Minutes

Ingredients:
- 2 tablespoons coconut oil, melted, plus additional for greasing
- 4 cups fresh blueberries
- Juice of ½ lemon
- 2 teaspoons lemon zest
- ¼ cup maple syrup
- 1 cup gluten-free rolled oats
- ½ cup chopped pecans
- ½ teaspoon ground cinnamon
- Sea salt, to taste

Directions:
1. Preheat the oven to 350ºF. Grease a baking sheet with coconut oil.
2. Combine the blueberries, lemon juice and zest, and maple syrup in a bowl. Stir to mix well, then spread the mixture on the baking sheet.
3. Combine the remaining ingredients in a small bowl. Stir to mix well. Pour the mixture over the blueberries mixture.
4. Bake in the preheated oven for 20 minutes or until the oats are golden brown.
5. Serve immediately with spoons.

Nutrition Info:
- Per Serving: Calories: 496;Fat: 32.9g;Protein: 5.1g;-Carbs: 50.8g.

Roasted Eggplant Hummus

Servings:4
Cooking Time:25 Minutes

Ingredients:
- 1 lb eggplants, peeled and sliced
- 1 lemon, juiced
- 1 garlic clove, minced
- ¼ cup tahini
- ¼ tsp ground cumin
- Salt and black pepper to taste
- 2 tbsp fresh parsley, chopped
- ½ cup mayonnaise

Directions:
1. Preheat oven to 350 F. Arrange the eggplant slices on a baking sheet and bake for 15 minutes until tender. Let cool slightly before chopping. In a food processor, mix eggplants, salt, lemon juice, tahini, cumin, garlic, and pepper for 30 seconds. Remove to a bowl. Stir in mayonnaise. Serve topped with parsley.

Nutrition Info:
- Per Serving: Calories: 235;Fat: 18g;Protein: 4.1g;Carbs: 17g.

Festive Pumpkin Cheesecake

Servings:6
Cooking Time:50 Min + Chilling Time

Ingredients:
- ½ cup butter, melted
- 1 cup flour
- 1 can pumpkin purée
- 1 ½ cups mascarpone cheese
- ½ cup sugar
- 4 large eggs
- 2 tsp vanilla extract
- 2 tsp pumpkin pie spice

Directions:
1. Preheat oven to 350 F. In a small bowl, combine the flour and melted butter with a fork until well combined. Press the mixture into the bottom of a greased baking pan. In a large bowl, beat together the pumpkin purée, mascarpone cheese, and sugar using an electric mixer.
2. Add the eggs, one at a time, beating after each addition. Stir in the vanilla and pumpkin pie spice until just combined. Pour the mixture over the crust and bake until set, 40-45 minutes. Allow to cool to room temperature. Refrigerate for at least 6 hours before serving. Serve chilled.

Nutrition Info:
- Per Serving: Calories: 242;Fat: 22g;Protein: 7g;Carbs: 5g.

Strawberry Parfait

Servings:2
Cooking Time:10 Minutes

Ingredients:
- ¾ cup Greek yogurt
- 1 tbsp cocoa powder
- ¼ cup strawberries, chopped
- 5 drops vanilla stevia

Directions:

1. Combine cocoa powder, strawberries, yogurt, and stevia in a bowl. Serve immediately.

Nutrition Info:
- Per Serving: Calories: 210;Fat: 9g;Protein: 5g;Carbs: 8g.

Pecan & Raspberry & Frozen Yogurt Cups

Servings:4
Cooking Time:10 Minutes

Ingredients:
- 2 cups fresh raspberries
- 4 cups vanilla frozen yogurt
- 1 lime, zested
- ¼ cup chopped praline pecans

Directions:

1. Divide the frozen yogurt into 4 dessert glasses. Top with raspberries, lime zest, and pecans. Serve immediately.

Nutrition Info:
- Per Serving: Calories: 142;Fat: 3.4g;Protein: 3.7g;Carbs: 26g.

Salmon-cucumber Rolls

Servings:4
Cooking Time:5 Minutes

Ingredients:
- 8 Kalamata olives, chopped
- 4 oz smoked salmon strips
- 1 cucumber, sliced lengthwise
- 2 tsp lime juice
- 4 oz cream cheese, soft
- 1 tsp lemon zest, grated
- Salt and black pepper to taste
- 2 tsp dill, chopped

Directions:

1. Place cucumber slices on a flat surface and top each with a salmon strip. Combine olives, lime juice, cream cheese, lemon zest, salt, pepper, and dill in a bowl. Smear cream mixture over salmon and roll them up. Serve immediately.

Nutrition Info:
- Per Serving: Calories: 250;Fat: 16g;Protein: 18g;Carbs: 17g.

Cinnamon Pear & Oat Crisp With Pecans

Servings:4
Cooking Time:30 Minutes

Ingredients:
- 2 tbsp butter, melted
- 4 fresh pears, mashed
- ½ lemon, juiced and zested
- ¼ cup maple syrup
- 1 cup gluten-free rolled oats
- ½ cup chopped pecans
- ½ tsp ground cinnamon
- ¼ tsp salt

Directions:

1. Preheat oven to 350 F. Combine the pears, lemon juice and zest, and maple syrup in a bowl. Stir to mix well, then spread the mixture on a greased baking dish. Combine the remaining ingredients in a small bowl. Stir to mix well. Pour the mixture over the pear mixture. Bake for 20 minutes or until the oats are golden brown.

Nutrition Info:
- Per Serving: Calories: 496;Fat: 33g;Protein: 5g;Carbs: 50.8g.

Choco-tahini Glazed Apple Chips

Servings:2
Cooking Time:10 Minutes

Ingredients:
- 1 tbsp roasted, salted sunflower seeds
- 2 tbsp tahini
- 1 tbsp honey
- 1 tbsp cocoa powder
- 2 apples, thinly sliced

Directions:

1. Mix the tahini, honey, and cocoa powder in a small bowl. Add 1-2 tbsp of warm water and stir until thin enough to drizzle. Lay the apple chips out on a plate and drizzle them with the chocolate tahini sauce. Sprinkle sunflower seeds.

Nutrition Info:
- Per Serving: Calories: 261;Fat: 11g;Protein: 5g;Carbs: 43g.

Traditional Pizza Margherita

Servings:4
Cooking Time:30 Minutes

Ingredients:
- 1 can diced San Marzano tomatoes with juices
- 16 oz pizza dough
- Salt to taste
- 1 tsp oregano
- 2 tbsp extra-virgin olive oil
- 10 mozzarella cheese slices
- 12 fresh basil leaves
- 6 whole black olives

Directions:

1. Preheat oven to 450 F. Place the dough on a floured surface and roll out it thinly. Place it on a lightly floured pizza pan and drizzle with some olive oil. Puree the tomatoes, a splash of olive oil and a sprinkle of salt until smooth. Spread the tomato sauce over the base, leaving a 1-inch border and sprinkle with oregano. Arrange the mozzarella cheese slices on top and bake for 8-10 minutes until the crust is golden. Top with basil and olives and serve.

Nutrition Info:
- Per Serving: Calories: 542;Fat: 21g;Protein: 26g;Carbs: 63g.

Apples Stuffed With Pecans

Servings:4
Cooking Time:55 Minutes

Ingredients:
- 2 tbsp brown sugar
- 4 apples, cored
- ¼ cup chopped pecans
- 1 tsp ground cinnamon
- ¼ tsp ground nutmeg
- ¼ tsp ground ginger

Directions:

1. Preheat oven to 375 F. Arrange the apples cut-side up on a baking dish. Combine pecans, ginger, cinnamon, brown sugar, and nutmeg in a bowl. Scoop the mixture into the apples and bake for 35-40 minutes until golden brown.

Nutrition Info:
- Per Serving: Calories: 142;Fat: 1.1g;Protein: 0.8g;Carbs: 36g.

Avocado & Dark Chocolate Mousse

Servings:4
Cooking Time:10 Min + Freezing Time

Ingredients:
- 2 tbsp olive oil
- 8 oz dark chocolate, chopped
- ¼ cup milk
- 2 ripe avocados, deseeded
- ¼ cup honey
- 1 cup strawberries

Directions:

1. Cook the chocolate, olive oil, and milk in a saucepan over medium heat for 3 minutes or until the chocolate melt, stirring constantly. Put the avocado in a food processor, then drizzle with honey and melted chocolate. Pulse to combine until smooth. Pour the mixture into a serving bowl, then sprinkle with strawberries. Chill for 30 minutes and serve.

Nutrition Info:
- Per Serving: Calories: 654;Fat: 47g;Protein: 7.2g;Carbs: 56g.

Chili & Lemon Shrimp

Servings:6
Cooking Time:10 Minutes

Ingredients:
- 24 large shrimp, peeled and deveined
- ½ cup olive oil
- 5 garlic cloves, minced
- 1 tsp red pepper flakes
- 1 lemon, juiced and zested
- 1 tsp dried dill
- 1 tsp dried thyme
- Salt and black pepper to taste

Directions:

1. Warm the olive oil in a large skillet over medium heat. Add the garlic and red pepper flakes and cook for 1 minute. Add the shrimp and cook an additional 3 minutes, stirring frequently. Remove from the pan, and sprinkle with lemon juice, lemon zest, thyme, dill, salt, and pepper. Serve.

Nutrition Info:
- Per Serving: Calories: 198;Fat: 6g;Protein: 9g;Carbs: 28g.

Greek Yogurt & Za'atar Dip On Grilled Pitta

Servings:6
Cooking Time:10 Minutes

Ingredients:
- 1/3 cup olive oil
- 2 cups Greek yogurt
- 2 tbsp toasted ground pistachios
- Salt and white pepper to taste
- 2 tbsp mint, chopped
- 3 kalamata olives, chopped
- ¼ cup za'atar seasoning
- 3 pitta breads, cut into triangles

Directions:

1. Mix the yogurt, pistachios, salt, pepper, mint, olives, za'atar spice, and olive oil in a bowl. Grill the pitta bread until golden, about 5-6 minutes. Serve with the yogurt spread.

Nutrition Info:
- Per Serving: Calories: 300;Fat: 19g;Protein: 11g;Carbs: 22g.

Charred Asparagus

Servings:4
Cooking Time:25 Minutes

Ingredients:
- 2 tbsp olive oil
- 1 lb asparagus, trimmed
- 4 tbsp Grana Padano, grated
- ½ tsp garlic powder
- Salt to taste
- 2 tbsp parsley, chopped

Directions:

1. Preheat the grill to high. Season the asparagus with salt and garlic powder and coat with olive oil. Grill the asparagus for 10 minutes, turning often until lightly charred and tender. Sprinkle with cheese and parsley and serve.

Nutrition Info:
- Per Serving: Calories: 105;Fat: 8g;Protein: 4.3g;Carbs: 4.7g.

Caramel Peach & Walnut Cake

Servings:6
Cooking Time:50 Min + Cooling Time

Ingredients:
- ¼ cup coconut oil
- ¼ cup olive oil
- 2 peeled peaches, chopped
- ½ cup raisins, soaked
- 1 cup plain flour
- 3 eggs
- 1 tbsp dark rum
- ¼ tsp ground cinnamon
- 1 tsp vanilla extract
- 1 ½ tsp baking powder
- 4 tbsp Greek yogurt
- 2 tbsp honey
- 1 cup brown sugar
- 4 tbsp walnuts, chopped
- ¼ caramel sauce
- ¼ tsp salt

Directions:

1. Preheat the oven to 350 F. In a bowl, mix the flour, cinnamon, vanilla, baking powder, and salt. In another bowl, whisk the eggs with Greek yogurt using an electric mixer. Gently add in coconut and olive oil. Combine well. Put in rum, honey and sugar; stir to combine. Mix the wet ingredients with the dry mixture. Stir in peaches, raisins, and walnuts.

2. Pour the mixture into a greased baking pan and bake for 30-40 minutes until a knife inserted into the middle of the cake comes out clean. Remove from the oven and let sit for 10 minutes, then invert onto a wire rack to cool completely. Warm the caramel sauce through in a pan and pour it over the cooled cake to serve.

Nutrition Info:
- Per Serving: Calories: 568;Fat: 26g;Protein: 215g;Carbs: 66g.

Date: _____

MY SHOPPING LIST

Recipe ....

From the kicthen of ....

Serves .... Prep time .... Cook time ....

☐ Difficulty   ☐ Easy   ☐ Medium   ☐ Hard

Ingredient

....

....

....

....

....

Directions ....

....

....

....

....

....

APPENDIX A: MEASUREMENT CONVERSIONS

BASIC KITCHEN CONVERSIONS & EQUIVALENTS

DRY MEASUREMENTS CONVERSION CHART

3 TEASPOONS = 1 TABLESPOON = 1/16 CUP

6 TEASPOONS = 2 TABLESPOONS = 1/8 CUP

12 TEASPOONS = 4 TABLESPOONS = 1/4 CUP

24 TEASPOONS = 8 TABLESPOONS = 1/2 CUP

36 TEASPOONS = 12 TABLESPOONS = 3/4 CUP

48 TEASPOONS = 16 TABLESPOONS = 1 CUP

METRIC TO US COOKING CONVERSIONS

OVEN TEMPERATURES

120 °C = 250 °F

160 °C = 320 °F

180° C = 350 °F

205 °C = 400 °F

220 °C = 425 °F

LIQUID MEASUREMENTS CONVERSION CHART

8 FLUID OUNCES = 1 CUP = 1/2 PINT = 1/4 QUART

16 FLUID OUNCES = 2 CUPS = 1 PINT = 1/2 QUART

32 FLUID OUNCES = 4 CUPS = 2 PINTS = 1 QUART
 = 1/4 GALLON

128 FLUID OUNCES = 16 CUPS = 8 PINTS = 4 QUARTS = 1 GALLON

BAKING IN GRAMS

1 CUP FLOUR = 140 GRAMS

1 CUP SUGAR = 150 GRAMS

1 CUP POWDERED SUGAR = 160 GRAMS

1 CUP HEAVY CREAM = 235 GRAMS

VOLUME

1 MILLILITER = 1/5 TEASPOON

5 ML = 1 TEASPOON

15 ML = 1 TABLESPOON

240 ML = 1 CUP OR 8 FLUID OUNCES

1 LITER = 34 FL. OUNCES

US TO METRIC COOKING CONVERSIONS

1/5 TSP = 1 ML

1 TSP = 5 ML

1 TBSP = 15 ML

1 FL OUNCE = 30 ML

1 CUP = 237 ML

1 PINT (2 CUPS) = 473 ML

1 QUART (4 CUPS) = .95 LITER

1 GALLON (16 CUPS) = 3.8 LITERS

1 OZ = 28 GRAMS

1 POUND = 454 GRAMS

BUTTER

1 CUP BUTTER = 2 STICKS = 8 OUNCES = 230 GRAMS = 8 TABLESPOONS

WHAT DOES 1 CUP EQUAL

1 CUP = 8 FLUID OUNCES

1 CUP = 16 TABLESPOONS

1 CUP = 48 TEASPOONS

1 CUP = 1/2 PINT

1 CUP = 1/4 QUART

1 CUP = 1/16 GALLON

1 CUP = 240 ML

WEIGHT

1 GRAM = .035 OUNCES

100 GRAMS = 3.5 OUNCES

500 GRAMS = 1.1 POUNDS

1 KILOGRAM = 35 OUNCES

BAKING PAN CONVERSIONS

1 CUP ALL-PURPOSE FLOUR = 4.5 OZ

1 CUP ROLLED OATS = 3 OZ 1 LARGE EGG = 1.7 OZ

1 CUP BUTTER = 8 OZ 1 CUP MILK = 8 OZ

1 CUP HEAVY CREAM = 8.4 OZ

1 CUP GRANULATED SUGAR = 7.1 OZ

1 CUP PACKED BROWN SUGAR = 7.75 OZ

1 CUP VEGETABLE OIL = 7.7 OZ

1 CUP UNSIFTED POWDERED SUGAR = 4.4 OZ

BAKING PAN CONVERSIONS

9-INCH ROUND CAKE PAN = 12 CUPS

10-INCH TUBE PAN =16 CUPS

11-INCH BUNDT PAN = 12 CUPS

9-INCH SPRINGFORM PAN = 10 CUPS

9 X 5 INCH LOAF PAN = 8 CUPS

9-INCH SQUARE PAN = 8 CUPS

APPENDIX B : RECIPES INDEX

Made in the USA
Middletown, DE
17 December 2023

46037723R00068